D1236415

Beyond Boredom and Anxiety

The Experience of Play in Work and Games

▲▲▲

Mihaly Csikszentmihalyi

With contributions by
Isabella Csikszentmihalyi
Ronald Graef
Jean Hamilton Holcomb
Judy Hendin
John MacAloon

▲▲▲

BEYOND BOREDOM AND ANXIETY

▲▲▲

Jossey-Bass Publishers
San Francisco • Washington • London • 1975

BEYOND BOREDOM AND ANXIETY
The Experience of Play in Work and Games
by Mihaly Csikszentmihalyi

Jossey-Bass, Inc., Publishers
615 Montgomery Street
San Francisco, California 94111
&
Jossey-Bass Limited
3 Henrietta Street
London WC2E 8LU

Library of Congress Catalogue Card Number LC 75-21751

International Standard Book Number ISBN 0-87589-261-2

Manufactured in the United States of America

JACKET DESIGN BY WILLI BAUM

FIRST EDITION

Code 7514

The
Jossey-Bass
Behavioral Science Series

Preface

▲▲

When Atys was king of Lydia in Asia Minor some three thousand years ago, a great scarcity threatened his realm. For a while people accepted their lot without complaining, in the hope that the times of plenty would return. But when things failed to get better, the Lydians devised a strange remedy for their problem. "The plan adopted against the famine was to engage in games one day so entirely as not to feel any craving for food," Herodotus writes, "and the next day to eat and abstain from games. In this way they passed eighteen years." And along the way they invented the dice, knuckle-bones, the ball, and "all the games which are common to them with the Greeks" (Herodotus, *Persian Wars,* Book 1, Chapter 94).

The account may be fictitious, but it points at an interesting fact: people do get immersed in games so deeply as to forget hunger and other problems. What power does play have that men relinquish basic needs for its sake? This is the question that the studies reported in *Beyond Boredom and Anxiety* were designed to answer. It is a question that cuts into some of the central issues with which the behavioral sciences deal.

Most theories of human motivation depend on a "deficit model," which assumes that only a limited number of pleasurable physiological states exist; according to this model, behavior is simply a set of innate and learned responses directed toward satisfying basic needs. This closed homeostatic model, which grew out of observations made in the laboratory or on the couch, has some important implications. It suggests that one can derive enjoyment only from a finite number of experiences and objects. Therefore, life must be inherently painful because scarce resources of enjoyment lead to competition and only a few can get more than intermittent satisfaction. For Freud, the libido is the source of all pleasure; but since the requirements of social life conflict with libidinal desires, discontent is the lot of civilized man. All theories of behavior that reduce enjoyment to the satisfaction of needs, whether they are held by economists or behaviorists, come to the same conclusion: the needs can never be fully satisfied.

But the study of play leads to a different picture of motivation. One sees people involved in a great variety of activities which provide none of the rewards that a closed model predicts must be there. One soon begins to realize that almost any object or any experience is potentially enjoyable. The task is to find out how this potential can be translated into actuality. If it is true that enjoyment does not depend on scarce resources, the quality of life can be greatly improved.

This book addresses also a second set of issues. The dominant assumption in the behavioral sciences is that observable actions are the only legitimate data. As a result, inner experience has been exiled to a scientific no-man's-land. Yet the crucial locus of psychological events is still the psyche; our thoughts and our feelings, not our "objective" behavior, give meaning to life. Play is a good example of this truism; here concrete behavior is an unreliable guide for understanding the phenomenon. It is not so much what people do but how they perceive and interpret what they are doing that makes the activity enjoyable.

And it makes a great deal of difference to a person whether his acts are enjoyable or not, even though the difference is not noticeable to an outside observer. When a person acts because his behavior is motivated by the enjoyment he finds in the behavior itself, he increases his self-confidence, contentment, and feeling of solidarity with others; if the behavior is motivated by external pressures or external rewards, he may experience insecurity, frustration, and a sense of alienation. This is a vital distinction, yet one that is rarely made. At a time when psychology is developing means for controlling behavior through electronic implants, drugs, behavior-modification programs, and a whole armory of other intrusive techniques, it is vital to preserve an understanding of the active, creative, self-motivated dimensions of behavior. The study of play seems to offer one such opportunity.

Man at play, as thinkers from Plato to Sartre have observed, is at the peak of his freedom and dignity. If we can find out what makes play such a liberating and rewarding activity, we can start applying this knowledge outside of games as well. Perhaps Plato was right, and it is possible after all to "live life as play." But in this last quarter of the twentieth century, when despite unprecedented prosperity and control of the environment people seem to feel more destitute and unfree than ever before, the intuitive grasp of playfulness is difficult to recapture. Hence the studies reported here, which attempt to describe, as analytically and objectively as possible, the experience of enjoyment and the structural contexts in which it occurs.

One fact seemed clear from the beginning: the immersion into enjoyable experience which is typical of play occurs frequently outside of games. Indeed, the ideas presented here began to crystallize in my mind about a dozen years ago, as I was observing artists at work. One thing struck me as especially intriguing. Despite the fact that almost no one can make either a reputation or a living from painting, the artists studied were almost fanatically devoted to their work; they were at it night and day, and nothing else seemed to matter so much in their lives. Yet as soon as they finished a painting or a sculpture, they seemed to lose all interest in it. Nor were they interested much in each other's paintings or in great masterpieces. Most artists did not go to museums, did not decorate their homes with art, and seemed to be generally bored or baffled by talk about the aesthetic qualities of the works they or their friends produced. What they did love to do was talk about small technical details, stylistic breakthroughs—the actions, thoughts, and feelings involved in making art. Slowly it became obvious that something in the activity of painting itself kept them going. The process of making their products was so enjoyable that they were ready to sacrifice a great deal for the chance of continuing to do so. There was something about the physical activities of stretching canvas on wooden frames, of squeezing tubes of paint or kneading clay, of splashing colors on a blank surface; the cognitive activity of choosing a problem to work on, of defining a subject, of experimenting with new combinations of form, color, light, and space; the emotional impact of recognizing one's past, present, and future concerns in the emerging work. All these aspects of the artistic process added up to a structured experience which was almost addictive in its fascination.

Artists provided the clue for the importance of intrinsic motivation. Their acts implied that work can give enjoyment and meaning to life. It was a simple and obvious message, yet full of tantalizing implications. Did these artists enjoy their work because the subject matter was art or because the pattern of actions required by their work was in itself rewarding? In other words, is enjoyment of work unique to creative people doing creative tasks, or can everyone experience it if some set of favorable conditions is met? If everyone can experience such enjoyment, then boring everyday tasks might also be turned into enjoyable and meaningful activities.

In my search for answers, three main fields of psychological literature seemed most promising. Eventually all three proved helpful, although none resolved all questions. The first field was writings on self-actualization and peak experiences: the work of psychologists like Abraham Maslow or accounts of ecstatic experiences such as provided by Marghanita Laski. These works contain detailed descriptions of the subjective feelings with which I had become familiar through the reports of artists. But these writings do not provide concrete explanations of what makes peak experiences possible. A second promising field was the literature on intrinsic motivation. Robert White, D. E. Berlyne, Richard De Charms, and a number of other psychologists have been trying to isolate characteristics of stimuli that make them enjoyable (characteristics such as novelty) or states of the person that make him enjoy a situation (for instance, feelings of competence or personal causation). This approach abounds in concrete studies, but most of them are experimental in nature, and although they suggest important ideas, it is difficult to extrapolate from the findings to conditions of everyday life. Finally, there was the literature on play. Play provides peak experiences and intrinsic motivation; and I had, of course, noticed a playful quality in the work and concurrent experience of the artists whom I had observed. Perhaps the phenomenon of play could give the unifying concept needed to solve the riddle of why certain activities are enjoyable. But writings on play turn out to have their own limitation. Scholars in this field seem to assume that play is removed from "real" life; whenever an act has consequences that matter outside a playful context, it ceases to be play. To accept this assumption would have meant that the concept of play is useless for studying how everyday life can be made more enjoyable.

To escape from this impasse, I decided to begin a series of studies combining the three approaches. The goal was to focus on people who were having peak experiences, who were intrinsically motivated, and who were involved in play as well as real-life activities, in order to find out whether I could detect similarities in their experiences, their motivation, and the situations that produce enjoyment.

The results are reported in this volume. (For details about the study and the contents of the various chapters, see Chapter One.) The results suggest that anything one does can become rewarding if the activity is structured right and if one's skills are matched with the challenges of the action. In this optimal condition, people enjoy even work, extreme danger, and stress. To change a boring situation into one that provides its own rewards does not require money or physical energy; it can be achieved through symbolic restructuring of information.

So it appears that the sources of enjoyment are not finite and that life can be made infinitely more rewarding if we learn how to use the opportunities lying all around us. Of course, the task is full of difficulties. As the Italians say: *Tra il dire e il fare c'è di mezzo il mare*—"An ocean lies between saying and doing." But it is never too early to raise these issues, and perhaps it is not too late.

Acknowledgments

There are two sources without which this project would have been impossible to carry out. One is the Applied Research Branch, Social Problems Research Committee, of the National Institute of Mental Health, which provided the necessary financing. The other indispensable help came from the people interviewed; these people—more than three hundred in number—gave generously of their time to enable us to derive some conclusions about the dynamics of enjoyment.

This has been a collaborative enterprise, in which the contributions of several people were integrated in a joint product. Specifically, Gary Becker collected interviews with male chess players and basketball players. Paul Gruenberg interviewed rock climbers and some basketball players. John MacAloon also worked with rock climbers. Jean Hamilton Holcomb interviewed surgeons, and she analyzed the data with Isabella Csikszentmihalyi. Judy Hendin interviewed rock dancers, and Sonja Hoard interviewed modern dancers. Pamela Perun collected the data on women chess players. Henry Post interviewed composers. John Eggert provided statistical assistance at various points of the project. Geri Cohen and Ronald Graef ran the deprivation experiments, and the latter helped in writing up the results.

Several colleagues expressed interest in the ideas contained in this work, and their moral support was invaluable to me in pursuing the elusive concepts with which we are dealing. I must especially thank Donald Campbell of Northwestern University, Brian Sutton-Smith of Columbia University Teachers College, Gerald Kenyon of the University of Waterloo, and

Thomas Greening, editor of the *Journal of Humanistic Psychology*, for the encouragement they have been so generous with. At my own university, the enthusiasm of Victor Turner and Bernice Neugarten was always helpful. William E. Henry provided many useful suggestions which were incorporated in the revision of the manuscript. Finally, I must thank Alice Chandler for the expert administrative supervision she gave the project, and Gwen Stevenson for typing the manuscript.

Chapter Four of this volume is a modified version of an article which appeared in the *Journal of Humanistic Psychology* and is reprinted here with permission.

As is customary, the reader is asked to absolve the persons and institutions mentioned above of all blame and to hold me solely responsible for any shortcomings.

Chicago
September 1975

Mihaly Csikszentmihalyi

Contents

Beyond Boredom and Anxiety

The Experience of Play in Work and Games

▲▲▲

Chapter *1*

Enjoyment and Intrinsic Motivation

▲▲

In a world supposedly ruled by the pursuit of money, power, prestige, and pleasure, it is surprising to find certain people who sacrifice all those goals for no apparent reason: people who risk their lives climbing rocks, who devote their lives to art, who spend their energies playing chess. By finding out why they are willing to give up material rewards for the elusive experience of performing enjoyable acts, we hope to learn something that will allow us to make everyday life more meaningful. At present, most of the institutions that take up our time—schools, offices, factories—are organized around the assumption that serious work is grim and unpleasant. Because of this assumption, most of our time *is* spent doing unpleasant things. By studying enjoyment, we might learn how to redress this harmful situation.

To be sure, one may see the behavior of people dedicated to the pursuit of enjoyment as useless, the result of deviant socialization toward meaningless goals. Psychologists may account for it as sublimated variants of the pursuit of real needs which cannot be directly satisfied. Our interest in the matter relies on a different assumption: if we can learn more about activities which are enjoyable in themselves, we will find clues to a form of motivation that could become an extremely important human resource.

The management of behavior, as presently practiced, is based on the tacit belief that people are motivated only by external rewards or by the fear of external punishment. The stick and the carrot are the main tools by which people are made to pull their weight. From the earliest months of life, children are threatened or cajoled into conformity with parental demands; when they go on to school, grades and symbolic promotions are used to make them move along predetermined paths. Even the concepts of identification or internalization are based on the idea that the child is afraid of his parents or envies their status. By the time they grow to be adults, most people have been conditioned to respond predictably to external cues, usually represented by the symbolic rewards of money and status.

There is no question that this motivational system, evolved by societies over a long period of centuries, is quite effective. By objectifying incentives into money and status, societies have developed a rational, universal motivational system whereby communities can produce desired behaviors predictably and can allot precisely differentiated rewards to construct a complex social hierarchy. The standardization of external rewards, and the general acceptance of their value by most members of society, has created the "homo economicus" responsive to the laws of supply and demand and the "homo sociologicus" who is kept within bounds by the network of social controls.

The commonsense assumption is that extrinsic rewards like money and status are basic human needs—or, in behaviorist terms, primary reinforcers. If this were true, it would be quite hopeless to try substituting satisfaction with one's job for external rewards. But there are good reasons to believe that striving for material goods is in great part a motivation that a person learns as part of his socialization into a culture. Greed for possessions is not a universal trait. Anthropological evidence shows that there are cultures in which material goals do not have the importance we attribute to them (Polanyi, 1957). Even in our society, children have to learn "the value of a dollar"; only because every accomplishment in our culture has a dollar tag to it do children learn to appreciate financial rewards above all else. Other evidence that supports this view is the presence of people, within our society, who choose to expend energy for goals that carry no conventional material rewards. These are the people we deal with in the present study, hoping to learn from them the dynamics of intrinsic motivation.

But why should one worry about extrinsic rewards? If they are successful, why try to moderate their effect with recourse to intrinsic motives? The fact is that the ease with which external rewards can be used conceals real dangers. When a teacher discovers that children will work for a grade, he or she may become less concerned with whether the work itself is meaningful or rewarding to students. Employers who take for granted the wisdom of external incentives may come to believe that workers' enjoyment of the task is irrelevant. As a result, children and workers will learn, in time, that what they have to do is worthless in itself and that its only justification is the grade or paycheck they get at the end. This pattern has become so general in our culture that by now it is self-evident: what one *must* do cannot be enjoyable. So we have learned to make a distinction between "work" and "leisure": the former is what we have to do most of the time against our desire; the latter is what we like to do, although it is useless. We therefore feel bored and frustrated on our jobs, and guilty when we are at leisure. Among the consequences of such a state of affairs is the deep-seated alienation of workers in industrial nations (Keniston, 1960; Ginzberg, 1971; Ford, 1969; Gooding, 1972; Terkel, 1974). This conflict cannot be dismissed as just a temporary result of affluence. Some writers seem to think that workers are dissatisfied only when their jobs are safe; during periods of scarcity or unemployment, people are glad enough to make a living even if their jobs are dull and meaningless. It is more likely that workers threatened in their jobs will vent their frustration in even more destructive ways. Although German workers during the Great Depression did not agitate for job enrichment, they were glad to take a chance on conquering the world.

There is another serious problem with using extrinsic rewards as the only incentive for reaching desirable goals. Extrinsic rewards are by their nature either scarce or expensive to attain in terms of human energy. Money and the material possessions it can buy require the exploitation of natural resources and labor. If everything we do is done in order to get material rewards, we shall exhaust the planet and each other. Admittedly, people will always need possessions based on resources and physical energy. The waste begins when these are not used only to meet necessities but mainly as symbolic rewards to compensate people for the empty drudgery of life. At that point a vicious circle seems to begin; the more a person complies with extrinsically rewarded roles, the less he enjoys himself, and the more extrinsic rewards he needs. The only way to break the circle is by making the roles themselves more enjoyable; then the need for a *quid pro quo* is bound to decrease.

The same sort of argument holds for the other main class of extrinsic rewards, which includes power, prestige, and esteem. Although these are in many ways very different from each other, they are all based on an invidious comparison between persons. There is no question that people are different and that some deserve recognition above others in certain respects. But status differentials tend to follow a zero-sum pattern: the psychic benefits to those who get recognition are paid for by the decreased self-respect of those who do not.

Therefore, when a social system learns to rely exclusively on extrinsic rewards, it creates alienation among its members, and it places a drain on material resources which eventually may prove fatal. In the past, a more diversified set of incentives apparently reduced the monopoly of material goals; in many societies men seemed to enjoy thoroughly what they had to do to make a living (Arendt, 1958; Carpenter, 1970), or they hoped to be rewarded with eternal bliss, or they found rewards in the approval of their peers (Weber, 1947; Polanyi, 1957). When these other reward systems are operative, demands on the ecology are less pressing.

The goal of this study was to begin exploring activities that appear to contain rewards within themselves, that do not rely on scarce material incentives—in other words, activities that are ecologically sound. For this reason, we started to look closely at such things as rock climbing, dance, chess, and basketball. Of course, while these activities may be intrinsically rewarding and hence ecologically beneficial, they are also unproductive. A society could not survive long if people were exclusively involved in playful pursuits. We assumed, however, that there is no unbridgeable gap between "work" and "leisure." Hence, by studying play one might learn how work can be made enjoyable, as in certain cases it clearly is. To make sure that the bridge between the two activities does exist, we included in our study members of a few occupations which one would expect to be enjoyable: composers of music, surgeons, and teachers. By understanding better what makes these leisure activities and satisfying jobs enjoyable, we hoped that we might also learn how to decrease dependence on extrinsic rewards in other areas of life as well.

Because modern psychology is concerned mainly with behavior and performance, rather than the reality of inner states of experience, psychologists largely ignore the distinction between extrinsic and intrinsic motivation. Because the only scientific way to control a person's behavior is to manipulate concrete rewards or punishments from outside the organism, most researchers focus on the motivating effects of extrinsic factors—pellets of food, M&M candies, tokens, or electric shocks. They often seem to forget that behavior appears closely dependent on external rewards simply because experimental conditions have necessitated the use of external rewards. Outside the laboratory people often have quite different reasons for acting. They may, for instance, suddenly find great value or meaning in a previously neutral stimulus simply because it is important for them to create value and meaning. The importance of inner sources of motivation may be obvious enough in real life, but as long as they cannot be harnessed in an experiment they have no chance of being generally recognized. Until that day comes—if it comes—the accepted convention is to believe that people behave or learn only in response to external events.

Admittedly, some psychologists—people like Murphy (1958), Rogers (1961), and Maslow (1962, 1965, 1971)—have tried to return the focus of psychological investigation to the psyche, the inner events experienced by a person. But those researchers who are currently working on intrinsic motivation approach the problem from a much more molecular level. They are interested in establishing the reinforcing properties of single stimuli (Day, Berlyne, and Hunt, 1971; Deci, 1973), or they attempt to assess the effects of extrinsic rewards on simple, enjoyable, experimental tasks (Deci, 1971; Lepper, Greene, and Nisbett, 1973). These approaches generally equate enjoyment with "pleasure" (Berlyne and Madsen, 1973). But although much behavior is motivated by physiological stimulation which produces a positive response (Olds, 1969; Olds and others, 1972), the simple hedonistic model fails to account for a wide range of human action. The crucial question is why patterns of stimulation which under some conditions are neutral or even aversive can suddenly become enjoyable. Rock climbing, for instance, is an activity that most people try to avoid and that even committed climbers sometimes dread—when the choice of climbing is not voluntary, for example. Yet under the right conditions it is an exhilarating experience. To understand how this is possible, it is not enough to know the objective characteristics of the external stimuli involved, or the pattern of the person's learned associations to pleasant experiences. What one needs is a holistic approach which takes into account a person's goals and abilities and his subjective evaluation of the external situation. It is the complex interaction of these subjective processes that determines whether an experience is enjoyable, as opposed to being simply pleasurable.

When it comes to complex activities like the ones studied here, there are very few precedents to draw from. Among the most significant work done in this area is the theoretical contribution of Callois (1958), who uses anthropological examples to construct a typology of games and, by implication, a typology of intrinsic motives. The growing literature on play, ably reviewed by Ellis (1973), and studies of games (Avedon and Sutton-Smith, 1971) contain some useful insights into the operation of intrinsic motives. For instance, Kenyon (1968, 1970) has studied attitudes toward physical activity among young people in various cultures; and Sutton-Smith has done much to explain the reasons for play in children (Roberts and Sutton-Smith, 1962; Sutton-Smith, 1971a, 1973) and in adults (Sutton-Smith and Roberts, 1963; Sutton-Smith, 1971b). Even these studies, however, are more interested in the social or psychological *function* of intrinsically rewarding activities rather than in the enjoyable experience itself. As an example, when games involve risk, as in mountain climbing or gambling, the usual explanations given are that the activity is enjoyed because of a masochistic release from guilt about sexuality and aggression (Bergler, 1970). In other words, the usual psychological account of intrinsic enjoyment is based on reductionistic, deficit assumptions: nothing is enjoyable except the simplest physiological needs and the reduction of anxieties generated by them. Here too, there are exceptions, such as Kusyszyn's (1975) refreshing study of the psychology of gambling. On the whole, however, because the discipline of psychology, despite its ultimate roots in philosophy, counts the natural sciences and the medical approach to mental illness among its more immediate ancestors, the study of human behavior is colored by a mechanistic orientation which often fails to do justice to the phenomena it seeks to explain.

This intellectual heritage is most obtrusive when psychology deals with the kinds of behavior that are least predictable in terms of species-specific survival needs: creativity, religion, and the enjoyment people derive from complex activities. The leading natural science branch of psychology, behaviorism, explains these phenomena in terms of the same stimulus-response paradigm it uses to account for any other human action. A person paints a picture or plays chess because each step of the process becomes linked to an originally rewarding stimulus; eventually the whole behavior pattern is built up, and painting or chess becomes rewarding in its own right (Skinner, 1953). Psychoanalysis, which in its various forms is the main descendant of the clinical approach to behavior, explains creativity or enjoyment as the disguised manifestation of a conflict between basic instinctual needs and social constraints. People paint pictures because they cannot directly indulge their libidinal curiosity, and they play chess because in that game they can vicariously kill their father (the opponent's king) and thus release the oedipal tension which frustrates them in real life (Jones, 1931; Fine, 1956).

These forms of reductionism are, however, ultimately unsatisfactory. Let us take, for instance, the psychoanalytic account of why people enjoy chess. If chess is pleasurable only because it satisfies libidinal needs, then how can one explain why the game is so difficult, abstract, and elegant? The libido is notoriously uninterested in such qualities. It would be much better pleased if the father were quickly dispatched without all the rigamarole. So one must explain the complexity of the game as a concession to the suspicious superego. In this abstract disguise, the desire to kill goes unrecognized and hence will not produce guilt. But why *this* particular disguise? A man could express such a libidinal desire in a million forms at least as convincing as chess and much less demanding of energy. It seems more plausible to assume that the main rewards of the game are independent of whatever release its symbolism may bring to the libido. To stay within a Freudian framework, one would suppose that people go to the trouble of playing chess because it appeals to some function of the ego. Sublimation may also be involved, but by itself it is not an adequate explanation.

There is nothing wrong with the behaviorist or psychoanalytic accounts, as long as they are understood to be *as-if* models of the phenomena they deal with. But psychologists and laymen often assume that a likely explanation of a behavior is the only explanation, that the explanatory model exhausts the reality in question. The model then ceases to be *as if* and becomes *nothing but*. Chess playing becomes *nothing but* sublimated oedipal aggression, and mountain climbing is reduced to sublimated penis worship. The problem with such reductionistic explanations is not that they do not work. In fact, they do give a reasonably consistent account of human phenomena; but this account—like all accounts—makes sense only within a particular set of assumptions.

Scientific explanations in the natural sciences are always of the *as-if* kind. They do not presume to stand for the reality explained. They are just models which help to simplify the behavior of the reality under study; they do not claim to represent the wholeness of that reality in the abstract form. If natural scientists, upon discovering gravitational properties, had assumed that the laws of gravity suffice to account for the dynamics of matter, they would have missed other significant forces, such as electromagnetism and atomic energy. Similarly, it seems clear that excessive reliance on the currently paramount reductionistic models will hinder our understanding of things such as creativity or enjoyment.

Therefore, we need a new model of intrinsically rewarding behavior—not to substitute it for the reductionistic ones but to complement them. Scholars who impute death wishes or latent homosexuality to rock climbers may be perfectly correct in their ontogenetic analysis. But such an analysis fails to address the most intriguing question: Why is climbing enjoyable? We shall not be concerned with questions of origin, of psychic compensation, of phylogenetic function. Very possibly, as ethologists have suggested (Beach, 1945; Jewell and Loizos, 1966; Eibl-Eibesfeldt, 1970; Bekoff, 1972, 1974; Fagen, 1974), playful activities enable the species to develop flexible behavior which is adaptive in the long run.

But that is not what we are interested in demonstrating. The simple goal of this study is to understand enjoyment, here and now—not as compensation for past desires, not as preparation for future needs, but as an ongoing process which provides rewarding experiences in the present. Therefore, the model used in this investigation requires a subtle shift in assumptions. Instead of approaching enjoyment as something to be explained away in terms of other conceptual categories like "survival function" or "libidinal sublimation," we try to look at it as an autonomous reality that has to be understood in its own terms.

The way we originally approached this study was to contact people in as many different autotelic activities as possible and simply ask them why they were performing these activities. An activity was assumed to be autotelic (from the Greek *auto* = self and *telos* = goal, purpose) if it required formal and extensive energy output on the part of the actor, yet provided few if any conventional rewards. First, we conducted pilot interviews with about sixty respondents, including hockey and soccer players at a college, spelunkers and explorers, a mountain climber of international reputation, a champion handball player, and a world-record long-distance swimmer. From these interviews we developed a questionnaire and a more structured interview form.*

With these instruments we approached a number of other respondents involved in autotelic activities: thirty rock climbers, including experts as well as a few beginners; thirty male chess players, ranging from beginners to grand masters; twenty-three of the top female chess players in the United States; twenty-two professional composers of modern music; twenty-eight female modern dancers, ranging from beginners to professionals; and forty basketball players from two Boston-area championship high school teams. A number of other respondents were also interviewed, but most of this additional information is not included in this volume.

In general, the respondents filled out the questionnaire, and the interviewer filled out the open-ended questions of the interview. Some interviews were tape-recorded and transcribed later. The female chess players, who were contacted by mail, filled out the interview form as well as the questionnaire. A total of nine interviewers—five male, four female—were involved, each experienced in the same activity as the respondents

*A full technical report of these studies, including questionnaire and interview forms, is available from the author to researchers working in this field.

were. Several joint training sessions were held to ensure a neutral approach to the interviews and accuracy of transcription.

Chapters Two and Three are based on the responses of this core group of 173 subjects. In Chapter Two the questionnaire answers are used to provide some clues to the kinds of rewards people derive from autotelic activities. In Chapter Three we begin to show what characteristics make an activity enjoyable. A new model of intrinsic rewards, derived from the questionnaire and interview answers, is presented in Chapter Four. It describes the *flow* experience, which, according to our reading of the interviews, is the crucial component of enjoyment; we also develop a model of flow processes, to describe the common structure of activities that are experienced as enjoyable. Chapters Five through Eight focus on four selected autotelic—or flow—activities: chess, rock climbing, rock dancing, and surgery.

Out of this welter of material—some quantitative, some qualitative—emerges a clear description of what enjoyment consists of and how it comes about. The flow model used to explain enjoyment is admittedly just another *as-if* construct that cannot do justice to the phenomenon studied. As Steiner (1974b, p. 106) has recently remarked, "Analytic thought has in it a strange violence. To know analytically is to reduce the object of knowledge, however complex, however vital it may be, to just this: an object" (see also Brown, 1959). To a certain extent, our attempt to formalize the experience of enjoyment and the activities that allow it to occur results in a relative impoverishment of the object of knowledge. However, as long as one remembers that we are talking about a model and not the real thing, not much harm will be done. And one hopes that the model, which is both comprehensive and relatively precise, will make it easier for us to build intrinsic rewards into everyday life.

In Part III of this volume, we try to describe patterns of enjoyable behavior that individuals perform during a normal day. Instead of the "deep-flow" activities discussed in the preceding chapters, Chapter Nine describes microflow events such as watching television, stretching one's muscles, or taking a coffee break. Chapter Ten reports on what happens to people when they stop their microflow—how their physical feelings, their intellectual performance, and their self-concepts are affected by flow deprivation. For this latter part of the study twenty additional subjects were tested according to a complex experimental procedure described in Chapter Nine.

Because of the exploratory nature of our work as a whole, and because of the elusive character of the phenomenon investigated, the methodology of this report is not as neat and consistent as one would expect from an experimental study. Some of the respondents in Parts I and II did not fill out a questionnaire, and some were unavailable for interviews. Some questions were rephrased or added as the study went on. The method by which the respondents were chosen was neither random nor stratified, although in most cases we obtained the best practitioners of a given activity, plus a roughly equal number of beginners and of persons with intermediate skills. On the whole, we believe that our respondents and their responses are representative and that the results do not distort unduly the reality studied. The one exception to the rather free-wheeling procedures is the material contained in Part III. Here rigor was essential, and accordingly the experimental design of that section reflects the appropriate controls.

Our study describes the components of enjoyment quite concretely, but it stops short of giving detailed instructions for bringing intrinsic rewards into usually boring situations like classrooms, jobs, or unstructured everyday life. However, the implications of the flow model outlined in this study are not difficult to draw. Plato has said that a sound education consists in training people to find "pleasure and pain in the right objects" (*Laws,* II; see also Aristotle, *Ethics,* II, 3). In the *Bhagavad Gita,* Krishna explains that "They all attain perfection when they find joy in their work" (18: 45). In Chapter Eleven we attempt to draw out some of the practical implications of this study of intrinsic rewards, and we explore the significance of its findings for the behavioral sciences in general.

Chapter 2

Rewards of Autotelic Activities

▲▲▲

All the groups studied had one thing in common: they consisted of people who devote much energy to some activity which yields minimal rewards of a conventional sort. The absence of conventional incentives, however, does not imply an absence of rewards. Clearly, people are motivated to pursue these activities because they derive some satisfaction from them, and this satisfaction itself acts as a reward. The purpose of our study was to understand better what these intrinsic rewards are that people derive from a variety of different activities not rewarded extrinsically.

The first step in this direction was to ask respondents to rank eight "reasons for enjoying" the particular activity in which they were engaged. The eight items, derived from pilot interviews with college soccer and hockey players (Csikszentmihalyi and Gruenberg, 1970), range from reasons that appear to be almost purely intrinsic ("enjoyment of the experience and use of skills"; "the activity itself: the pattern, the action, the world it provides") to reasons that are definitely more extrinsic ("competition, measuring self against others"; "prestige, regard, glamor"). A factor analysis of the data confirmed that the eight reasons were relatively independent of each other. Only the two "intrinsic" items tended to load on the same factor; the remaining six each loaded on a separate one. Hence, the eight reasons evidently represent exhaustive and nonredundant incentives for participating in activities which lack conventional rewards.

If our expectations were correct, respondents in each group would rate intrinsic reasons for enjoying the activity as being more important than extrinsic ones. This hypothesis was amply confirmed (see Table 1). When the scores of the five baseline groups were combined ($N = 145$), the two intrinsic reasons emerged as most important—significantly more so than each of the six remaining reasons. In fact, twenty-four of the twenty-eight possible contrasts between the eight items were significant (86 percent), generally at the .005 level of probability or beyond. The pattern reflects the fact that, across widely different activities, a very strong consensus exists as to why the activity is enjoyable.

The main reasons for devoting time and effort to playing chess, dancing, or composing music are that the experiences are rewarding in themselves, and that the activities provide little worlds of their own which are enjoyable. Of course, Table 1 merely states what we already expected; the data give no clues to what precisely is rewarding about these activities and the experiences derived from them. The answer to that question will have to wait, since it is the purpose of the study as a whole to disentangle the sources of intrinsic motivation. In the meantime, it is encouraging to note that respondents on the whole did indeed regard intrinsic rewards as most important. Of course, since we did not include control groups involved in boring activities, we cannot say with complete assurance that only autotelic activities are rated high on intrinsic rewards. It is theoretically possible that people involved in repetitive activities would also rank the two intrinsic items first. This is, however,

Table 1. Rankings Given to Reasons for Enjoying Activity
(rock climbers, composers, modern dancers, chess players, basketball players; $N = 173$)

Rank		Mean	SD	Differs significantly from ranks (t test)*							
1	Enjoyment of the experience and use of skills	5.99	1.83	X	NS	3,	4,	5,	6,	7,	8
2	The activity itself: the pattern, the action, the world it provides	5.78	1.93		X	3[a],	4,	5,	6,	7,	8
3	Development of personal skills	5.38	1.91			X	4[a],	5,	6,	7,	8
4	Friendship, companionship	4.77	2.74				X	5,	6,	7,	8
5	Competition, measuring self against others	4.22	2.78					X	NS	NS	8
6	Measuring self against own ideals	3.81	2.03						X	NS	8
7	Emotional release	3.75	2.00							X	8
8	Prestige, regard, glamor	2.49	1.72								X

*Numbers marked [a] are significant at the .05 level; all others are significant at the .005 level.

extremely unlikely, since research indicates that workers derive little if any enjoyment from their occupations (see Walker and Guest, 1952; Chinoy, 1955; Berger, 1964; Ford, 1969; Gooding, 1972).

A further inspection of Table 1 indicates that "prestige, regard, glamor," which we considered the most extrinsic item, was also listed least important, significantly lower than the remaining seven items. "Competition," however, was in fifth rather than the anticipated seventh place. The respondents felt that "emotional release" and "measuring self against own ideal" were less important than competition as sources of reward. As will become clear later, competition presents a complex problem: for some activities it is definitely an important reward, while for others it is perceived as a negative feature.

After the two "intrinsic" reasons, the one that received the highest score was "development of personal skills." Each activity apparently allows the participant to refine his abilities in a particular area, to increase his control of a given aspect of the environment. The importance of this feature will be stressed again and again by the findings in the following sections. In fourth place among the sources of reward was the "friendship and companionship" that one experiences in the activity; again, this is a concomitant of situations which are satisfying, although there are large differences among activities in this respect.

Despite the very strong agreement in the sample as a whole about what provides enjoyment, some activities offer relatively more rewards of one kind than others. For instance, camaraderie is important in a team sport like basketball, or in rock climbing, where one person's life is in the hands of his companions; it is less salient to dancers or to composers, who work in solitude. Table 2 shows how the various groups ranked the sources of enjoyment which the activity offers. Five of the six rated the two intrinsic rewards highest; the sixth group, the basketball players, rated competition and the development of skills more highly. In light of recurring differences between basketball players and the other five groups, it should be mentioned that they were both the youngest (17 years on the average, versus 26 years for male chess players and modern dancers,

Table 2. Ranking of Mean Rank Scores Given to Reasons for Enjoying Activity, by Groups*

	Rock Climbers	Composers	Dancers	Male Chess	Female Chess	Basketball
1. Enjoyment of the experience and use of skills	1a	1.5a	1.5a	1a	1a	5a′
2. The activity itself: the pattern, the action, the world it provides	2a	1.5a′	1.5b	2b′a	2	4b′a
3. Friendship, companionship	3a	6.5a′b′	6a′b	4a	4.5a	3a
4. Development of personal skills	4a	3a	3a′	3	3a′	2
5. Measuring self against own ideals	6a	4ba	5a	6a	6.5a′	6b′
6. Emotional release	5a	5a	4c	7bc′	6.5a′c′	8a′b′c′
7. Competition, measuring self against others	7ab′	8b	8b	5a′cb′	4.5a′b′d′	1a′c′b′d′
8. Prestige, regard, glamor	8a	6.5a′b	7a′b	8a′b	8a′b	7a′b′
Total Autotelic Rank	3a	1a	2a	4a′b	5a′b	6a′b′

*Mean ranks marked *a* are significantly different from those marked *a′*, *b* from *b′*, and so on, by *t* test. For instance item 1 (Enjoyment . . .) was ranked the same way by the first five groups, but significantly lower by the basketball players. On item 2 (The activity . . .), rock climbers, male chess players, and basketball players were significantly different from composers; dancers were significantly different from basketball players.

28 for rock climbers, 37 for composers, and 39 for female chess players) and the lowest in socioeconomic status. Because the tendency to find intrinsic enjoyment is positively related to age, to father's income, and to education (as reported below), the deviant pattern of the basketball players might be explained by their youth and their relative economic deprivation. Possibly, however, the pattern reflects the activity, rather than the players' background. In other words, basketball, or other competitive sports, may provide a reward structure in which enjoyment comes from measuring oneself against others and from developing one's skills, rather than from experiencing the activity itself. Which of these two explanations fits the facts better is a question for future research.

Returning to Table 2, we note a number of further differences. Friendship is perceived as significantly less enjoyable by composers and dancers than by the four other groups; composers are further differentiated from dancers in holding friendship less important. Again, perhaps these two artistic activities attract people who are less interested in companionship; or perhaps composing and dancing do not offer opportunities for camaraderie. Both explanations are in accord with what is known about artists in general (Csikszentmihalyi and Getzels, 1973).

Development of skills, which is very important for basketball players relative to the rest of their scores, does not differentiate this group from the others. The female chess players and dancers—the two groups of women, in fact—rated this aspect of their activity as more enjoyable than rock climbers and composers did. Perhaps for women who are expert in a public activity, the ability to develop skills is relatively more important, since traditional feminine roles are usually private (Arendt, 1958) and offer few opportunities for demonstrating skills in a universalistic context.

Emotional release is most enjoyable to dancers and least enjoyable to basketball players. This finding may reflect the relatively regimented environment in which basketball is practiced in high school.

Competition is the least important feature to the two

artistic groups, while it is the most salient one for basketball players. The two chess groups also enjoy competition, although it is relatively less important for them. This item clearly reflects the structure of the various activities: basketball and chess are zero-sum activities; that is, every victory must be paid for with a defeat. The other three activities do not depend on loss to balance success, at least not directly.

To get an overall rating of intrinsic rewards, we added the scores on the two first items ("enjoyment of the experience" and "the activity itself") and then subtracted the last two items ("competition" and "prestige") from that sum. The resulting "autotelic" score represents the relative importance of intrinsic rewards for the various groups. As Table 2 (bottom line) shows, the two artistic groups are highest on the autotelic component, and rock climbers are third. The three groups involved in zero-sum activities are lower, and the basketball players are in turn significantly less autotelic than chess players of either sex.

These internal differences among the groups should not obscure the fact that *all* the participants in the various activities are motivated primarily by intrinsic rewards. It is only in comparison with composers or climbers that chess players prove to be significantly less autotelic. They are, however, still motivated to devote time to chess because the activity provides an enjoyable experience. The case of basketball players is less clear. Their involvement may be at least partly motivated by hope of upward social mobility, to which their game is a means. This possibility was confirmed by the interviews. In this context of external reinforcement, enjoyment seems to come more from the acquisition of concrete skills tested in a competitive framework than from within the activity itself.

Another way of comparing the sources of reward offered by the various activities is to correlate the rankings in Table 2. When this is done, it becomes clear that male and female chess players perceive the rewards of their game in almost identical terms. The mean ranks of the two groups correlate $r = .98$ ($p < .005$). A similar identity of views obtains between composers and dancers ($r = .96$, $p < .005$). Rock climbers are most similar in their rankings to male chess players and dancers ($p < .01$), and are somewhat similar to female chess players and composers ($p < .05$). The rankings of basketball players are different from those of the other five groups (no significant correlations). These patterns of relationship again suggest that there is a considerable overlap in what makes widely different autotelic activities enjoyable.

If the ability to derive autotelic rewards from an activity is one of the keys to intrinsic motivation, then it becomes important to know what characteristics of the respondent are related to this ability. The task of finding replicable correlations to an autotelic orientation, however, proved to be almost impossible. The pattern within each group was different enough to preclude overall generalizations. A few tentative findings that hold true across the groups are that older people, females, and those with higher socioeconomic backgrounds and education will tend to perceive intrinsic rewards as more important. The correlation coefficients between age, sex, father's occupation, and respondent's highest academic degree, on the one hand, and the tendency to rank autotelic rewards higher, on the other, had probability values of less than .01, .05, .005, and .01, respectively. This pattern may indicate simply a social-acceptability factor, according to which a higher-SES respondent will be sophisticated enough to stress the more autotelic answers because these are deemed more appropriate. A more likely explanation is that autotelic reasons for involvement do in fact become stronger as one grows older and more affluent. Such a relationship fits a "hierarchy of needs" theory like the one advanced by Maslow (1954, 1962), which states that a person cannot become concerned with self-actualization until more basic needs—safety, esteem, and so forth—are satisfied. Our data suggest that one can more easily respond to intrinsic rewards when one has not been deprived of extrinsic rewards.

Other variables tended to show more complex relationships with the ability to obtain autotelic rewards. The competence of the person in the given activity, for instance, was generally not associated with intrinsic satisfactions, although the better male chess players and composers rated "competition" as significantly more enjoyable than the less proficient ones did.

We also asked the respondents whether their involvement in the activity was presently decreasing, staying the same, or increasing. Composers whose involvement was increasing rated enjoyment of the activity as more important ($p < .05$), and competition as less important ($p < .025$), compared with those who were decreasing their involvement. By contrast, basketball players who were becoming more active rated enjoyment of the experience and the use of skills to be *less* important ($p < .005$), and measuring themselves against their own ideal more important rewards ($p < .005$), than their less active colleagues. Apparently, to become more involved in a basically autotelic activity such as composing, a person needs to be responsive to intrinsic rewards; the opposite may be true for increased participation in an activity which is relatively less autotelic to begin with.

The data presented thus far suggest a number of points which must be kept in mind if one is to understand intrinsic motivation. In the first place, it seems useful to make a distinction between autotelic *activities*, autotelic *personalities*, and autotelic *experiences*. These three concepts empirically overlap, but they should be separated at least at the level of analysis.

Autotelic activities are patterns of action which maximize immediate, intrinsic rewards to the participant. While presumably one may derive enjoyment from *any* activity, some forms are much more suited to the purpose. The six groups dealt with in this chapter were expected to be outstanding examples of the sort, and the data have confirmed this fact. The data have also indicated, however, that activities are located on an autotelic continuum. A sport or an occupation is neither absolutely autotelic nor absolutely exotelic; rather, it provides a variable amount of intrinsic and extrinsic rewards. Among our groups composing seems to provide the strongest intrinsic rewards, high school basketball the weakest; yet both are pursued for their own sake and are hence essentially autotelic.

In many cases the same activity may provide strong extrinsic rewards in addition to strong intrinsic ones. In our sample the composers were the most autotelic people, but they were also the only ones who could earn money and prestige from their work. A similar group are surgeons, on whom we shall report later. Some researchers have recently argued that experimental subjects who are rewarded extrinsically for an enjoyable task take less pleasure in the activity and become less involved in it (Lepper, Greene, and Nisbett, 1973). Their findings suggest that enjoyment can be turned into drudgery if someone from the outside rewards behavior which was formerly pursued for its own sake—presumably because the reward indicates that someone besides the actor is evaluating, and is hence in control of, the actor's behavior (Deci, 1973). The present data suggest, however, that in real-life situations extrinsic and intrinsic rewards need not be in conflict. Money, status, or a sense of service can certainly enhance the enjoyment derived directly from the activity. The intrinsic dimension, however, also can be a powerful source of motivation, either alone or in conjunction with external rewards. And because intrinsic rewards are, at least potentially, less expensive and scarce than extrinsic ones, it is vital to understand what they are and how they work.

In addition to autotelic activities, we may speak of autotelic people. An autotelic person is one who is able to enjoy what he is doing regardless of whether he will get external rewards for it. In general, the amount of intrinsic pleasure a person derives from what he does depends on the structure of the activity. But some people apparently can enjoy the least autotelic of activities, whereas others need external incentives even to do things rife with intrinsic rewards. Therefore, we can assume that there is an autotelic personality variable which is orthogonal to the autotelic structure of the activity. So far, the data have shed very little light on what such a personality trait may look like. It seems, however, that age, sex, and social class affect one's ability to enjoy activities for their own sake. In addition, presumably a large number of other factors are involved. What these are we do not know. But it is important to find out, for the same reason that it is urgent to understand autotelic activities: a community that knows how to create autotelic personalities will be more happy and more efficient than one that relies only on external motivation.

It is true that, strictly speaking, autotelic *activities* and autotelic *personalities* are conceptual abstractions without independent ontological status. An activity is autotelic only insofar as people derive intrinsic satisfaction from it, and a person can be called autotelic only if he enjoys an activity. The only real empirical datum that bridges activities and people is the autotelic *experience.* An autotelic experience is a psychological state, based on concrete feedback, which acts as a reward in that it produces continuing behavior in the absence of other rewards. The reality of this experience permits us to conceive of autotelic activities and persons. So, we might say, an autotelic activity is one that usually provides autotelic experiences, and an autotelic person is one who tends to have such experiences. We cannot assume, however, that even the most universally enjoyable activity will be experienced as autotelic at any given time, or that a person who is usually most responsive to intrinsic rewards will enjoy a given experience.

This first foray into the nature of intrinsic rewards has begun to outline the dimensions of the phenomenon. We know that certain activities are differentially able to provide direct enjoyment and that different people are more or less able to derive enjoyment from the same activity. But we have not yet touched on the central questions: What are autotelic experiences? How do activities make autotelic experiences possible? A systematic answer to these questions will have to wait until Part II of this volume, where the analysis of the interview material is presented.

In the meantime, the following chapter describes the structure of intrinsically rewarding activities, as revealed by the participants' answers to the questionnaire. It is a further step in trying to understand why some patterns of action are able to give people enjoyment out of all proportion to conventional rewards.

Chapter 3

Structure of Autotelic Activities

▲▲▲

Much has been written about intrinsic motivation, but very little is known about what exactly produces it. For centuries men have found enjoyment in chess, in tennis, in singing, and in hundreds of other activities. Is there a common experience of "fun" that all these activities produce? Or is each activity the source of its own unique experience, unrelated to others? What is even more basic, we do not know how various activities make the experience of enjoyment possible.

One of the earliest answers to this last question was proposed by Groos (1901) and elaborated by Bühler (1930). They advanced the concept of *Funktionlust,* the pleasurable sensation that an organism experiences when it is functioning according to its physical and sensory potential. This is also the kind of explanation implicit in Piaget's writings. Murphy (1947, p. 425) describes this form of enjoyment as a sensory experience involving sight, sound, or muscle sense and prompting delight and curiosity; he posits the existence of *sensory* and *activity drives* to account for the feeling of pleasure. Any activity, then, will be experienced as rewarding if it allows one to use his sensory and physical potential in a novel or challenging way.

The notion that a stimulus—and, by extension, an activity—must contain novelty in order to be enjoyable has been developed by Hebb (1955) and Berlyne (1960). From their work arose the concept of an optimal level of stimulation which organisms seek to attain. According to this position, a person will enjoy an activity if it offers a pattern of stimulation not ordinarily available in the person's environment. Novel stimuli provide enjoyable sensations to a nervous system that is burdened by repetitive information.

White (1959) and De Charms (1968) explain intrinsic motivation somewhat differently. According to these authors, the basic issue is whether a person feels that he himself has originated an act, or whether he feels forced to do it because of external constraints. In the former case, he will enjoy the activity; in the latter, he will experience it as drudgery. There is research support for this hypothesis (Deci, 1971; Lepper, Greene, and Nisbett, 1973), and it certainly fits what philosophers have said in the past; namely, that freedom is the essential criterion of an enjoyable act. It is for this reason that thinkers like Heraclitus, Plato, Nietzsche, and Sartre have held play in such high esteem: play is activity that one is free to enter and free to leave.

None of these approaches—*Funktionlust,* need for an optimal level of stimulation, or the desire to be a cause—really explains specifically why some things are enjoyable and others are not. With their help we know that an enjoyable activity must involve a person's physical, sensory, or intellectual skills; and it must give the actor a feeling of being in control of his actions. But these criteria are still too abstract and too general to help us describe autotelic activities, let alone understand them.

One writer who has tried to develop a classification of autotelic activities is the French anthropologist Roger Callois.

On the basis of extensive readings in historical and ethnological sources, he concludes that intrinsically rewarding activities are ways to satisfy four central human needs (Callois, 1958). One is competition; hence the popularity of all the games, sports, and various religious or political rituals in which men pit themselves against each other. A second need, the need to control the unpredictable, generates games of chance, forms of divination, astrology, and other ways of trying to beat the odds. A third dimension is the human desire to transcend limitations through fantasy, pretense, disguise; these efforts, which Callois calls "mimicry," are manifested in the dance, the theater, and the arts in general, as well as by the little girl playing with her doll or by her brother pretending to be a cowboy. Finally, in a "vertigo" category, Callois classifies activities involving danger or loss of consciousness; such activities–skiing, mountain climbing, and various forms of intoxication–allow man to transcend his limitations by altering his state of consciousness. Most activities are not "pure" examples of any one category but a mixture of two or more. Downhill skiing, for instance, fits both the competitive and the vertigo needs at the same time.

In some ways Callois's model shares the assumptions of the other explanations of intrinsic rewards. He also believes that pleasure comes from exercising one's skills in novel situations and in freedom. But his model is given philosophical coherence by the underlying assumption that all such activities are ways for people to test the limits of their being, to transcend their former conception of self by extending skills and undergoing new experiences. His use of the four categories is elegant and thought-provoking; but, like any neat typology, such a system might close off investigation instead of stimulating it.

Our own attempt to describe the structure of autotelic activities was to a certain extent influenced by Callois's categories. We started by developing a list of twenty items, each consisting of a common activity. Then we asked respondents to check whether their feelings during a typical bout of their own activity were very similar, neutral, different, or very different with respect to the twenty experiences listed. The list included examples from Callois's four categories; for example "running a race" is competitive, "playing a slot machine" involves chance, "watching a movie" is mimicry, and vertigo is represented by items like "taking a high dive" and "taking drugs." In addition, some items not readily classified by Callois's scheme were added—items such as "assembling equipment," "exploring a strange place," and "designing or discovering something new." We devised this checklist to find out whether participants in each autotelic activity would agree about the kinds of experiences that their activity provides. Would climbers emphasize vertigo experiences? Would composers and dancers emphasize mimicry? Would chess and basketball players emphasize competitive experiences? Or perhaps all our groups would describe the same experience, or perhaps no patterns of any kind would emerge.

Our first step, however, was to do a factor analysis to find out whether the respondents differentiated the twenty items into meaningful groupings. The five factors that emerged lent support to Callois's typology but also suggested some important changes. The strongest grouping (36 percent of the variance) was a cluster which brought together items like "being with a good friend" and items like "watching a good movie" and "reading an enjoyable book." In other words, warm interpersonal experiences were seen as similar to reading, listening to music, and watching movies. The whole cluster in turn was perceived to be different from the remaining items. We called this first factor *Friendship and Relaxation,* although it contains items that Callois might classify as mimicry. The second factor combines items that Callois would classify under vertigo and chance. "Taking drugs" is seen as similar to "playing a slot machine," and both are like "exposing oneself to radiation to prove one's theory" and "entering a burning house to save a child." We called this factor *Risk and Chance.* The next cluster contains four items which we labeled *Problem Solving,* since they deal with purposeful, goal-directed action: "solving a mathematical problem," "assembling equipment," "playing poker," and "exploring a strange place." Two items related to *Competition* load on the next factor. The last contains only one item, "designing or discovering something new," which appears to be a unique experience, different from the others; this item represents a *Creative* dimension. Our factor analysis, then, showed that participants in autotelic activities do discriminate among various forms of experience and that they order the range of such experiences in five main clusters, which overlap to a certain extent with the categories that Callois constructed.

But which of these categories reflect the experiences of the various activities, and which do not? Table 3 shows the rankings of the eighteen items which loaded in the factor analysis. Although there are some strong similarities among the groups (the rankings of dancers and rock climbers are correlated .76, $p < .005$; male and female chess players .73, $p < .005$), the differences are even more noticeable. This is as one would expect, since the respondents were describing very different activities. Rock climbers, for instance, see their experience as being most like exploring a strange place, designing or discovering something new, and being with a good friend. Basketball players find what they are doing most comparable to playing a competitive sport, running a race, and listening to music.

In general, the pattern fits rather well what one might expect. Each group listed "cramming for a boring course" (an item not included in Table 3 because it did not load on any factor) as the experience most unlike the one they are usually involved with; "playing a slot machine" was the next most unlikely experience for most of the groups. The chess players and the basketball players ranked "playing a competitive sport" among the three most similar experiences, reflecting the common competitive nature of their activity; but the chess players listed "solving a mathematical problem" in second place, whereas the basketball players ranked "running a race," thereby differentiating the intellectual from the athletic dimensions. Composers and dancers agreed in ranking "designing or discovering something new" and "listening to good music" among the top three, but they differed in their remaining choice: "solving a mathematical problem" for composers; "exploring a strange place" for dancers.

Perhaps the most striking agreement is about the creative and problem-solving dimensions, which were marked high by all

Table 3. Ranking of Similarity of Experience Items Within Each Autotelic Activity (Based on Mean Rank Scores)

Factors	Rock Climbers $N = 30$	Composers $N = 22$	Dancers $N = 27$	Male Chess $N = 30$	Female Chess $N = 22$	Basketball $N = 40$
1. *Friendship and Relaxation*						
Making love	6	6.5	4.5	16.5	17.5	14
Being with good friend	3	9	4.5	9	14.5	8
Watching a good movie	15.5	5	9	12	17.5	6
Listening to good music	6	3	2	10	12.5	3
Reading an enjoyable book	8	8	6.5	5	12.5	15.5
2. *Risk and Chance*						
Swimming too far out on a dare	13	13.5	15	14	7	17.5
Exposing yourself to radiation to prove your theory	17	10	12	12	10	9.5
Driving too fast	10	16.5	12	12	10	6
Taking drugs	10	13.5	15	15	14.5	9.5
Playing a slot machine	18	18	15	18	16	17.5
Entering a burning house to save a child	13	11	12	16.5	10	4
3. *Problem Solving*						
Solving a mathematical problem	4	2	9	1.5	2	12
Assembling equipment	13	6.5	17	7.5	7	15.5
Exploring a strange place	1	4	3	4	4	12
Playing poker	15.5	13.5	18	6	5	12
4. *Competition*						
Running a race	6	16.5	9	7.5	7	2
Playing a competitive sport	10	13.5	6.5	1.5	3	1
5. *Creative*						
Designing or discovering something new	2	1	1	3	1	6

groups except basketball players. Rock climbing is supposed to provide the experience of vertigo, dance that of mimicry; yet both groups ranked "designing or discovering something new" as a closer experience to their activity than anything related to vertigo or mimicry. "Exploring a strange place" and "solving a mathematical problem" also were ranked high in similarity by most of the groups. The underlying similarity that cuts across these autotelic activities, regardless of their formal differences, is that they all give participants a sense of discovery, exploration, problem solution—in other words, a feeling of novelty and challenge.

It would be difficult to overemphasize the importance of this finding. The fact that some people climb mountains whereas others make up tunes at a piano or push chess pieces across a board is in a sense incidental to the fact that they are all exploring the limits of their abilities and trying to expand them. Whatever the specific structure of an autotelic activity is like, it seems that its most basic requirement is to provide a clear set of challenges. These can be of two types: the challenge of the unknown, which leads to discovery, exploration, problem solution, and which is essential to activities like composing, dancing, climbing, and chess; or the most concrete challenge of competition, which is important in activities like basketball.

One finding that deserves comment is the relative importance of the interpersonal items which load high on Factor 1. "Making love" and "being with a good friend" are seen as quite similar to the experiences of climbing, composing, and dancing. Apparently a warm feeling of closeness to others, or a loosening of ego boundaries, is important in at least some autotelic activities. This is not an unexpected finding, since the experience we are trying to describe is typically present in the state that Turner (1974) has called *communitas,* a state that exists when social roles are temporarily abolished and spontaneous interactions among people are encouraged—as in certain religious rituals, feasts, or initiation rites. The importance of this feeling of friendship, and consequent loss of self-centeredness, in the total structure of the autotelic experience will be illustrated in Part II, especially in the chapter devoted to rock climbing (Chapter Six).

As was shown in Chapter One, some activities, like composing and dancing, are perceived to give more intrinsic rewards than others, such as chess or basketball. Table 3 shows that this difference in the sources of reward corresponds to differences in the structure of the activities, as perceived by the participants. When the mean similarity scores for the eighteen items were contrasted by *t* tests across the six activities, 113 of the 153 possible comparisons, or 74 percent, showed a significant difference at least at the .05 level of probability. Thus, the groups varied considerably in their ranking of the items. For instance, the two groups of chess players and the basketball players (the three zero-sum activities) consistently rated the five items in the Friendship and Relaxation factor as resembling significantly less what they are doing than did the composers, dancers, and climbers (the three non-zero-sum activities). In other words, "making love" was seen as rather similar to the experience of composing, dancing, and climbing but as significantly less similar to playing chess and basketball. The least friendly and relaxing activity appears to be chess as practiced by women. This is not surprising, since women have to play chess under severe pressures in essentially all-male tournaments, where they are often patronized or condescended to. For the same reason, female chess players see their activity as much more risky than males do.

It might seem curious that rock climbing is perceived as less risky than basketball, since climbers routinely risk their lives and limbs. Perhaps the comparatively low risk rating is due to denial of the danger, which may be psychologically useful in order to pursue the sport. But climbing actually may be less risky, because the objective dangers force the participant to be more in control of his actions.

To find out whether there is a relationship between (a) the way a person perceives an activity and (b) the kind of reward he or she derives from it, we correlated the "autotelic" reward score (see Table 2, Chapter Two) with the items which describe the experience during performance of the activity. People who enjoy intrinsic rewards describe what they are doing as significantly less competitive and more creative than those who rely to a greater extent on external incentives. For instance, a person's autotelic reward score is positively related to his perception of the activity as being like "designing or discovering something new" ($p < .01$) and negatively related to "playing a competitive sport" ($p < .005$). People who enjoy intrinsic rewards also see their activity as more like "exploring a strange place" and less risky—although more like "taking drugs."

These results point to the convergence of autotelic activities, experiences, and people. Those who are involved in more creative and less competitive activities enjoy intrinsic rewards more. However, regardless of the activity, people who perceive what they are doing as primarily creative, rather than competitive, are also motivated by intrinsic rewards. The data at hand cannot elucidate these relationships more precisely. There is no way of knowing whether, for instance, a predisposition to enjoy intrinsic rewards precedes or follows the experience of an autotelic activity. All that can be said is that autotelic experiences tend to occur more frequently to people who are responsive to intrinsic rewards while they are engaged in activities which maximize such rewards. Personal-background variables do not affect appreciably the way a participant describes the activity, with a few scattered exceptions. For instance, older chess players feel that chess involves significantly less risk and chance than younger players do. Dancers as they grow older rate dancing as more like "solving a mathematical problem" ($p < .005$). But the effects are not consistent: rock climbers from higher-status families experience climbing as less like "solving a mathematical problem" ($p < .005$) than do climbers whose family origin is lower class, while the opposite is true of female chess players ($p < .005$) and composers ($p < .05$): for both these groups socioeconomic status is positively related to seeing their activity as being similar to "solving a mathematical problem."

In conclusion, the data tend to support the existing theories of intrinsic motivation. Most people describe the autotelic experience as involving creative discovery and exploration. The *Funktionlust* and the need-for-novelty models are congruent with this emphasis. Intrinsically rewarding experience requires involvement and active participation—even though of a sedentary intellectual kind, as in chess. The kind of interaction that produces autotelic experience is open-ended, and its outcome can be determined by the participant. It is not as predictable as a routine job, nor is it as unpredictable as reckless driving or slot machine playing. The outcome of an autotelic activity is uncertain ("like exploring a strange place"), but the actor is potentially capable of controlling it. This last characteristic relates our findings to De Charms's theory of inner causation.

Discovery and exploration imply transcendence, a going beyond the known, a stretching of one's self toward new dimensions of skill and competence. One direction in which transcendence is possible involves physical skill. Progress in this area can most easily be measured by competition; this is the route of basketball players. A more subtle way of establishing physical competence is by matching one's skill against a physical obstacle or against the boundaries of one's own competence. Rock climbers take this option. Another way of going beyond the given is by confronting intellectual problems. Again, one can do so competitively, as chess players do, or by struggling against internal obstacles, as composers do.

To this extent, Callois's typology seems to hold: autotelic experiences are based on activities which allow people to surpass their limitations in some domain of reality. But the detailed categories that Callois develops seem to need some revision. For instance, rock climbers ought to feel that what they do involves risks—the vertiginous alteration of consciousness of those who expose themselves to danger. Yet they place much more emphasis on discovery, problem solving, and relaxing interpersonal experiences. In fact, Callois's typology misses these three dimensions, which, at least in the samples we studied, are considered the main components of the autotelic experience.

If we summarize the means in Table 3 across the six groups, the five items with the highest overall scores are "designing or discovering something new," "exploring a strange place," "solving a mathematical problem," "playing a competitive sport," and "listening to good music." It would be rash to conclude that those items are the main components of all autotelic experiences. We did not get samples of people who enjoy gambling or other forms of chance, and a larger representation of competitive participants would almost certainly have changed the results. Also, and perhaps more important, respondents in a different culture or another historical period might have described the experience very differently.

Despite these qualifications, the outlines of intrinsically rewarding experience are becoming clearer. In Chapters Four through Eight the picture will become even more visible. There we present a theoretical model that specifies the essential characteristics of autotelic activities, and we use the interview material to illustrate the applicability of the model.

Chapter 4

A Theoretical Model for Enjoyment

▲▲▲

The interviews with participants in autotelic activities confirmed the questionnaire results. With near unanimity, respondents (even those who received extrinsic rewards for their activity: composers, chess champions, and surgeons) stated that they devoted time and effort to their activity because they gained a peculiar state of experience from it, an experience that is not accessible in "everyday life." In each case, intrinsic rewards appeared to overshadow extrinsic ones as the main incentives for pursuing the activity.

But what is this autotelic experience that motivates people to pattern their lives in ways so inimical to conventional wisdom? It is easier, at first, to say what the experience is not like. It is not boring, as life outside the activity often is. At the same time, it does not produce anxiety, which often intrudes itself on awareness in "normal" life. Poised between boredom and worry, the autotelic experience is one of complete involvement of the actor with his activity. The activity presents constant challenges. There is no time to get bored or to worry about what may or may not happen. A person in such a situation can make full use of whatever skills are required and receives clear feedback to his actions; hence, he belongs to a rational cause-and-effect system in which what he does has realistic and predictable consequences.

From here on, we shall refer to this peculiar dynamic state—the holistic sensation that people feel when they act with total involvement—as *flow.** In the flow state, action follows upon action according to an internal logic that seems to need no conscious intervention by the actor. He experiences it as a unified flowing from one moment to the next, in which he is in control of his actions, and in which there is little distinction between self and environment, between stimulus and response, or between past, present, and future. Flow is what we have been calling "the autotelic experience." There are two reasons for our changing names in midcourse. The first is relatively trivial: flow is less awkward than the former label. The second is more substantive: in calling an experience "autotelic," we implicitly assume that it has no external goals or external rewards; such an assumption is not necessary for flow. Later we shall see that one of the main traits of flow experiences is that they usually are, to a lesser or greater extent, autotelic—that is, people seek flow primarily for itself, not for the incidental extrinsic rewards that may accrue from it. Yet one may experience flow in any activity, even in some activities that seem least designed to give enjoyment—on the battlefront, on a factory assembly line, or in a concentration camp.

Flow is most readily experienced, however, in certain kinds of activities. The pursuits we studied—climbing, chess, basketball—are *flow activities* that seem to provide the corresponding (flow) experience. Games are obvious flow activities,

*The term *flow* is what anthropologists call a native category—a word frequently used by the informants themselves to describe the experience.

and play is the flow experience *par excellence.* Yet playing a game does not guarantee that one is experiencing flow, just as reciting the pledge of allegiance is no proof of patriotic feelings. Conversely, the flow experience can be found in activities other than games. One such activity is creativity in general, including art and science. The composers and dancers in our sample described their feelings in ways that did not differ substantially from the descriptions of climbers or chess players. Surgeons involved in medical research and mathematicians working on the frontiers of their field answered the interviews in terms that were almost interchangeable with those used by players. Almost any description of the creative experience (see, for example, Montmasson, 1932; Ghiselin, 1952; Dillon, 1972; Getzels and Csikszentmihalyi, 1975) includes experiential accounts that are in important respects analogous to those obtained from people at play.

Besides play and creativity, experiences analogous to flow have been reported in contexts usually called "transcendental" or "religious." Maslow's (1962, 1965, 1971) peak experiences and De Charms's (1968) "origin" state share many distinctive features with the flow process. The same is true of accounts of collective ritual (Deren, 1953; Worsley, 1968; Turner, 1969); of the practice of Zen, Yoga, and other forms of meditation (Herrigel, 1953, 1960; Eliade, 1969; Naranjo and Ornstein, 1971); or of practically any other form of religious experience (Laski, 1962; Rahner, 1967; Moltmann, 1972).

In a variety of human contexts, then, one finds a remarkably similar inner state, which is so enjoyable that people are sometimes willing to forsake a comfortable life for its sake. In many cases, the importance of this experience is blurred by what appear to be the external goals of the activity—the painting that the artist wants to create, the theory that the scientist strives to prove, or the grace of God that the mystic seeks to attain. On a closer look, these goals lose their substance and reveal themselves as mere tokens that justify the activity by giving it direction and determining rules of action. But the doing is the thing. We still have to hear of an artist who packed up his brushes after completing a painting, or even paid much attention to a canvas after it was finished; or of a scientist who felt rewarded enough by a discovery to cease his investigations. Achievement of a goal is important to mark one's performance but is not in itself satisfying. What keeps one going is the experience of acting outside the parameters of worry and boredom: the experience of flow.

Elements of Flow Experience

Perhaps the clearest sign of flow is the merging of action and awareness. A person in flow has no dualistic perspective: he is aware of his actions but not of the awareness itself. A tennis player pays undivided attention to the ball and the opponent, a chess master focuses on the strategy of the game, most states of religious ecstasy are reached through complex ritual steps; yet for flow to be maintained, one cannot reflect on the act of awareness itself. When awareness becomes split, so that one perceives the activity from "outside," flow is interrupted. Therefore, flow is difficult to maintain for any length of time without at least momentary interruptions. Typically, a person can maintain a merged awareness with his or her actions for only short periods, which are broken by interludes when he adopts an outside perspective. These interruptions occur when questions flash through the actor's mind: "Am I doing well?" "What am I doing here?" "Should I be doing this?" When one is in a flow episode (*in ludus* as opposed to *inter ludes*), these questions simply do not come to mind.

Steiner (1972, p. 94) gives an excellent account of how it feels to get out of the state of flow in chess, and then back into it again:

> The bright arcs of relation that weld the pieces into a phalanx, that make one's defense a poison-tipped porcupine shiver into vague filaments. The cords dissolve. The pawn in one's sweating hand withers to mere wood or plastic. A tunnel of inanity yawns, boring and bottomless. As from another world comes the appalling suggestion . . . that this is, after all, "only a game." If one entertains that annihilating proposition even for an instant, one is done for. (It

> seemed to flash across Boris Spassky's drawn features for a fraction of a second before the sixty-ninth move of the thirteenth game.) Normally, the opponent makes his move and in that murderous moment addiction comes again. New lines of force light up in the clearing haze, the hunched intellect straightens up and takes in the sweep of the board, cacophony subsides, and the instruments mesh into unison.

For action to merge with awareness to such an extent, the activity must be feasible. Flow seems to occur only when tasks are within one's ability to perform. That is why one experiences flow most often in activities with clearly established rules for action, such as rituals, games, or participatory art forms like the dance.

Here are a few quotes from our interviews with people engaged in flow-producing activities. Their words illustrate what the merging of action and awareness means in different cases.

An outstanding chess player: "The game is a struggle, and the concentration is like breathing—you never think of it. The roof could fall in and, if it missed you, you would be unaware of it."

An expert rock climber: "You are so involved in what you are doing [that] you aren't thinking of yourself as separate from the immediate activity. . . . You don't see yourself as separate from what you are doing."

A dancer describing how it feels when a performance is going well: "Your concentration is very complete. Your mind isn't wandering, you are not thinking of something else; you are totally involved in what you are doing. Your body feels good. You are not aware of any stiffness. Your body is awake all over. No area where you feel blocked or stiff. Your energy is flowing very smoothly. You feel relaxed, comfortable, and energetic."

A basketball player from a state-champion high school team: "The only thing that really goes through my mind is winning the game. I really don't have to think, though. When I am playing, it just comes to me. It's a good feeling. Everything is working out—working smooth." And one of his teammates: "When I get hot in a game . . . like I said, you don't think about it at all. If you step back and think about why you are so hot, all of a sudden you get creamed."

In some activities, the concentration is sustained for incredible lengths of time. A woman world-champion marathon swimmer has this to say: "For example, I swam in a twenty-four-hour race last summer. You dive in at 3 P.M. on Saturday and you finish at 3 P.M. on Sunday, it's 49 degrees in the water, and you are not allowed to touch the boat or the shore. . . . I just keep thinking about keeping my stroke efficient . . . and, you know, thinking about the strategy of the race and picking up for a little while and then ease off, things like that. . . . Every once in a while, just because of the long time, your mind wanders. Like I'll wake up and say, 'Oh, I haven't been thinking about it for a while!' "

This merging of action and awareness is made possible by a second characteristic of flow experiences: a centering of attention on a limited stimulus field. To ensure that people will concentrate on their actions, potentially intruding stimuli must be kept out of attention. Some writers have called this process a "narrowing of consciousness," a "giving up the past and the future" (Maslow, 1971, pp. 63-65). One respondent, a university professor in science who climbs rock, phrased it as follows: "When I start on a climb, it is as if my memory input has been cut off. All I can remember is the last thirty seconds, and all I can think ahead is the next five minutes."

This is what various chess experts say: "When the game is exciting, I don't seem to hear nothing—the world seems to be cut off from me and all there is to think about is my game." "I am less aware of myself and my problems . . . at times, I see only the positions. I am aware of spectators only in the beginning, or if they annoy me." "If I am busting a much weaker player, I may just think about the events of the day. During a good game, I think over various alternatives to the game—nothing else." "Problems are suspended for the duration of the tournament except those that pertain to it. Other people and things seem to have less significance."

The same experience is reported by basketball players: "The court—that's all that matters. . . . Sometimes on court I think of a problem, like fighting with my steady girl, and I think that's nothing compared to the game. You can think about a problem all day but as soon as you get in the game, the hell with it!" "Kids my age, they think a lot . . . but when you are playing basketball, that's all there is on your mind—just basketball . . . everything seems to follow right along."

A dancer describes this centering-of-attention experience in the following way: "I get a feeling that I don't get anywhere else. . . . I have more confidence in myself than at any other time. Maybe an effort to forget my problems. Dance is like therapy. If I am troubled about something, I leave it out the door as I go in [the dance studio]."

And a woman composer of modern music says virtually the same thing: "I am really quite oblivious to my surroundings after I really get going. I think that the phone could ring, and the doorbell could ring, or the house burn down, or something like that. . . . When I start working, I really do shut out the world. Once I stop, I can let it back in again."

In games, rules define the relevant stimuli and exclude everything else as irrelevant. But rules alone are not always enough to get a person involved with the game. Hence, the structure of games provides motivational elements which will draw the player into play. Perhaps the simplest of these inducements is competition. The addition of a competitive element to a game usually ensures the undivided attention of a player who would not be motivated otherwise. When being "beaten" is one of the possible outcomes of an activity, the actor is pressured to attend to it more closely. Another inducement is the possibility of material gains. It is usually easier to sustain flow in simple games, such as poker, when gambling is added to the rules. But the payoff is rarely the goal of a gambler. As Dostoevsky (quoted in Freud, 1959) clearly observed about his own compulsion in a letter to A. M. Maikov (Aug. 16, 1867), "The main thing is the play itself, I swear that greed for money has nothing to do with it, although heaven knows I am sorely in need of money." Finally, certain play activities rely on physical danger to produce centering of attention, and hence flow. Such is rock climbing, where one is forced to ignore all distracting stimuli by the knowledge that survival is dependent on complete concentration.

The addition of spurious motivational elements to a flow activity (competition, gain, danger) makes it also more vulnerable to intrusions from "outside reality." Playing for money may increase concentration on the game, but paradoxically one can also be more easily distracted from play by the fear of losing. A Samurai swordsman concerned about winning will be beaten by an opponent who is not thus distracted. Ideally, flow is the result of pure involvement, without any consideration about results. In practice, however, most people need some inducement to participate in flow activities, at least at the beginning, before they learn to be sensitive to intrinsic rewards.

In occupations, as opposed to flow activities, extrinsic rewards are usually of the foremost importance. Most jobs would not be done unless people were paid for doing them. But occupations can be greatly enriched if the pattern of action they require provides flow experiences. The best example of such an occupation is surgery, reported in Chapter Eight. When a "job" has some of the characteristics of a flow activity, intrinsic motivation to perform it seems to become a powerful incentive added to that provided by extrinsic rewards.

A third characteristic of flow experiences has been variously described as "loss of ego," "self-forgetfulness," "loss of self-consciousness," and even "transcendence of individuality" and "fusion with the world" (Maslow, 1971, pp. 65, 70). When an activity involves the person completely with its demands for action, "self-ish" considerations become irrelevant. The self (Mead, 1934) or the ego (Freud, 1927) has traditionally been conceived of as an intrapsychic mechanism which mediates between the needs of the organism and the social demands placed upon it. A primary function of the self is to integrate one person's actions with that of others; hence, it is a prerequisite for social life (Berger and Luckmann, 1967). Activities which allow flow to occur (activities such as games, rituals, or art), however, usually do not require any negotiation. Since they are based on freely accepted rules, the player does not need to use a self to get along in the activity. As long as all the participants follow the same rules, there is no need to negotiate roles. The participants need no self to bargain with about what should or should not be done. As long as the rules are respected, a flow situation is a social system with no deviance (Csikszentmihalyi and Bennett, 1971).

Self-forgetfulness does *not* mean, however, that in flow a person loses touch with his own physical reality. In some flow activities, perhaps in most, one becomes more intensely aware of internal processes. This heightened awareness obviously occurs in Yoga and many religious rituals. Climbers report a great increase in kinesthetic sensations, a sudden increase in ordinarily unconscious muscular movements. Chess players are very aware of the working of their own minds during games. What is usually lost in flow is not the awareness of one's body or of one's functions, but only the self *construct,* the intermediary which one learns to interpose between stimulus and response.

Here are some quite different ways in which rock climbers describe this state:

> The task at hand is so demanding and rich in its complexity and pull that the conscious subject is really diminished in intensity. Corollary of that is that all the hangups that people have or that I have as an individual person are momentarily obliterated. . . . It's one of the few ways I have found to . . . live outside my head.

> One tends to get immersed in what is going on around him, in the rock, in the moves that are involved . . . search for handholds . . . proper position of body—so involved he might lose the consciousness of his own identity and melt into the rock.

> It's like when I was talking about things becoming "automatic" . . . almost like an egoless thing in a way—somehow the right thing is done without . . . thinking about it or doing anything at all. . . . It just happens . . . and yet you're more concentrated. It might be like meditation, like Zen is a concentration. One thing you are after is one-pointedness of mind, the ability to focus your mind to reach something.

> You become a robot—no, more like an animal. It's pleasant. There is a feeling of total involvement. . . . You feel like a panther powering up the rock.

The same experience is reported by people involved in creative activities. An outstanding composer has this to say about how he feels when he is writing music: "You yourself are in an ecstatic state to such a point that you feel as though you almost don't exist. I've experienced this time and time again. My hand seems devoid of myself, and I have nothing to do with what is happening. I just sit there watching it in a state of awe and wonderment. And it just flows out by itself." And a chess player says: "Time passes a hundred times faster. In this sense, it resembles the dream state. A whole story can unfold in seconds, it seems. Your body is nonexistent—but actually your heart pumps like mad to supply the brain."

Still another characteristic of a person in flow is that he is in control of his actions and of the environment. He has no active awareness of control but is simply not worried by the possibility of lack of control. Later, in thinking back on the experience, he will usually conclude that, for the duration of the flow episode, his skills were adequate for meeting environmental demands; and this reflection might become an important component of a positive self-concept.

A dancer expresses well this paradoxical feeling of simultaneously being in control and being merged with the environment: "If I have enough space, I am in control. I feel I can radiate an energy into the atmosphere. It's not always necessary that another human being be there to catch that energy. I can dance for walls, I can dance for floors. . . . I don't know if it's usually a control of the atmosphere. I become one with the atmosphere." Another dancer says: "A strong relaxation and calmness comes over me. I have no worries of failure. What a powerful and warm feeling it is! I want to expand, hug the world. I feel enormous power to effect something of grace and beauty."

In chess, basketball, and other competitive activities the feeling of control comes both from one's own performance and from the ability to outperform the opponent. Here are a few chess players: "I get a tyrannical sense of power. I feel immensely strong, as though I have the fate of another human in my grasp. I want to kill!" "I like getting lost in an external situation and forgetting about personal crap—I like being in control." "Although I am not aware of specific things, I have a general feeling of well-being, and that I am in complete control of my world."

In nonflow states, such a feeling of control is difficult to sustain for any length of time. There are too many imponderables. Personal relationships, career obstacles, health problems —not to mention death and taxes—are always to a certain extent beyond control.

Even when the sense of control comes from defeating another person, the player often sees it as a victory over his own limitations, rather than over the opponent. A basketball player says: "I feel in control. Sure. I've practiced and have a good feeling for the shots I can make. . . . I don't feel in control of the other player—even if he's bad and I know where to beat him. It's me and not him that I'm working on." An ace handball player also stresses this notion of control over self: "Well, I have found myself at times when I have super concentration in a game whereby nothing else exists—nothing exists except the act of participating and swinging the ball. [The other player must] be there to play the game, but I'm not concerned with him. I'm not competing with him at that point. I'm attempting to place the ball in the perfect spot, and it has no bearing on winning or losing."

Flow experiences occur in activities where one can cope, at least theoretically, with all the demands for action. In a chess game, for instance, everything is potentially controllable. A player need not fear that the opponent's move will produce any threats except those allowed by the rules.

The feeling of control and the resulting absence of worry are present even in flow situations where "objectively" the dangers to the actor are quite real. The famous British rock climber Chris Bonington describes the experience very well: "At the start of any big climb I feel afraid, dread the discomfort and danger I shall have to undergo. It's like standing on the edge of a cold swimming pool trying to nerve yourself to take the plunge; yet once [you are] in, it's not nearly as bad as you have feared; *in fact, it's enjoyable. . . . Once I start climbing, all my misgivings are forgotten.* The very harshness of the surroundings, the treacherous layer of verglas covering every hold, even the high-pitched whine of falling stones, all help build up the tension and excitement that are ingredients of mountaineering" (Quoted in Unsworth, 1969; italics added).

Although the dangers in rock climbing and similar activities are genuine, they are foreseeable and hence predictable and manageable; a person can work up to mastering them. Practically every climber says that driving a car is more dangerous than the incredible acrobatic feats on the rock, and in a sense it may be true: when one is driving a car, the elements outside his control are more numerous and dangerous than in climbing. In any case, a sense of control is definitely one of the most important components of the flow experience, whether or not an "objective" assessment justifies such feeling.

Another quality of the flow experience is that it usually contains coherent, noncontradictory demands for action and provides clear, unambiguous feedback to a person's actions. These components of flow, like the preceding ones, are made possible because one's awareness is limited to a restricted field of possibilities. In the artificially reduced reality of a flow episode, one clearly knows what is "good" and what is "bad." Goals and means are logically ordered. A person is not expected to do incompatible things, as he is in real life. He or she knows what the results of various possible actions will be. A climber describes it as follows: "I think it's one of the few sorts of activities in which you don't feel you have all sorts of different kinds of demands, often conflicting, upon you. . . . You aren't really the master, but are moving with something else. That's part of where the really good feeling comes from. You are moving in harmony with something else, the piece of rock as well as the weather and scenery. You're part of it and thus lose some of the feeling of individual separation." In this description several elements of flow are combined: noncontradictory demands for the activity, the issue of control, and the feeling of egolessness.

But in flow, one does not stop to evaluate the feedback; action and reaction have become so well practiced as to be automatic. The person is too involved with the experience to reflect on it. Here is the clear account of a basketball player: "I play my best games almost by accident. I go out and play on the court and I can tell if I'm shooting O.K. or if I'm not—so I know if I'm playing good or like shit—but if I'm having a super game I can't tell until after the game. . . . Guys make fun of me because I can lose track of the score and I'll ask Russell what the score is and he'll tell me and sometimes it breaks people up—they think 'That kid must be real dumb.' " In other words, the flow experience differs from awareness in everyday reality because it contains ordered rules which make action and the evaluation of action automatic and hence unproblematic. When contradictory actions are made possible (for instance, when cheating is introduced into a game), the self reappears to negotiate between the conflicting definitions of what needs to be done, and the flow is interrupted.

A final characteristic of the flow experience is its "autotelic" nature. In other words, it appears to need no goals or rewards external to itself. Practically every writer who has dealt with play (for instance, Huizinga [1939] 1950; Piaget, 1951, 1965; Callois, 1958) has remarked on the autotelic nature of this activity. In the *Bhagavad Gita,* Lord Krishna instructs Arjuna to live his whole life according to this principle: "Let the motive be in the deed and not in the event. Be not one whose motive for action is the hope of reward."

A young poet who is also a seasoned climber describes the autotelic experience in words that would be difficult to improve on. It is from this person's interview that we borrowed the word *flow* to describe the autotelic experience—a word which we noticed recurring spontaneously in other respondents' reports. "The mystique of rock climbing is climbing; you get to the top of a rock glad it's over but really wish it would go forever. The justification of climbing is climbing, like the justification of poetry is writing; you don't conquer anything except things in yourself. . . . The act of writing justifies poetry. Climbing is the same: recognizing that you are a flow. The purpose of the flow is to keep on flowing, not looking for a peak or utopia but staying in the flow. It is not a moving up but a continuous flowing; you move up only to keep the flow going. There is no possible reason for climbing except the climbing itself; it is a self-communication."

A top woman chess player in the United States, although she receives a certain amount of fame and money, is still motivated primarily by the experience itself rather than by the extrinsic rewards: "The most rewarding thing is the competition, the satisfaction of pitting your mental prowess against someone else. . . . I've won . . . trophies and money . . . but considering expenses of entry fees, chess associations, et cetera, I'm usually on the losing side financially."

A medical doctor who has participated in many expeditions to the highest mountains on earth reflects on the need for extrinsic rewards: "The world has to look for a star, the whole time. . . . You don't look at the Milwaukee Bucks, you look at Jabbar, which is so wrong. It's so understandable, it's so childlike. It seems to me that an expedition should be totally beyond that. If I had my way, all expeditions would go secretly and come back secretly, and no one would ever know. Then that would have a sort of perfection about it, perhaps, or be more near to perfection."

A famous composer explains why he composes (after a long and hearty laugh at the "inanity of the question"): "One doesn't do it for money. One does it for, perhaps, the satisfaction it gives. I think the great composers, all the great artists, work for themselves, period. They don't give a damn for anybody else. They primarily satisfy themselves. . . . If you get any fame out of it, it's when you are dead and buried, so what the hell's the good of it. . . . This is what I tell my students. Don't expect to make money, don't expect fame or a pat on the back, don't expect a damn thing. Do it because you love it."

As the quoted statements show, the various elements of the flow experience are linked together and dependent on each other. By limiting the stimulus field, a flow activity allows people to concentrate their actions and ignore distractions. As a result, they feel in potential control of the environment. Because the flow activity has clear and noncontradictory rules, people who perform in it can temporarily forget their identity and its problems. The result of all these conditions is that one finds the process intrinsically rewarding.

Structure of Flow Activities

Some people can start a flow episode just by directing their awareness to conform with the requirements of flow, like limiting the stimulus field so as to allow the merging of action and awareness. But most people rely on external cues for getting into flow states, so we might speak of flow activities as those structured systems of action which usually help to produce flow experiences. Although one can enter flow while engaged in any activity, some situations (such as games, art, and rituals) appear to be designed almost exclusively to provide the experience of flow. It is therefore useful to begin a formal analysis that will answer the question: How do some activities make possible the experience of flow?

Despite vast differences among them, flow activities seem to share certain characteristics. More specifically, activities that reliably produce flow experiences are similar in that they provide opportunities for action which a person can act upon without being bored or worried. A more formal way of presenting this idea is illustrated in Figure 1. The model is based on the

Figure 1. Model of the Flow State. When a person believes that his action opportunities are too demanding for his capabilities, the resulting stress is experienced as anxiety; when the ratio of capabilities is higher, but the challenges are still too demanding for his skills, the experience is worry. The state of flow is felt when opportunities for action are in balance with the actor's skills; the experience is then autotelic. When skills are greater than opportunities for using them, the state of boredom results; this state again fades into anxiety when the ratio becomes too large.

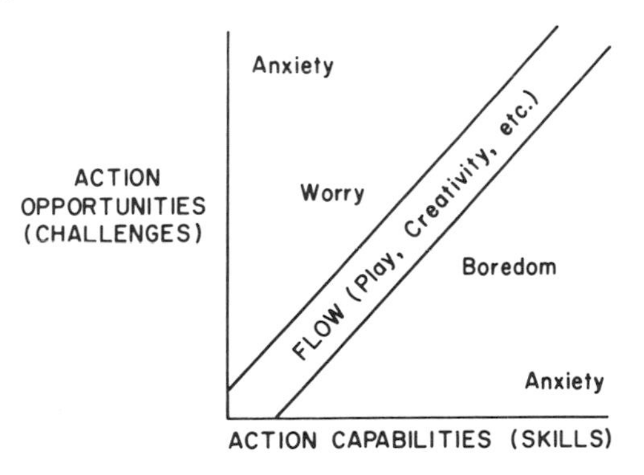

axiom that, at any given moment, people are aware of a finite number of opportunities which challenge them to act; at the same time, they are aware also of their skills—that is, of their capacity to cope with the demands imposed by the environment. When a person is bombarded with demands which he or she feels unable to meet, a state of anxiety ensues. When the demands for action are fewer, but still more than what the person feels capable of handling, the state of experience is one of worry. Flow is experienced when people perceive opportunities for action as being evenly matched by their capabilities. If, however, skills are greater than the opportunities for using them, boredom will follow. And finally, a person with great skills and few opportunities for applying them will pass from the state of boredom again into that of anxiety. It follows that a flow activity is one which provides optimal challenges in relation to the actor's skills.

From an empirical point of view, there are some clear limitations to the model. The problem is that a state of flow does not depend entirely on the objective nature of the challenges present or on the objective level of skills; in fact, whether one is in flow or not depends entirely on one's *perception* of what the challenges and skills are. With the same "objective" level of action opportunities, a person might feel anxious one moment, bored the next, and in a state of flow immediately afterward. In a given situation, therefore, it is impossible to predict with complete assurance whether a person will be bored or anxious or in a state of flow. Before the flow model can be empirically applied, then, we will have to identify those personality characteristics which make people underestimate or overestimate their own skills as well as the "objective" demands for action in the environment. In other words, we will have to acquire an understanding of the autotelic personality makeup, which we still lack. For a preliminary understanding of the flow experience, however, it is enough to consider the "objective" structure of the situation.

An example of one such situation is shown in Figure 2. In rock climbing, the challenge consists in the difficulties of the rock face—or pitch—which one is about to climb. Each climb,

Figure 2. Example of Flow and Nonflow Situations in Rock Climbing. Confronted with a rock face whose difficulty factor is classified F^7, climber A (a rock climber with F^4 skills) will feel worried; climber C (with F^{10} skills) will feel bored; and climber B (with F^6 skills) will experience flow. On a rock whose difficulty factor is F^{10}, A will feel anxious, B worried, and C in flow.

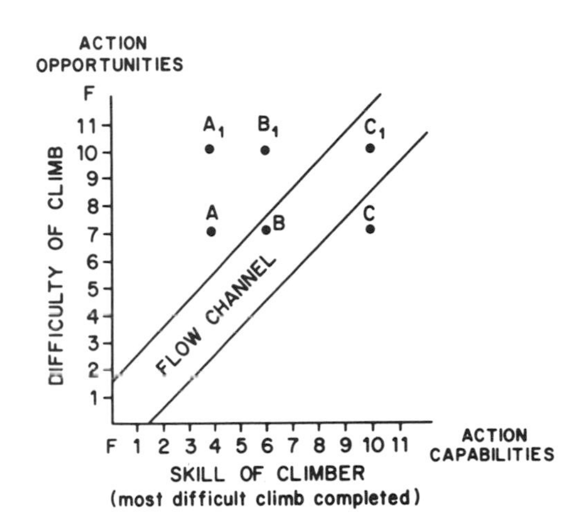

and each move in a climb, can be reliably rated in terms of the objective difficulties it presents. The generally adopted system of ratings ranges from F^1 (a scramble) to F^{11} (the limits of human potential). A climber's skills can also be rated on the same continuum, depending on the difficulty of the hardest climb he has completed. If the hardest climb a person ever did is rated F^6, skill level can also be expressed as F^6. In this case, we have fairly "objective" assessments of both coordinates. Figure 2 suggests some of the predictions one might make about the experiential state of a climber if one knows the rating of both the rock and the climber.

It should be stressed again that the prediction will be accurate only if the individuals involved perceive the difficulties and their own capabilities "objectively." Although this is never completely the case, it is a useful assumption. For instance, as Figure 2 suggests, F^4 climbers on an F^7 pitch will tend to be worried; on an F^{10} pitch they will be anxious. Similarly, people with F^{10} skills will be bored climbing an F^7 pitch—unless they decide to raise its challenges by adopting some tacit rule such as using only one arm, doing the climb without protection, or focusing their attention on new action possibilities (for instance, teaching a novice how to climb).

Rock climbing is a good flow activity because no single individual can master all the F^{11} pitches in the world and because even the same climb can be rendered more challenging by weather conditions or self-imposed handicaps. Athletics in general have theoretically unreachable ceilings, although record-breaking performances are nearing the asymptote. Other flow activities—such as art, creativity, and religious ecstasy—also have infinite ceilings and thus allow an indefinite increase in the development of skills or in the ability to organize experience.

Another type of flow activity is the game of chess. The skill of chess players is objectively measured by the United States Chess Federation ratings which each person earns as a result of performing in tournaments and championships. Chess, unlike rock climbing, is a competitive activity. In a chess game, therefore, the challenges a person faces do not originate in some material obstacle, like the difficulty of a rock face, but mainly in the skill of the opponent. A player with a USCF rating of 2000 when matched against one rated 2150 will be confronted with action opportunities in excess of capabilities of the order of 7.5 percent. Whether such a discrepancy in the challenge/skill ratio is enough to make the weaker player worried and the stronger one bored is, of course, impossible to tell in advance. Since each individual undoubtedly has his own threshold for entering and leaving the state of flow, the bands that delimit the state of flow from those of boredom and worry, in Figures 1 and 2, are only illustrative. For certain activities and for certain persons the band might be much narrower or much wider. The diagrams show only the direction of relationships, not the precise limits. The transition points remain to be determined empirically.

People in a state of worry can return to flow through an almost infinite combination of two basic vector processes: decreasing challenges or increasing skills (see Figure 3). If they choose the latter, the resulting flow state will be more complex

Figure 3. Two Ways of Experiencing Flow. Chess player A, with x level of skills, playing against someone at level y, will be worried. A person in such a situation can choose a number of ways to reenter the state of flow. For instance, he can insist on playing only against opponents of skill level x, or he can increase his own skills to level y; or the opponent can handicap himself until challenges match A's skill level at x. Flow state A_{yy} is more complex than flow state A_{xx} since the former involves the use of greater skills in overcoming greater challenges.

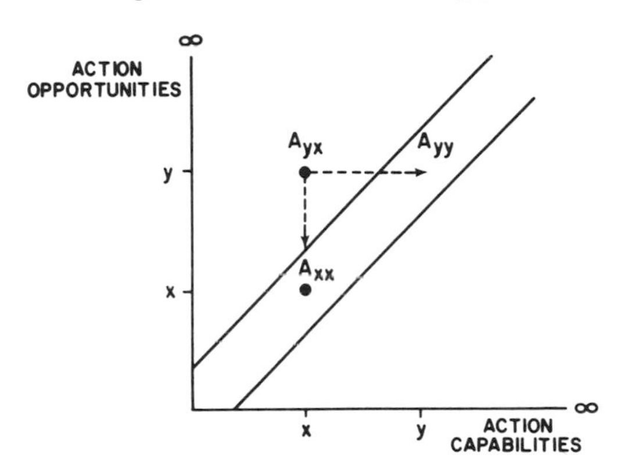

because it will involve more opportunities and a higher level of capabilities. Conversely, if one is bored one can return to flow either by finding a means to increase environmental challenges or by handicapping oneself and reducing the level of skills. The second choice is then less complex than the first.

It is to be stressed again that whether a person will experience flow at all and, if he does, whether it will be at a complex or at a simple level depends only in part on the objective conditions in the environment or the concrete structure of the activity. What counts even more is the person's ability to restructure the environment so that it will allow flow to occur. Artists, poets, religious visionaries, and scientists are among those who have learned to use cognitive techniques to order symbols so that they can "play" with them any time and anywhere, to a certain extent regardless of environmental conditions. Ideally, anyone could learn to carry inside himself the tools of enjoyment. But whether the structure is internal or external, the steps for experiencing flow are presumably the same; they involve the same process of delimiting reality, controlling some aspect of it, and responding to the feedback with a concentration that excludes anything else as irrelevant.

Figure 3 also suggests the relationship between flow and what is ordinarily meant by "pleasure"; that is, the satisfaction of basic needs—hunger, sex, and so forth. In the present model, the experience of pleasure tends to be one of low complexity, since it does not require the use of complex skills. One can think of flow as a continuum, ranging from repetitive, almost automatic acts (like doodling or chewing gum) to complex activities which require the full use of a person's physical and intellectual potential. Chapter Nine describes patterns of *microflow*, the simple unstructured activities that people perform throughout the day; these activities appear to give little positive enjoyment yet are indispensable for normal functioning. Chapters Five through Eight present examples of *macroflow*, the complex, structured activities that produce full-fledged flow experiences.

Chapter 5

Enjoying Games: Chess

▲▲

Chess, an ancient and universal game that provides an almost unlimited ceiling of challenges, is probably the leisure activity most often written about in Western countries. The psychological intricacies of the game have suggested plots to several novelists, Vladimir Nabokov and Stefan Zweig among them. Outstanding psychologists have analyzed the thinking required by chess (Binet, 1894; De Groot, 1965). Researchers also are investigating the similarities between problem solving in chess and computers (Newell, Shaw, and Simon, 1958; Tikhomirov and Terekhov, 1967); the relationship between physiological, cognitive, and emotional processes in chess (Pushkin, Pospelov, and Efimov, 1971; Chase and Simon, 1973); and the grammatical features of chess notation (Mason and Peterson, 1967).

Despite all this interest, very little has been done to explain the attraction of the game for the player. Although, virtually alone among behavioral scientists, some psychoanalysts (Jones, 1931; Fine, 1967) have attempted to unearth the sources of enjoyment derived from the game, their approach is based on a model which forces them to interpret the enjoyment in terms of displacement and sublimation. Whether true or not, that interpretation leaves much to be explained. The best attempts at describing the fascination of chess have been made by literate players such as Abrahams (1960) and Steiner (1974a).

Because of its complexity, chess is an ideal activity to investigate with the help of the flow model. In Chapter Four, the section describing the model, we noted that the opportunities for action in chess are given by the opponent's moves; hence, whether or not a person will be in flow depends on the ratio of skills between the two players. That description was meant to be a simplified, schematic illustration of what we considered the most salient structural element of the game, and hence the most typical form of experience in chess. How simplified that version of chess was became clear only later, after we started to analyze the chess players' answers.

The interviews and questionnaires show that chess is not only a difficult intellectual game but also an interlocking combination of quite different activities. It contains opportunities for action at several levels, each independent of the other. One can respond to the competitive setting of the game, to the purely cognitive challenges, to the interpersonal opportunities, to the pastime element, to the snob appeal, or to the chance for solitary study. A person can "play chess" at any one of these levels, or at all of them at different times. The game is complex enough to allow for a variety of flow experiences, depending on what mixture of action opportunities he or she decides to confront.

The example of chess illustrates that the possibilities of flow are not restricted by the obvious structural characteristics of the activity. Chess is a mock war based on the clash of opposing rational strategies. It is very competitive and very intellectual. Yet people find all sorts of other reasons for enjoying it; they may choose to stress challenges which to an outsider would not seem "essential" to the game. This flexibility suggests that different kinds of intrinsic rewards can be built into the same activity. The example of chess is instructive because it begins to show the potential for structuring flow into other activities. Chess itself has evolved over a period of well over a thousand years. During this time, it has been given a form which provides a variety of challenges, and hence of enjoyment. By understanding these, we may hope to learn how to create similar opportunities in play as well as in work.

Two groups of chess players were included in this part of the study. One consisted of thirty males in the Chicago area: nine beginners, eleven intermediate players, and ten outstanding players. They were approached through the Chicago Chess Club and two local colleges. Age varied from 17 to 63 years, with an average of 26.2 and a standard deviation of 11.1 years. The second group consisted of twenty-three female chess players who responded to a mailing addressed to forty-six women players. This group included twelve of the nineteen top female chess players in the country, as rated by the United States Chess Federation. The remaining eleven respondents were less highly rated players from the Chicago area. The average age of this group was 38.9 years, with a standard deviation of 15.9. The section below deals only with results obtained from the male sample; later sections include the women and compare male and female players' perceptions of the activity.

Forms of Involvement

Pilot interviews with chess players had alerted us to the fact that a person's involvement with the game can be measured along several dimensions. For instance, some people stress the amount of time they play; others stress the amount of time they study chess by themselves. Some people subscribe to a dozen chess journals and know everything about the latest games played in Tokyo or Buenos Aires. Some talk about tournaments all the time and act as if winning were the only reason for playing. All of these people are talking about chess; yet by emphasizing one dimension of the activity over another they seem to be describing entirely different things. To find out the relationship between the various aspects of the game, we took eight measures of involvement on each of the thirty male players. We wanted to know how these different ways of playing chess were related to each other, and whether each form of involvement corresponded to a different source of enjoyment derived from the activity. The eight indices were measured as follows:

1. *USCF Ratings.* These are the ranks assigned each player by the United States Chess Federation, on the basis of wins and losses in official tournament play. They represent the best estimate of a player's skill. The range is from below 1200 (unrated player) to over 2600 (grand master). The median rating in this sample was 1780 (A rank). There were nine unrated players; eleven rated C to A; eight experts, one master, and one senior master. Therefore, approximately one third of the sample were active beginners, one third were advanced players, and one third were outstanding players.
2. *Rank (USCF rating) of highest opponent.* This index was thought to express the competitiveness of the player. The median rank of highest opponent was 2300.
3. *Number of tournaments.* This index reflects participation in the official competitive structure of championship chess. The mean score on this variable was 3.58 on an eight-point scale; the median number was seventeen tournaments.
4. *Time spent playing chess.* An estimate of the number of hours per week spent playing. Mean score was 2.73 on a six-point scale; the median was six hours per week.
5. *Time spent studying chess.* An estimate of the number of hours per week spent studying. Mean score was 1.63 on a six-point scale; the median was between two and three hours per week.
6. *Club membership.* On the average, each subject belonged to 2.2 chess clubs; the range was from one to four memberships.

7. *Books on chess.* The number of chess books that a subject reported owning was recorded on an eight-point scale. The mean was 2.37; the median, twelve books.

8. *Chess magazines.* The number of subscriptions was recorded on a five-point scale. The median was between one and two subscriptions; the range, from zero to fourteen.

When the eight measures of involvement were entered into a correlation matrix, two relatively independent clusters emerged. USCF ratings, rank of highest opponent, number of tournaments, and subscriptions to chess magazines were all very significantly correlated. They seem to measure *competitive* achievement in the activity. Five of the six correlations between the remaining four variables were also significant: time spent playing, time spent studying, number of club memberships, and number of chess books owned. These items formed a second cluster; it suggests a basically *noncompetitive* form of involvement with the game.

All the variables in the first cluster and 83 percent of the variables in the second cluster are significantly correlated with each other; but only 38 percent of the correlations between the two clusters are significant. The two variables which cut across the clusters, and to a certain degree form a third intermediary grouping, are the number of chess books and chess magazines owned. Thus, although there are eight main ways that a person can operate within the structure of chess—by trying to improve his ratings, by devoting time to study, by participating in club activities, and so on—these various approaches tend to boil down to two basic issues: a person responds to the competitive opportunities for action, or he responds to the chance to play, study, relate to other players in a club, and read chess books.

Is there a relationship between a given form of involvement and the kind of reward one derives from it? Does a person with high ratings enjoy the same things about chess that one with low ratings does? Do people who play a lot and those who play infrequently get the same rewards from chess? To answer these questions, we correlated the eight indices of involvement with the ratings of the eight sources of enjoyment (reported in Tables 1 and 2). Table 4 reports partial correlations in which the common variance between the two main groups of involvement variables has been removed. The pattern suggests that each form of involvement in chess provides a somewhat different reward structure to the player. In general, people who enjoy the autotelic elements of the game (the experience, the activity) tend to be low on competitive achievement; people who enjoy the exotelic aspects (competition, prestige) are the ones involved at the competitive level. In other words, players who are successful within the competitive framework of chess tend to discount intrinsic rewards in favor of the enjoyment of competition.

But a closer inspection of Table 4 reveals a number of more subtle relationships. For instance, people who say that they enjoy the activity itself are those who play against opponents of a lesser caliber. Perhaps when a person confronts opponents far above himself in skill, the challenges become excessive and disrupt the flow activity by producing worry or anxiety. It is puzzling, however, that the two autotelic sources of reward are not correlated positively with any of the forms of involvement in chess. This finding suggests that one does not get to like chess better the more one plays it; those who do not find intrinsic rewards in it at the beginning are not likely to learn to find them later.

A clear pattern is shown in item 3. People who rank "friendship, companionship" as an important source of enjoyment also belong to more chess clubs. This is a predictable relationship but one that confirms the fact that chess gives opportunities to enjoy interpersonal relationships through the institution of clubs.

Players who list "measuring self against own ideals" as an important reward tend to play against stronger opponents. This finding may seem to be logically backward. Why should a person who enjoys measuring himself against his own ideals in fact measure himself against other players who are better than he is? But there is no necessary contradiction here: in chess the clearest way to know whether one has met one's own standards is by beating a stronger opponent.

Table 4. Partial Correlations Between Involvement and Sources of Reward in Chess ($N = 30$)*

Source of Reward	Form of Involvement							
	Competitive (noncompetitive held constant)				Noncompetitive (competitive held constant)			
Items	1	2	3	4	5	6	7	8
	Ratings	Opponents	Tourna-ments	Magazines	Time Play	Time Study	Number Clubs	Chess Books
1. Enjoyment of the experience	.13	.14	−.18	−.30	.08	.02	.17	.06
2. The activity itself	−.21	−.47[c]	.24	−.33[a]	−.07	.13	−.27	.20
3. Friendship, companionship	−.25	−.17	−.17	−.19	.06	−.22	.45[b]	−.14
4. Development of skills	−.01	.03	−.02	.06	.00	.25	.02	.15
5. Measuring self against own ideal	.18	.36[a]	.12	.23	−.13	.06	−.07	.01
6. Emotional release	−.23	−.12	−.06	.07	.39[a]	.08	−.08	.04
7. Competition	.36[a]	.15	.44[b]	.15	−.14	−.19	−.19	.06
8. Prestige, glamor	.09	.05	.19	.37[a]	−.27	−.16	−.26	−.36[a]

*Numbers marked [a] are significant at the .05 level; those marked [b] are significant at the .02 level; and those marked [c] are significant at the .01 level.

Those who enjoy "emotional release" also spend significantly more time playing the game. This finding suggests that the tendency to play a lot of chess, when isolated from competitive involvement, is a form of escape; the reward that it provides is insulation from the real world and its problems.

A person who enjoys competition is likely to participate in many tournaments and to achieve higher ranks as a player. Here again, one of the possible sets of challenges in the activity is matched with one kind of enjoyment. Competitive people respond to the competitive potential of the game. From a commonsense point of view, it may be said that competition *is* the reward of chess, because the better players respond more to it. But that would be an elitist prejudice, and in any case it runs contrary to the whole idea of intrinsic rewards. Even though some people do reach flow through beating strong opponents and advancing in the hierarchy of ratings, others achieve flow through interacting with friends, through playing when they feel like it, or through meeting self-imposed challenges. There is no objective reason why these latter forms of flow would be less valid than the ones derived from competition.

Enjoyment of prestige is positively related to the number of magazines subscribed to and negatively related to the number of chess books one owns. It seems that there is a kind of snob appeal in keeping up to date with the world of chess through reading journals; but people who collect books on the game are less likely to derive pleasure from this form of oneupmanship.

The results in Table 4, then, support the following conclusions: (1) The skill of the player, as measured by USCF ratings, is positively related to only one kind of reward: the one derived from competition. (2) Involvement with strong opponents decreases satisfaction with the game itself but increases the reward of matching oneself against one's own ideal. (3) To participate in many tournaments provides competitive rewards. (4) The possession of chess journals satisfies a desire for prestige. (5) Because chess can be played at almost any time and any place, people can easily use it as a form of escape. (6) Finally, chess clubs obviously offer opportunities for friendship and camaraderie.

Flow Structure and Flow Experience

The structure of the game of chess is so varied that it allows a great many forms of involvement, and hence of rewards. Those who play chess, however, see certain structural and experiential properties of the activity as being more essential than others. Chess is an intellectual and a competitive game. These are its primary characteristics. That it provides companionship, prestige, and so on, is a secondary consideration. This differentiation between primary and secondary dimensions does not imply a value judgment. In fact, from a theoretical point of view, the secondary elements are more interesting. They show that any activity—no matter what it is ostensibly about—can provide rewards that are very different from the primary ones; that is, even routine work and other necessary activities can be made to offer intrinsic rewards.

Still, if one wishes to describe chess in a proper perspective, one needs to focus on the primary rewards of the activity. We know from the rankings in Table 2 that chess players, like most other groups, report autotelic rewards as the most important source of enjoyment: "enjoyment of the experience" and "the activity itself" are listed highest. When chess players describe the experience, the strongest analogies they list are "solving a mathematical problem," "playing a competitive sport," "designing or discovering something new," and "exploring a strange place" (Table 3). Clearly, the activity is perceived primarily as a competitive, creative, intellectual problem-solving process. These adjectives serve as a bare outline of the game. To get a closer view, we shall turn to the interviews. In this section the twenty-three interviews with outstanding female players are used, since the males only filled out the questionnaire and were not interviewed.

When asked to describe the experience of playing a game that is going well, the players most frequently used the adjectives *exhilarating, exciting,* and *satisfying.* Several people mentioned the problem-solving and competitive elements: "It is exhilarating, like I'm succeeding at putting a very hard puzzle together." "A little like winning in any competitive sport, a little like solving a complicated problem." Some emphasized the increased sense of competence that one derives from playing a good game: "I feel as if I couldn't do a wrong move. Very, very happy feeling–I feel smarter, clever. Sadistical as it is, I can't stop a grin from breaking out on my face!" This feeling of elated power is moderated by a constant alertness. The players know that they cannot relax because the challenges are always present and must be constantly faced: "Exhilarating . . . and nerve-wracking because I know it is only a matter of time before I blunder." "When my game is absolutely 'won,' I am beside myself with tension. I have lost too many games from overconfidence." "[I] have to fight off the desire to stop struggling, because if I relax my determination I will lose my advantage and probably the game as well."

Flow in chess, as in other activities, depends on a very delicate balance between being in control and being overwhelmed. It is this tension that forces the player to attend to the game, with the resulting high pitch of concentration and involvement.

When asked to describe, in their own words, the best things about chess, seventeen respondents (74 percent) listed a variant of "intellectual challenge"; the others mentioned "unlimited variety," "it is another world," "it is always different." The two next largest clusters of responses included references to "camaraderie" or "neat people" (by six, or 26 percent, of the respondents) and "competition" (by four, or 17 percent). The remaining responses were quite idiosyncratic, ranging from "the opportunity to travel" to "notoriety."

Asked why they play the game, nineteen players (82 percent) answered that they "enjoy it," "love it," "it is a pleasure," or "it is fun." Two of the four exceptions said that it is a form of stimulation or mental exercise, one mentioned that she plays chess for companionship, and one in order "to get lost in an external situation and forget about personal crap."

The evidence is overwhelming that chess players are intrinsically motivated to play the game. The enjoyment that they derive from the activity is primarily an intellectual challenge; it produces exhilaration by giving the player a feeling of control in a difficult situation. The typical flow experience in chess depends on this precarious balance between challenges and skills.

The structure of chess is well adapted to induce the flow experience. The rules, equipment, and organization of the game provide a clear-cut separation between "normal life" and the activity. Therefore, a player can easily shut out irrelevant stimuli and concentrate on the limited world of the game. No player stated that she had problems with getting started in the activity; however, some rely more on the structure of the activity to get into the flow experience, while others need fewer structural supports. At one extreme, people said that they can enjoy chess any time and any place, as long as there is a board and an opponent. Others reported that the immersion starts immediately after they make their familiar opening move. Still others said that only after a few moves do they really enter what we call the flow state: "I start a game fairly indifferently, don't really get started until after the opening takes an individual turn that tells me something about the opponent's level of skill." This is a point that all respondents stress: flow cannot be maintained unless the skills of the opponent are well matched. We shall return later to this issue. Finally, a few players seem to need the structure of a competitive tournament to enter the flow experience: "The quiet, clocks ticking, points at stake."

Once a person is immersed in the activity, the rest of the world disappears from awareness. Concentration on the game excludes thoughts that are irrelevant, and perceptions of events outside the board are held in abeyance. The sense of time is suspended: "Usually someone says, 'Wanna play?' and the next thing I know several hours have gone by." Twenty-one of the twenty-three players (91 percent) reported that time goes by much faster or that it "does not exist"; one said that time goes slower, and one found no difference.

The element that maintains the intensity of concentration is the basic move-countermove structure of chess. Within a limited time, a person must respond to every move of the opponent without endangering his own position, and he must endeavor to make the opponent unable to move his king under check. Any move can be the crucial one, and hence there is no occasion to relax at any point—provided the opponent is reasonably competent and hence able to present challenges.

When asked whether they have to make an effort to concentrate on the game, 91 percent of the players gave an unequivocal "no" for an answer. "No effort—the game is a struggle, and concentration is like breathing: you never think of it. The roof could fall in and, if it missed you, you would be unaware of it." Some, however, qualified their answers by saying that one might get distracted at the beginning of a game, or if there is excessive noise around (52 percent mentioned noise), or if people crowd too closely (32 percent), or if hunger, headache, or bladder pressure becomes too intense. One player said that she has difficulties in concentrating "only in the very beginning or when it is clear to me that either my opponent or myself is in trouble, and when I get tired. Or if I have personal worries. Distractions are people talking, their various nervous habits, or my own thoughts. I have to ask others to stop making noise, and for my own thoughts it requires determination and I struggle to 'dig in.' " This statement illustrates the precarious permeability of the flow state. Intrusions are always possible from within or without. But when the flow situation is optimal (when the challenges match skills), the activity becomes all-absorbing.

Asked whether they think about other things while they are playing a good game, 74 percent said that they do not: "I generally do not think of other things while playing, but am wholly concentrating on the game." Some mentioned that as soon as their mind wanders, they lose. An additional 13 percent said that they think of things outside the game only when they play against a less qualified opponent: "If busting a much weaker player, I may just think about the events of the day. During a good game, I think over various alternatives to the game—nothing else." Only two players said that they usually think about other things while playing, and one did not answer the question.

The intensity of concentration is partly due to the clear feedback one gets to every move. There is no excuse for getting distracted because everything needed for acting in the situation is available—all the information is there, all the tools are at hand. A player learns early that it does no good to grasp for straws or entertain wild hopes. The only way to meet challenges effectively is to apply the rules in the most appropriate ways. One player explains: "[The best things about chess are] being in control of a situation and having all the evidence right there. . . . In chess everything is in front of you to see. No other variables . . . can control it." As this statement suggests, chess is a self-contained universe which one can control. And that is true of all flow activities. The components of the universe can vary (the world of chess is different from the world of rock climbing), and the skills needed to control a particular universe are diverse. But the flow experience is similar across the various activities.

When asked whether their experience in chess can be duplicated in other situations, 38 percent of the players said that it cannot. Of those who said "yes," several qualified their answer in one way or another: "Sometimes—but not in the concentrated way, divorced from life, as it does in chess." Yet the same person, later in the interview, stated: "*Nothing* comes close to chess in providing beauty or pleasure." The experiences mentioned as most similar to chess were competitive sports, artistic activities like painting and music, research into new problems, bridge, and "the army or politics."

The primary reward of the activity is clearly the flow experience which results from the intellectual challenge of the game itself. Yet again one must keep in mind that there are other dimensions which provide secondary opportunities for action, and hence different kinds of flow experiences. For instance, 58 percent of the sample mentioned at one point or another in the interview that the camaraderie of other players is important to them. Chess provides a common focus of interest and a topic of conversation—in short, a form of social bonding: "Most of my social life is centered around chess players." "Most of my friends are players." "I enjoy other chess players and the social life around chess, which is unique." For many of the women in this sample, chess is an activity which they pursue in common with their husbands and children.

Still others mentioned the rewards of traveling to tournaments or working as officers in chess clubs. One person edits a biweekly chess bulletin, another is a club treasurer, a third directs tournaments for a small compensation. Some find rewards in studying the games of past masters and trying to find new winning combinations in them. All these forms of involvement are in a way parasitic on the essentially competitive structure of the game, but are nevertheless important sources of intrinsic rewards.

It would not be fair to conclude this section without mentioning the price that one has to pay for the enjoyment of the flow experience. In chess, as in other flow activities, the need to be always ready to act to meet challenges produces mental and physical strain. Tournament play is especially debilitating. People emerge from a series of games exhausted, and the demands of the body rush into awareness. To play well enough to experience flow consistently, one must devote a great deal of time and energy to the game. When asked to list the worst things about chess, 18 percent said that they could think of nothing wrong with it; 46 percent admitted that it consumes too much time; 23 percent complained about fatigue or tension; and the remaining 13 percent said that playing badly and losing are the worst.

Although some women expressed guilt about the amount of time and effort they devote to the game, they all felt that the game is worth what they put into it. The intrinsic rewards of the activity apparently more than compensate for the very real expenditures of energy it demands.

Chess: Male and Female

Flow activities are not equally available to everyone. Age puts severe limits on the practice of most sports. Social class influences the activities available to a person: polo is strictly for the affluent and boxing is primarily for the disadvantaged; playing Bach on a cello or watching a roller derby is almost as class-determined as where one lives or which school one goes to. The rewards present in different cultures may facilitate or inhibit flow in the same activity. For instance, in Canada or the United States hockey players earn considerable money and prestige, while soccer players until recently could look forward to neither. The opposite is true in countries like France or Italy. It is therefore easier to play soccer for intrinsic rewards in North America, and hockey in southern Europe.

A person's sex also helps to determine the flow activity he or she will enter, and the kind of experience he or she will get from the activity. The flow experience depends on skills; therefore, if persons of one sex are not trained to have certain skills, they are unlikely to get intrinsic rewards from an activity that requires those skills. Chess is a good case in point. It is well known that men are, on the whole, better players than women. The best woman player at this writing has a USCF rating of only 1907, while Bobby Fischer's is over 2700. Our female group included twelve of the nineteen top women players in the country; yet the average rating of the group was still 100 points below that of the male sample, which did not include any top-ranked men. This consistent difference between the sexes has been often commented upon; the favorite explanation for it is that women are simply unable to use analytic thinking (Maccoby, 1963, 1966) or to excel at spatial visualization (Garai and Scheinfeld, 1968).

While the difference is real, the data on the background of chess players suggest that its origin may be explained just as well by early socialization as by sex-linked genetic differences. On the average, for instance, the male players in our sample had learned the game at age ten; the women had learned it when they were twice that age. All the men had learned the game from another male, whereas only 23 percent of the women had learned it from a female. Furthermore, 73 percent of the women reported that even now they play exclusively against males; 94 percent play chess with their husbands or boyfriends, and 81 percent said that their male companions are better players than they themselves are.

This pattern suggests that in our culture chess has become so strongly sex-typed that it is very difficult for a young girl, whatever potential skills she may have, to develop them early enough to become fully competitive with males. She is born into an environment where the knowledge of chess is in the hands of males. Her brother may be taught the game before his teens, but she has to wait for the relative independence of young adulthood before she has a chance to learn it, usually from an older male with whom she has a culturally defined dependent relationship, such as her father, husband, or lover. If she gets to play in a tournament, her competition will be almost exclusively male. It is likely that she will be condescended to and patronized, if not ridiculed or harassed. Among the "three most significant experiences in chess," one respondent sarcastically listed "getting propositioned at the Chicago Chess Club during a game." To the same question another player replied: "winning games against men or boys who have given me the feeling that they expect to win just because I am a female." One respondent put it all together when she wrote: "Preparation for the female role in society begins very early; therefore, when the female is exposed to the game, at whatever age, and finds she likes it, she is so completely indoctrinated with the requirements of her role that she simply cannot spare the time necessary to become a truly great player. Example: Bobby Fischer has devoted his entire life to the perfection of his game. Any woman attempting to do the same thing would have been committed to an institution for the insane."

Under these conditions it is not surprising that few women become top players, and so the vicious circle is maintained from generation to generation. Of course, we have no data to demonstrate that the difference in skills is the result of training rather than genetics. The findings simply show that it is impossible to prove the contrary as long as social conditions make it so difficult for women to equal the performance of men.

But the point of this analysis was not to explain why women chess players get lower ratings than men. Instead, we were interested in learning whether men and women—considering the different conditions under which they play chess—experience the activity in the same way. In other words, does it make sense to think of chess as being the same activity regardless of who plays it, or is male chess in some respects different from female chess? One way to answer this question is by comparing male and female responses to the questionnaire that describes the experience of playing chess (see Table 3). Every item in the Friendship and Relaxation factor was rated higher (more similar to chess) by male players than by female players; and every item in the Risk and Chance factor was rated higher by female players than by male players. The same activity produces different levels of alienation and anxiety in the two sexes, probably because of the unequal socialization and unequal conditions under which the game is played. The largest difference ($p < .001$) was on the item "entering a burning house to save a child." Male players thought that this is definitely not an experience similar to chess; female players saw a significantly greater similarity. Again, women more than men thought that "swimming too far out on a dare" is close to the experience of playing chess ($p < .05$). Male monopoly of the game apparently makes a competitive woman player feel not unlike Joan of Arc as she tried to win her stripes in the French army.

A further relationship between the acceptance of a feminine role and the perception of the activity has been illustrated by Perun (1973). She administered a "femininity scale" to a group of female chess players and found that those who thought of themselves as more feminine, more traditional, and more dependent tended to experience chess as significantly more risky and less like a problem-solving activity. The more that women internalize their role, it seems, the less sure they become that they can cope with this "masculine" activity, and the more their anxiety increases.

At the same time, women who succeed at chess despite the odds against them may feel a higher sense of accomplishment than males. The crucial item "designing or discovering something new" was rated significantly more like playing chess by females ($p < .01$). These suggestive findings are echoed by the interviews. Female players see themselves as pioneers in a strange territory, almost overwhelmed by the odds but proud and excited to have survived.

Conclusions

Structurally chess is a self-contained meaning system which provides a rational set of action opportunities for those who learn the skills to act within the system. Although the challenges are primarily intellectual, a person can respond to a variety of secondary opportunities (interaction, esteem, competition, scholarship) that chess makes available. By the nature of the social organization of the activity, women are faced with a different structure; hence, their experiences are somewhat different from those of male chess players.

Because of the structure of the game, the primary rewards people derive from it are autotelic. For the actor, the enjoyment of acting in a flow activity justifies the expenditure of time and energy.

Although the *content* of chess experiences is unique to that game, the *modality* of experience is shared with other intrinsically rewarding experiences. Like climbers, dancers, or surgeons, chess players shift into a common mode of experience when they become absorbed in their activity. This mode is characterized by a narrowing of the focus of awareness, so that irrelevant perceptions and thoughts are filtered out; by loss of self-consciousness; by a responsiveness to clear goals and unambiguous feedback; and by a sense of control over the environment. These are the salient features of that modality of experience we have called "flow." They appear, time and again, in the most diverse activities. And in each case it is this common flow experience that people adduce as the main reason for performing the activity.

As we learn more about the various ways that flow can be induced, we also realize, by contrast, why average life experiences are rarely enjoyable in and of themselves. For one thing, most of life is not even made up of experiences, in Dewey's (1934) sense of the term—interactive sequences with a beginning, a middle, and an end, which provide a clear cognitive or emotional resolution. Even when we do go through a real "experience," it is rarely a flow experience; in real life there is no way to make sure that challenges will match one's skills. Games like chess, religious rituals, and artistic forms were developed to provide finite enjoyable experiences within the interstices of real life. By learning how these activities achieve their purpose, we may finally be able to begin structuring more and more of our normal experiences into forms that will provide enjoyment.

Chapter 6

Deep Play and the Flow Experience in Rock Climbing

▲▲▲

Because it involves physical danger and no discernible external rewards, rock climbing is an outstanding example of a particular class of flow activities. Furthermore, the artificial, sheltered universe of climbing can assume a reality of its own more meaningful to the actor than the reality of everyday life. In this sense, the analysis of rock climbing shows how flow activities can serve as models for societal transformation and provide experiences that motivate people to implement change.

The presence of risk places rock climbing squarely in what Jeremy Bentham, the eighteenth-century British philos-

This chapter was written by John MacAloon and Mihaly Csikszentmihalyi.

opher, called "deep play." He used that phrase with misgivings, to describe "play in which the stakes are so high that it is, from his [Bentham's] utilitarian standpoint, irrational for men to engage in it at all" (Geertz, 1973, p. 432). And certainly, if one thinks in terms of economic utility and the support of existing cultural values, deep play is useless, if not subversive. But that is exactly why it interests a student of human nature. Why are people attracted to an activity that offers no "rational" rewards? That is the question we shall try to answer with the help of the flow model. The second issue, concerning the effects that playful activities may have on "real" life, has been often mentioned in the past but with very few concrete examples. This study of rock climbers may help to redress the lack of empirical information on the topic, for rock climbing is a form of deep play in the sense of involving an extreme wager which acts as a vehicle for the deeper personal and cultural interests of the participants who risk it.

Climbing and Climbers

Rock climbing is an autonomous sport which developed out of the older and more general activity of mountaineering. The separation began roughly half a century ago, when in the 1920s some mountain climbers in the Alps perfected the use of equipment and techniques to make *direttissima* (most direct rather than roundabout) ascents of mountain faces previously thought to be unassailable. The two sports still overlap; but there is now a clearly established group of "technical climbers," interested not in reaching summits but in climbing the sheerest faces, as opposed to traditional climbers (Csikszentmihalyi, 1969).

Climbers consider their sport one of the purest forms of human activity, partly because achievement in it is a private experience rather than a public event. Feats of rock climbing are impervious to inclusion in the Guinness *Book of Records*: neither speed nor height nor any other measurable dimension is meaningful to assess performance. Only the initiated can appreciate the blend of objective difficulty and the artistry of the climber; however, climbing is usually done without an audience, and no one but the climber himself knows what he has accomplished and how well. Rock climbing is the exact antithesis of the American preoccupation with spectator sports.

Advances in technology and physical conditioning, together with the conquest of all the major summits, have led to the pursuit of ever more challenging rock walls, regardless of their location. More and better climbers regularly queue up at local climbing areas or jet about the world seeking new challenges. But the basic nature of the activity as a form of deep play has not changed. As far back as 1854, Thomas Murray confidently noted in his *Handbook for Travellers in Switzerland* that mountaineers suffer "of a diseased mind" (quoted in Lukan, 1968, p. 43). Contemporary opinions of rock climbers are not too different. We have undertaken to question what there is in the activity itself which leads men to engage in it despite its "irrationality." Historical and literary references are employed where helpful, but the bulk of the material comes from the climbers we interviewed.

Informants

Thirty rock climber/mountaineers were personally interviewed, by researchers who themselves are rock climbers, in Boulder, Colorado; Chicago, Illinois; and Devil's Lake, Wisconsin. Informants were selected to provide a range of experience, involvement, and skill. The mean age of the group was 28, with a range from 19 to 53. Five were female; twenty-five were male. The educational level ranged from high school equivalency to Ph.D., with most at or near the B.A. level. Place of birth, father's occupation and income, and personal financial status varied widely.

Mean length of experience was five years of technical rock climbing and eight years of general mountaineering, with the range in each case being from one to thirty-six years. In the summer, most of those interviewed climb once every two weeks, though some get out as often as four times a week and others as infrequently as once a month. During the winter, the activity level is approximately halved for most of the sample. Mean investment in rock-climbing gear—rope and hardware—approximated $138 at 1972 prices. Five climbers owned no equipment of their own; two had equipment worth more than $400.

A word on the international rating system is necessary, since this system permits a fairly accurate absolute and comparative estimate of the climbers' skills. In the last two decades a system of numerical ratings has been devised to describe the strenuousness of individual climbs. The rating expresses the most arduous move or series of moves to be encountered, taking into account such factors as type of move; degree of strength and gymnastics required; size and number of holds; and shape, inclination, friability, and exposure of the rock. The rating is established by the climber who makes the first ascent, although it may later be revised by a more recognized expert or by subsequent alteration of the rock itself. This rating system seems very subjective and mysterious, especially to the beginner; in practice, however, it is remarkably objective and consistent.

Serious rock climbs are termed "fifth-class" climbs, further broken down into a decimal range from 5.0 to 5.11. Climbs which are made "free"—that is, via the natural footholds and handholds provided by the rock alone—are rated by this system. An additional numerical value, from A-1 to A-6, describes direct-aid or "high-tension" climbs, in which artificial holds are created with the help of equipment designed for this purpose. The climbers interviewed in the course of this study ranged in ability from 5.3 to 5.11/A-6, from moderate skill to the limit of human potential, as it is currently estimated. Mean ratings indicate a slight skew toward the upper reaches of the spectrum (5.8/A-2).

On fifth-class climbs, climbers must be protected by ropes anchored to the rock by lashes, pitons, or chockstones. Such climbs generally involve two or more individuals and proceed in inchworm fashion. The first climber up the pitch, the "leader," is belayed from below and places his own protective anchors when he reaches a convenient perch. The skill ratings just mentioned for the climbers in the sample are for "following." Because a leader's fall is likely to involve more serious consequences than a follower's, separate ratings are kept for leading, according to the same numerical schema. The mean grade of rock led by the informants is 5.5/A-1, representing a more even distribution. Two climbers had led at the 5.11/A-6 level, while five had not led at all.

In addition to the quantitative skill ratings, attention was paid to the qualitative reputation of the individuals from the standpoint of the climbing population. Three of our respondents are quite well known to the American climbing community. Each has international experience and first ascents to his credit, and is known as a local hero in his home climbing area. Two others have made important first ascents, and one other has made a name for himself locally. The remaining twenty-four are not publicly distinguished.

Throughout the interview the accent was placed on obtaining the climber's own interpretation of his involvement in the activity. A common set of directed questions was asked of all informants, but the individual was allowed, even encouraged, to commandeer the interview vehicle to his own purpose. Many of the individuals whom we approached were initially reluctant to be interviewed. For the two most renowned climbers, this skepticism reflected past experience with journalists and psychologists; for others, with friends and family. Still others were generally (and understandably) leery of exposing the deeper layers of their personalities and social relationships. These misapprehensions (discussed freely and fully after they had been overcome in the interview process) reflected the desire to protect the integrity of the deep-play sphere from the perennially reductive glosses of the outsider.

Characteristics of Flow Experience

From the viewpoint of the outsider who uses the utilitarian calculus of normal life, climbing is indeed an irrational activity which needs to be explained by reducing it to a subtle form of mental derangement. But the previous results of this study have alerted us to the fact that certain forms of experiences are their own reward. We know that climbers, when they describe what they do, note "exploring a strange place" as the closest experience to climbing, followed by "designing or discovering something new," "being with a good friend," and "solving a mathematical problem" (Table 3). We also know that the intrinsic rewards of climbing are the ones rated highest by the respondents. But how exactly does the activity provide this creative, enjoyable experience? To answer this question, we turn to an analysis of the structural components of rock climbing and the associated experiences they stimulate, within the framework of the flow model.

Opportunities for action. Rock climbing provides an unlimited range of action challenges—both "horizontally," in the sense of progression from easy to difficult, and "vertically," in that, like chess, it permits the actor to be involved in the activity on a variety of dimensions. By Dember's (1960) definition, climbing offers "high complexity values" with "graduated pacers." A 5.5 climber may select the increased challenges of a 5.7 route, or he may choose to decrease the demands with a 5.3 climb: "It depends on the mood I'm in. There are days when you're not up to perfection, when you want to mellow out on some easy rock; others when you're quite willing to maim yourself for all time."

To a large degree one can choose in advance the level of challenge that best suits one's level of skills. Moreover, within each class of climbs, variability is potentially infinite; no two climbs are ever exactly alike: "The rock changes with a kind of psychological ecology. Depending on that ecology, which is to say where your head is, the 5.4 move you did yesterday might be a 5.10 ass-buster today." Differences in the kinds of moves required, texture of the rock, length of the route, quality of protection, and so on, render the hundreds of available climbs at, for instance, the 5.7 level into thousands of novel and interesting action opportunities. In addition, less predictable factors—weather, conditioning, mood, partner's performance, equipment failure—can always provide unexpected challenges.

The climber may also recomplexify a familiar route by adding new goals to the obvious central one of safely and successfully completing the climb. He may lead others to their limits; or he may change the demands upon himself by focusing on aesthetic criteria, such as the elimination of wasted motion or the reduction of reliance upon equipment; or he may increase the danger by eliminating equipment altogether on a solo climb. As one climber puts it, "When you run into something you've either done before or experienced the equivalent to, . . . you're going to be concentrating more on form than achievement. When you get up to 5.9, you get more into the achievement side of things. You just want to live through the son of a bitch. 5.4 is achievement, but in the form sense. It's achievement of as close to perfect balance, perfect gracefulness as you can get."

By a variety of such measures, the individual in effect "changes the rules" and alters the evaluative criteria. Climbers may return time and again to the same route and find it freshly interesting. Whether one chooses progression to higher objective ratings, or increased aesthetic and emotional achievement at a set skill level, climbing offers perpetual novelty: "Obviously you're not going to reach any perfection in climbing because your mind is always one step ahead. . . . You can always think of one step more perfect than you can do. Each time you move up, your present flow is imperfect. . . . It's an endless moving up."

Good flow activities, like chess and rock climbing, offer a wide range of "flow channels" at various levels of skill and commitment. As in all forms of deep play, control over the choice of challenge levels—the calculation of the "odds," so to speak—is extremely important. At the same time, a degree of uncertainty is always implicit and necessary to the process: "The uncertainty factor is the flow factor. Uncertainty is the existence of a flow, whereas certainty is static, is dead, is not flowing. . . . You can't have a certain flow any more than an uncertain staticness. They cancel each other out."

Centering of attention on limited stimulus field. In contrast to normative everyday life, the action of rock climbing is narrow, simplified, and internally coherent. From all the actions an individual might undertake, sensations he might process, thoughts he might entertain, the parameters of the activity define a narrow subset as relevant—a man climbing a rock. The remainder of the human repertoire is rendered irrelevant and irritant and is screened out from this simplified, manageable stimulus field. The physical and mental requirements involved in staying on the rock act as a screen for the stimuli of ordinary life—a screen maintained by an intense and focused concentration. Our informants universally recognize this effect, as these sample comments indicate.

> When I start on a climb, it's as if my memory input had been cut off. All I can remember is the last thirty seconds, and all I can think ahead is the next five minutes. . . . With tremendous concentration the normal world is forgotten.
>
> When you're [climbing] you're not aware of other problematic life situations. It becomes a world unto its own, significant only to itself. It's a concentration thing. Once you're into the situation, it's incredibly real, and you're very much in charge of it. It becomes your total world.
>
> It's a centering thing, being absolutely in the here and now, in the present. It's the most important part of climbing.
>
> You're moving in harmony with something else, you're a part of it. It's one of the few sorts of activities in which you don't feel you have all sorts of different kinds of conflicting demands on you.
>
> One thing you're after is the one-pointedness of mind.
>
> You're into an entirely different universe that the usual daily things don't really affect that much.

An expert and sensitive climber, Doug Robinson, in an article entitled "The Climber as Visionary," refers to this limited stimulus field as "the sensory desert of the climb." "To climb with concentration," he writes, "is to shut out the world, which, when it reappears, will be as a fresh experience, strange and wonderful in its newness" (Robinson, 1969, pp. 7-8). As in any "desert," there is less to look at, but what there is is seen more intensely.

How do climbers maintain this intense concentration? First of all, climbing problems attract the individual's interest, pique his curiosity, and titillate his desire for a decision: "One of the nicest things about climbing is figuring out the potentials of any one position. Each has an infinite number of balance potentials, and figuring out the best moves from among all those potentials, both moving from the position you're in and what the next move is going to be from the position you will be in, is really wild!" Some compare this intrinsic interest to problem solving in mathematics or engineering: "The satisfaction of working out a problem . . . like a math problem. You keep trying till you find a solution. It seems like there's always a solution." Others relate it to artistic creativity: "It's almost like an art, putting different combinations of moves together in order to get to the top"; "It's an aesthetic dance"; "It's a physical poem on the rock." This is the aspect of the activity which prompted the climbers to rate "designing or discovering something new" and "solving a mathematical problem" as experiences similar to their own.

But in rock climbing, as in most forms of deep play, a heightened concentration and enforcement of attention boundaries is achieved through the addition of risk to the intellectually engaging aspects of the activity. Whatever subsequent meanings the informants attach to physical danger in rock climbing, it functions principally as a compelling motivation to attend to the immediate situation. Any lapse of concentration, any opening of the postern gate to the concerns of ordinary life, is always potentially disastrous: "Mind wandering is dangerous. The more competent you get, the less your mind wanders." "If you're thinking about your old lady, you're not thinking about where your hand's going. You'll be back with your old lady soon enough, but right now you've got to put your hand in a place where it's going to stay. . . . Death's always on the mat with you."

Feelings of competence and control. In his attitude toward deep play, as we have seen, the outsider systematically misestimates the role played by the "irrational" counters of the activity, either by mistaking them for an end rather than a means or by assuming the player's obsession with them. As Geertz (1973) has shown for the Balinese cockfight, money is not *all that* paramount in the minds of the bettors. Similarly, in rock climbing, physical danger, while a very real and structurally crucial aspect of the activity, stands neither as an end in itself nor as a dominant preoccupation of the climbers. Only one respondent claimed that he climbs "for cheap thrills," and his statement was extremely qualified. No one else gave any indication of pursuing danger for its own sake. "Danger" as one put it, "is not a kick." Rather, danger is accepted and utilized as a part of the gestalt of climbing, in which feelings of control and competence predominate over voluntary risk in the figure-and-ground relationship. Indeed, when asked directly whether they consider climbing dangerous, twenty-one of the thirty informants responded negatively. Sample comments include these:

> No I don't think it's too dangerous, if you take a little precaution and use your head.
>
> No more dangerous than driving a car. You just can't let it affect you.
>
> No, emphatically. I did snow skiing since childhood; it's twice as dangerous. Climbing is only dangerous if you climb in a dangerous way.
>
> Very rarely, once in a while I do something insane but most of the time I'm safety conscious.
>
> No, I don't consider it dangerous. . . . I'm belayed and I'm sure of the people I go with, mainly because I trained them myself.
>
> You get so absorbed in the climb that you no longer think about danger.
>
> No, I consider it as dangerous as driving a car.
>
> The sport itself is safe, safer than driving a car.
>
> Most of it isn't dangerous, not more dangerous than walking in Hyde Park.
>
> The press and popular media overemphasize the danger. They generalize from the carelessness of irresponsible climbers. People see climbers as risqué, danger-loving daredevils—all misconceptions.

> Climbing may be less dangerous than walking down the street, because I haven't got control over the latter; there are more variables that can't be calculated.
>
> The degree of danger is in a way determined by you.
>
> Not really. The most things happen out of ignorance; the better climber you are, the more you can judge what's ahead.
>
> I like being up and looking down. When I look down, I look at the view, not the danger; I know I'm protected from that.
>
> No, I don't consider it that dangerous. The variables are subject to evaluation.

The intriguing recurrence of the statement that rock climbing is less dangerous than everyday activities, such as driving a car or walking down a street, is a point to which we shall later return. For the moment it is sufficient to note the objective correlates of the feelings of control: experience, training, precaution, anticipation, protection, judgment, responsibility, evaluation. All these qualities unite into the "discipline" of mind and body in climbing and allow the degree of danger to be managed by the individual. Most informants would concur with the climber who summarized it this way: "There's risk, to be sure, but it's a highly calculated risk, much more so than driving a car. You relate the risk involved to your own experience and that suggests the number and kinds of precautions you must take. If you do, you'll feel in control. Beyond that, there is always the unknown which simply is there and nothing can be done about it, so you can't worry about it." "Control," said another, "is just a feeling, but it's a very accurate feeling. That's what climbing depends on, how accurate that analysis is."

Unambiguous and immediate feedback. Along with its function as a device for centering and intensifying attention, physical danger provides the clear and immediate feedback requisite of a good flow activity. Eleven informants imagined that it is possible ideally for a good climber to always feel in control; nineteen did not. But in the actual experience of all informants, control feelings are not always present. In figure-

and-ground relations, control feelings sometimes give way to anxiety feelings. The climber knows he is "doing well" if he feels in control of his actions, whereas the arousal of fear signals immediately that he is "doing poorly" and must make adjustments. In the course of the average climb, this feedback loop, regulated by differential control/fear signals of varying intensity, is continuously operating. In those rare moments when the climber enters the deep-flow channel, control feelings intensify and stabilize to the point of presumption.

Merging of action and awareness: Transcendence of ego boundaries. If the ego is taken as that construct we learn to interpose between self and environment (Freud, 1927; Mead, 1934), as a broker for competing demands and an arbiter of ambiguities, we may begin to grasp the origins of that "egolessness" reported by our informants. When the actor's attention is highly focused in a limited stimulus field which provides noncontradictory demands for action appropriate to the actor's resources, with clear and immediate feedback in the form of control feelings, a state may be reached in which the ego has, so to speak, nothing to do, and awareness of it fades. The extremely processual nature of climbing—the continuous alternation between balance and movement, homeostasis and change, from position to position—is nicely expressed in one informant's statement: "It's self-catalyzing. . . . The moves . . . create each other. The move you're planning to do is also the genesis of the move you're going to do after you've done that one. It's an indefinite interrelationship, a kind of crystalline hookup."

This fluid process of movement-balance-perception-decision-movement-balance . . . forms the internal dynamic of climbing. One might visualize it as a strip of movie film. Each synchronic slice of the action (balance, decision, movement, and so on) is like a frame of that film. When the action is too easy or too difficult, the film stutters and the actor is very aware of the black borders of each frame, the negotiation of the ego construct. But when the difficulty is just right, action follows action in a fluid series, and the actor has no need to adopt an outside perspective from which to consciously intervene. Awareness of the individual frames disappears in the unbroken flow of the whole. "Your moves," as one respondent noted, "become one move." Action merges with awareness. The actor is immersed in the flow of his movement. The flow experience emerges as the psychological correlate of this kinesthetic-cognitive process.

Dennis Eberl (1969, p. 13), recounting a trying Matterhorn ascent, expresses this point clearly: "Just as we reached the base of a small icefield, the clouds enveloped us. I resigned myself to the fight and even began to hope that our struggle would be a classic one. What followed was one of *those rare moments of almost orgiastic unity as I forgot myself and became lost in action*. . . . At the top of the icefield I placed a rock piton, and as I reached to clip in, I was surrounded by a blue flash as a two-foot spark jumped from the rock to my hand. Unhurt, I traversed away from the rock and then down-climbed the ice. When I reached Gray, the *moment of unity between my thoughts and actions* was already over" (emphasis added).

But one need not turn to accounts of heroic success or retreat to find validation of this aspect of the flow experience in climbing. Our informants' statements are replete with it.

> You don't feel like you're doing something as a conscious being; you're adapting to the rock and becoming part of it.
>
> You feel more alive; internal and external don't get confused. The task at hand is so rich in its complexity and pull [that] your intensity as a conscious subject is diminished; a more subtle loss of self than mere forgetfulness.
>
> It's a pleasant feeling of total involvement. You become like a robot . . . no, more like an animal . . . getting lost in kinesthetic sensation . . . a panther powering up the rock.
>
> When things are going poorly, you start thinking about yourself. When things go well, you do things automatically without thinking. You pick the right holds, equipment, and it is right.
>
> You're so involved in what you're doing [that] you aren't thinking about yourself as separate from the immediate activity. You're no longer a participant observer, only a participant. You're moving in harmony with something else you're part of.

> When you first start climbing, you're very aware of capabilities. But after a while you just do it without reflecting on it at the time.
>
> When you're climbing, you have to devote yourself totally to the climb; you fuse your thinking with the rock. It's the ultimate in participation sports, participation endeavors.
>
> It's the Zen feeling, like meditation or concentration. One thing you're after is the one-pointedness of mind. You can get your ego mixed up with climbing in all sorts of ways and it isn't necessarily enlightening. But when things become automatic, it's like an egoless thing, in a way. Somehow the right thing is done without you ever thinking about it or doing anything at all. . . . It just happens. And yet you're more concentrated.
>
> If you can imagine yourself becoming as clear as when you focus a pair of binoculars, everything's blurred and then the scene becomes clear, as you focus them. If you focus yourself in the same way, until all of you is clear, you don't think about how you're going to do it, you just do it.
>
> The right decisions are made, but not rationally. Your mind is shut down and your body just goes. It's one of the extremes of human experience.

Strongly correlated with the merging of action and awareness is an altered time sense, a distortion in the congruence of chronological and psychological time. The climber who finds himself in a fearful predicament may feel time speeded up and may consistently misestimate the duration of his strain. Similarly, in periods of boredom, when time drags along, the subject often overestimates its passage. In both cases, self-consciousness or ego awareness is accented. In the flow experience, however, where ego awareness is decreased, the climber loses track of time altogether. Later he may even feel that for the duration of his flowing he was lifted out of time entirely, disattached from internal and external clocks. The temporal aspect of the deep-flow experience is characteristically reported with such oxymorons as "an eternal moment." In Robinson's words (1969, p. 6): "It is said to be only a moment, yet by virtue of total absorption he is lost in it, and the winds of eternity blow through it."

Transcendent Aspects of Deep-Flow Experience

Thus far we have stressed the narrow, contracted nature of the activity frame of rock climbing, its irrelevance to the concerns of normative life, its literal and figurative "away-from-it-all" qualities, the internal focusing of attention and merging of action and awareness on a severely restricted field of action and cognition. But within this intense contraction, indeed on account of it, there occurs a grand expansion, an opening out to the basic concerns of the human condition, a blossoming invisible to the flatland observer but real and compelling in the minds of the climbers. As one informant said about the pursuit of the useless in this human "miniature": "That one thing [climbing] is a complexity as great as the whole."

Before discussing these extraordinary aspects of the climbers' deepest experiences, for which adjectives such as *transcendent, religious, visionary,* or *ecstatic* are traditionally employed, we must make two important qualifications.

The first is that by no means all of the climbers in our sample reported these deep-flow experiences; only nine out of thirty consistently did. Others apparently had brushed with them at one time or another but either paid them little attention or even denounced them as mystical tommyrot.

> I just don't feel that. I can't say much about its importance because it doesn't affect me.
>
> I don't feel it really. I'm always conscious of the decisions I make on rock.
>
> Bullshit. Of course, you're very self-conscious. At least many people are. I am.
>
> God only knows [what such people are talking about]. Sounds mighty strange because in climbing you're most aware of yourself. I think somebody must be trying to be spectacular. Sounds like Greek to me.
>
> I don't think it's important to me, I don't think that's why I climb. My main reason for climbing is the physical exercise. Well, I supposc it would be a different experience without it [the feeling of egolessness]; it's part of the total experience.

We find ourselves faced with the same phenomenon which afflicted Maslow (1964) in his work on "peak experiences" and led him to divide the human population into "peakers" and "nonpeakers." While this radical bisection might be premature, it is important to search out the reasons for the difference. At the present stage of our work it is not yet possible to say anything systematic about why some people report deep-flow experiences, value them absolutely, and pursue them with vigor, while others do not. However, the climbers themselves offer some hints. One climber who does have deep-flow experiences suggests the inhibiting effects of ego intrusions: "You can get your ego mixed up with climbing in all sorts of ways, and it isn't necessarily enlightening." Another climber, who does not have deep-flow experiences but wishes she did, explains why she does not: "I'm too into competition with myself to feel that. I haven't done it long enough and am not in good enough shape."

To slip into the flow channel at all, then, an individual must attain certain levels of experience, skill, and conditioning appropriate to the challenges before him. Some simply have not climbed long enough, with the right companions, or under the right circumstance to have happened upon the experience or to be able to preselect situations in which it is likely to occur. Then again, various personality and sociocultural factors may interpose themselves between the individual and the flow experience through a process of selective attention. "Getting one's ego mixed up with climbing" may involve overemphasis on one of its structural features, such as competition with self and others. The transformation of conscious attention requisite to the flow experience may thus be inhibited.

The second point is that our informants' accounts of deep-flow experiences are translations of great emotions made after the fact—"emotion recollected in tranquility," as the poet would have it. As with any report of religious, creative, or visionary experiences, more is left behind than crosses the border of speech. Geertz (1973, p. 449) writes, "What the cockfight says it says in a vocabulary of sentiment." So too with rock climbing. While language is the only instrument we have to communicate these emotions and to discover their meaning, the emotions themselves are valued for their own sake as significant messages. Rock climbing, like the cockfight, is finally in this sense a form of art, though one which produces events and not objects. George Mallory, in "The Mountaineer as Artist," speaks to this point: "Artists . . . are not distinguished by the power of expressing emotion but by the power of feeling that emotional experience out of which Art is made. . . . Mountaineers are all artistic . . . because *they cultivate emotional experience for its own sake*" (quoted in Robinson, 1969, p. 4; emphasis added).

As we have seen, the merging of action and awareness which typifies the flow state does not allow for the intrusion of an outside perspective with such worries as "How am I doing?" or "Why am I doing this?" or even "What is happening to me?" In the moments of flow the individual does not even consciously acknowledge that he is flowing, much less elaborate and comment on the experience and its meaning. Realization, translation, and elaboration take place when the action has ceased: briefly at a belay stance, when the summit is finally reached, or after the climber is back on level ground. The processual structure of rock climbing not only produces great emotions but also offers regular opportunities to elaborate and solidify the experiences through reflection. Robinson (1969, pp. 7-8) describes this aspect of the activity very clearly:

> The concentration is not continuous. It is often intermittent and sporadic, sometimes cyclic and rhythmic. After facing the successive few square feet of rock for a while, the end of the rope is reached and it is time to belay. The belay time is a break in the concentration, a gap, a small chance to relax. The climber changes from an aggressive and productive stance to a passive and receptive one, from doer to observer, and in fact from artist to visionary. The climbing day goes on through the climb-belay-climb-belay cycle by a regular series of concentrations and relaxations. . . . When the limbs go to the rock and muscles contract, then the will contracts also. And at the belay stance, tied in to a scrub oak, the muscles relax; and the will also, which has been concentrating on moves, expands and takes in the world again, and the world is bright and new. It is freshly created, for it really had ceased to exist. . . . We

> notice that as the cycle of intense contractions takes over, and as this cycle becomes the daily routine, even consumes the daily routine, the relaxations on belay yield more frequent and intense visionary experiences. . . . The summit, capping off the cycling and giving final release from the tension of contractions, should offer the climber some of his most intense moments.

Most climbers, at one time or another, experience aspects of the entwined formal and affective features of the flow experience on a lowered level of intensity. The deep-flow or visionary experience is by all accounts rarer: "It is a state that one flows in and out of, gaining it through directed effort or spontaneously in a gratuitous moment. . . . It is at its own whim momentary or lingering suspended in the air, suspending time in its turn, forever momentarily eternal, as, stepping out on the last rappel you turn and behold the rich green wonder of the forest" (Robinson, 1969, p. 9).

One may say quite properly that the structured behavioral and thought processes involved in climbing point to and manipulate richer referents in the wider realm of cultural interest. But it would be a mistake to assume that climbers ordinarily are concerned with, or even aware of, the symbolic nature of their enterprise. However many symbolic relations are coalesced and condensed by the activity, in the deep-flow experience a sense of participation and immediacy, rather than condensation and displacement, is the key feature. The deep-flow experience is, as one informant said, "particle, wave, and source at the same time." The objects of perception in the sensory desert of climbing are transformed in this way into what Blake called the "minute particulars." The universe is not merely symbolized in these "grains of sand." The microcosm does not simply *stand for* the macrocosm; it *is* the macrocosm, fully experienced and assented to.

> With the more receptive senses we now appreciated everything around us. Each individual crystal in the granite stood out in bold relief. The varied shapes of the clouds never ceased to attract our attention. For the first time, we noticed tiny bugs that were all over the walls, so tiny that

> they were barely noticeable. While belaying, I stared at one for fifteen minutes, watching him move and admiring his brilliant red color.
>
> How could one ever be bored with so many good things to see and feel! This *unity with our joyous surroundings*, this *ultra-penetrating perception*, gave us a feeling that we had not had for years [Yvon Chouinard on El Capitan; quoted in Robinson, 1969, p. 6; emphasis added].

With the intense seeing, the *vision* induced by the activity, comes the transformation of material objects and the generalized "oceanic feeling of the supreme sufficiency of the present," "oceanic feelings of clarity, distance, union, and oneness" (Robinson, 1969, pp. 6, 8).

> After one prolonged climb in bad weather without food, I had this experience of having always climbed, always will. Once on top I felt as if I could open my arms and merge with the whole surroundings. I felt part of the greater whole—oneness.

> It's a physical transcendence, adapting to an unchangeable reality. You merge with it rather than change it.

> You could get so immersed in the rock, in the moves, the proper position of the body, that you'd lose consciousness of your identity and melt into the rock and the others you're climbing with.

> I would begin to look at it in religious terms. Certain natural settings represent some intensity or eternity. You can lose yourself in that. It's linked to the idea of creation, intense wonder, and realization.

> Your mind is more likely to be integrated with your body and you with the rocks and mountains themselves. . . . I like them so much. I feel really high in a way, grateful that I'm up there and not just drudging along in life below.

> The only religious feelings I ever have stem from the mountains. I feel that the mountains make one aware of spiritual matters. . . . I'm fortunate because I can appreciate these places where you can appreciate nature, the minisculeness of man and his aspirations, which can elevate one. Spiritually, religiously I can see in many ways the same thing.

> Climbing is unbelievably solo, [yet] the flow is a multitude of one. Climbing is dreamlike. When you're climbing, you're dealing with your subconscious as well as conscious mind. . . . You're climbing yourself as much as the rock. . . . If you're flowing with something, it's totally still. . . . There's no possibility of judging from the inside of a car whether the car is moving or the freeway. So you're not quite sure whether you are moving or the rock is, for the same reason, being inside yourself as you usually are. So it becomes very still. . . . Lack of self-awareness is totally self-aware to me. If the whole is self-awareness, you can have a lack of self-awareness because there's nothing else there.

Like all numinous experiences, deep flow "elevates and humiliates simultaneously" (Jung, 1963, p. 154). At once critical and synergic, these experiences provide new modes of evaluation and acceptance. The normative order, until now carefully screened out from the deep-play sphere, is made subject to new interpretation and criticism.

Metasocial Commentary: Antistructure and Protostructure

The Dutch historian Huizinga first elaborated the paradox that play forms are "good for nothing" in terms of existing economic, biological, or psychological needs, but are "good for everything" because they serve as experiments for new ways of living. "For many years," he wrote, "the conviction has grown upon me that civilization [*Cultuur*] arises and unfolds in and as play" (Huizinga, [1939] 1950, p. i). He went on to suggest that the main patterns of human society—arts, religions, science, law, government—had their historical origins in playful activities; after proving themselves enjoyable and viable, these activities then became accepted and institutionalized to give structure to "real" life. From this evolutionary point of view, deep play and other complex flow activities are like laboratories in which new patterns of experience are tested. Although this analogy misses the fact that the "testing" is enjoyable in itself, it may have more truth in it than one would ordinarily expect.

Recently the anthropologist Victor Turner (1969, 1974)

has looked at certain symbolic and ritual activities which are "antistructural" in the sense of breaking down utilitarian norms and status roles, but are in a deeper sense "protostructural" because they suggest ways of reformulating the normative order that gives pattern to everyday life. The connection between the rituals studied by Turner and the protostructural potential of games has been noted by Sutton-Smith (1973).

A classic example of the relationship between the world of play and the world of the normative order is Geertz's recent description of cockfighting in Bali. The Balinese spend a great deal of time and money training and wagering on roosters, and social status is briefly gained or lost depending on how one handles the game. Yet, Geertz concludes, the Balinese cockfight is finally useless in terms of economic utility or status concerns; the deep play provides, above all, a *metasocial commentary*. "Its function, if you want to call it that, is interpretive—it is a Balinese reading of Balinese experience, a story they tell about themselves" (Geertz, 1973, p. 448).

How can an autotelic activity like rock climbing provide a base from which one can perceive culture more clearly? And are the interpretations of society thus obtained protostructural as well as antistructural; in other words, do they point toward new structures or simply ignore or countermand the existing ones? Does rock climbing produce metasocial commentary? These questions are addressed in a single text of one informant's deep-flow experience:

> You see who the hell you really are. It's important to learn about yourself, to open doors into the self. The mountains are the greatest place in the twentieth century to get this knowledge. . . . [There's] no place that more draws the best from human beings . . . [than] a mountaineering situation. Nobody hassles you to put your mind and body under tremendous stress to get to the top, there's nobody there to hassle you, force you, judge you. . . . Your comrades are there, but you all feel the same way anyway, you're all in it together. Who can you trust more in the twentieth century than these people? People after the same self-discipline as yourself, following the deeper commit-

ment. The façades come rolling off. A bond like that with other people is in itself an ecstasy.

... The investment is bigger. It's exhilarating to come closer and closer to self-discipline. You make your body go and everything hurts; then you look back in awe of the self, at what you've done, it just blows your mind. It leads to ecstasy, to self-fulfillment. If you win these battles enough, that battle against yourself, at least for a moment, it becomes easier to win the battles in the world. Sometimes I think it's my only survival in the space age; without that I wouldn't last a week out here. It gives you courage you can't draw in the city. . . .

Too many stimuli in the world, it's a smog, a quagmire. Up there the clouds lift . . . the façades are all gone. Down here people live a sheltered reality, a false security arranged by extracurricular thoughts. The self-consciousness of society is like a mask. We are born to wear it. . . . Up there you have the greatest chance of finding your potential for any form of learning. Up there the false masks, costumes, personae that the world puts on you—false self-consciousness, false self-awareness—fall away. People miscommunicate all the time . . . find it impossible to break through the fog of façades, begin to lose their identity. In civilization man doesn't live reality. One never thinks about the universe and man's place in it . . . you think about cars, schools, parties.

There is great potential when man is on the mountain. People are always searching, through booze, drugs, whatever. The closest man can come to it is through nature. Mountaineering builds up body and mind while learning about the deepest chasms of man. Up there you see man's true place in nature, you feel one with nature.

The mountains and nature bombard the mind with the question of what man is meant to be doing. The fact that one's mind freaks out in civilizations shows how unhealthy and abnormal they can be. We are the animals that have been most fucked up in the last thousand years. Up there you know you're right, down here you think you're right. How could so many things come from nature if we did not belong there? . . . We consume natural resources at a rate greater than at any time in history. Once resources are gone, that's it. The Indians have a simple life. They will survive. They live as nature teaches and know so much about the environment and world . . . a religious knowing.

> They know far better who they are . . . they are who they are. I want most of all to learn something deep about the animal man; then I can get my ticket and check out. I just have a better chance to find it in the mountains.

Although our informants differ somewhat in their choice of issues and values, and in their degree of concern with them, they reinforce the points made in this extended statement. Taken together, our climbers' statements clearly offer a meta-social commentary along the lines suggested by Geertz. The recurrent themes of this critique are summarized in Table 5. The listing could, of course, be expanded, but it includes the most consensual topics discussed by our informants. Several of

Table 5. Deep-Flow Experience in Rock Climbing

Normative Life	Rock-Climbing Experience
Informational noise: distraction and confusion of attention	One-pointedness of mind
Nebulosity of limits, demands, motivations, decisions, feedbacks	Clarity and manageability of limits, demands, decisions, feedbacks
Severing of action and awareness	Merging of action and awareness
Hidden, unpredictable dangers; unmanageable fears	Obvious danger subject to evaluation and control
Anxiety, worry, confusion	Happiness, health, vision
Slavery to the clock; life lived in spurts	Time out of time: timelessness
Carrot-and-stick preoccupation with exotelic, extrinsic material and social reward; orientation toward ends	Process orientation; concern for autotelic, intrinsic rewards; conquest of the useless
Dualism of mind and body	Integration of mind and body
Lack of self-understanding; false self-consciousness; war between the selves	Understanding of the true self, self-integration
Miscommunication with others; masks, statuses, and roles in an inegalitarian order; false independence or misplaced dependency	Direct and immediate communication with others in an egalitarian order; true and welcomed dependency on others

Normative Life	Rock-Climbing Experience
Confusion about man's place in nature or the universe; isolation from the natural order; destruction of the earth	Sense of man's place in the universe; oneness with nature; congruence of psychological and environmental ecology
Superficiality of concerns; thinness of meaning in the flatland	Dimension of depth "up there"; encounter with ultimate concerns

these items may be found to overlap with the Balinese example or with other deep players if fieldwork focusing on cross-cultural descriptions of flow experience was available. Other items in Table 5 are perhaps more tied to our own society and peculiar level of culture.

Both the Balinese and the rock climbers' "tales" are antistructural in Turner's sense because they involve the experience and portrayal of values, themes, and relations which are underplayed, repressed, or ignored in "real" life. According to Geertz, the Balinese find true but unsettling what they see of themselves in the cockfight. For the rock climbers, on the contrary, the alternative vision induced by climbing is intensely critical of the normative order. As one informant stated, "The self-consciousness of society is like a mask. . . . We are born to wear it." When society is "unmasked" in climbing, he much prefers its novel visage.

The cockfight, in Geertz's view, displays the social order in a new light, and the matter seems to end there. Comparing the cockfight to another genre in which metasocial commentary regularly appears, Geertz (1973, p. 443) writes: "Poetry makes nothing happen, Auden says in his elegy of Yeats. 'It survives in the valley of its saying . . . a way of happening, a mouth.' The cockfight too, in a colloquial sense, makes nothing happen." What about the climbers who must reenter the realm of facades, social and chemical smog, and worries about money and spouses, jobs and school? Do real changes take place as a result of their climbing experiences?

The climber-poet Guido Rey in *Peaks and Precipices* (1914, quoted in Knight, 1970, p. 44) answered the question in a pessimistic vein: "If climbers remained as good and as pure in the plains as they were in their ideal moments on the summit, other men, seeing them return, would believe them to be a troop of angels descended from heaven. But climbers, when they go home, become once more prey to their weaknesses, resume their bad habits, and write their articles for alpine journals." But for our informants, notably those who have deep-flow experiences, climbing does make things happen. They would, it might be said, send out Shelley as their champion against Auden, for they consciously attempt to use the discoveries generated by their "physical poems on the rock" as legislative protostructures for the redesign of daily life.

For some of our respondents, climbing itself forms the center of any new road map of life. They may, as two of our informants have done, exchange lucrative positions for carpentry jobs in the mountains, so that they can climb every day. One of these subjects explains: "I would have made a great deal of money in corporate life, but I realized one day that I wasn't enjoying it. I wasn't having the kind of experiences that make life rewarding. I saw that my priorities were mixed up, spending most of my hours in the office. . . . The years were slipping by. I enjoy being a carpenter. I live where it's quiet and beautiful, and I climb most every night. I figure that my own relaxation and availability will mean more to my family than the material things I can no longer give them." Other informants also have cross-cut traditional financial, educational, and status pathways to stay close to climbing. For some of these, climbing has become "a bloody drug," generally because it is the only activity in which they regularly have the experiences they have come to prize most highly.

Most, however, believe that the proper course lies not in the intensification of activity within this one narrowed field but in the *internalization* of the properties and characteristics of the structure that produced these experiences. The experiences can then be *generalized* to whatever other situations the individual is forced into or chooses to enter. Some climbers report that they use climbing as a paradigm to which they refer situations from other realms of life for clarity and decision. Others recognize that their goal is to learn to flow in any given situation they find themselves in. Any number of citations could be offered here to show the conscious transfer of formal and affective components from climbing into ordinary life. It seems that the deeper the flow experiences reported by the individuals, the greater effort they put forth in this protostructural cause. It cannot be contested that rock climbing has altered the lives of many individuals; at the same time, no one would suggest that the course of American culture has been seriously affected by the small band of visionaries climbing has produced. However, when we understand the importance of flow experiences in the lives of people in a wide range of activities—particularly those activities classed as "work," where flow experiences might be least expected—we may find ourselves in possession of a new set of analytical tools with which to approach a class of phenomena too often overlooked. An important new set of questions and insights, perhaps even programs for change, could result.

Conclusions

Like any flow activity, rock climbing has structural elements which produce in the actor a set of intrinsically enjoyable experiences. In chess the structure involves the actor through intellectual competition; in climbing, danger draws the actor into physical and mental concentration. In each case, the person discovers a state of being which is rare in normative life. For a climber this state of being includes a heightened sense of physical achievement, a feeling of harmony with the environment, trust in climbing companions, and clarity of purpose. These experiences are in some ways different from what one gets from chess or from other flow activities. Yet what is common to all experiences is the total involvement of body and mind with a feasible task which validates the competence, indeed the very existence, of the actor. It is this that makes the activity worthwhile, despite the absence of utilitarian rewards.

A person who has attained this state of being inevitably compares it with the experiences of normative life. The comparison affords a relativizing perspective on the culture in which one is usually immersed. Deep flow is an ecstatic experience, in the sense that ecstasy means "standing out from" the ordinary. Whether this comparative glimpse will be liberating, and result in personal or social change, depends on many internal and external factors. But it seems appropriate to consider the heightened mental state of flow a prerequisite for the development of new cultural forms.

The practical consequences of what one can learn about intrinsic rewards from rock climbers are suggestive but difficult to apply to concrete social change. Our interest in this topic has been both antistructural and protostructural. We are aware of the amount of worry and boredom that people experience in schools, factories, and their own homes. We are concerned about the meaninglessness and alienation in daily activities, and hence the constant efforts we make to get extrinsic rewards which will serve as symbolic counters to compensate for the barrenness of experience. It is for this reason that we have turned to flow activities, to learn from them the mechanisms by which ordinary life could be made more enjoyable.

The most general conclusion to be drawn from this analysis is that to make tasks more enjoyable to a significant proportion of the population, there should be a variety of graduated activities available, covering the range of native and acquired skills. In his novel *Island,* Aldous Huxley made rock climbing mandatory for all the adolescents of that happy utopian society. But since the same challenges are unlikely to produce flow in people of very different skills, prescribing rock climbing to all is no solution to the problem of alienation. By the same token, our compulsory and uniform educational system is a sure guarantee that many, perhaps a majority in each generation, will spend their youth in meaningless unrewarding tasks. To provide intrinsic rewards, an activity must be finely calibrated to a person's skills—including his physical, intellectual, emotional, and social abilities. Such a personalized concern for each individual is antithetical to the structure of mass society with its rigidly bureaucratic forms of production, education, and administration.

If nothing else, the study of flow has produced some

concepts and methods for working more purposefully toward institutions that provide growth and enjoyment. Besides the utilitarian calculus of productivity and material gains, we can set up a criterion of personal satisfaction. Once we succeed in defining flow operationally, we may be able to use it as a benchmark of societal progress, complementing the one-sided indicators of material achievement currently in use.

Chapter 7

Measuring the Flow Experience in Rock Dancing

▲▲▲

That chess and rock climbing conform to the theoretical model of flow presented in Chapter Four was confirmed by the interviews with participants in those activities. Yet the support for the theory was based on impressionistic reports rather than clearly operationalized data. Our next step was to develop a simple questionnaire and an interview coding system that would permit us to estimate (a) the number of elements of the flow experience a person derives from an activity and (b) the ratio of skills to challenges perceived by a person in a given activity. To perfect these instruments, we interviewed a small number of

This chapter was written by Judy Hendin and Mihaly Csikszentmihalyi.

people involved in rock dancing. All our respondents had about equal experience in this form of dance, but half were actively enjoying the activity and the other half were participating only with reluctance. By comparing the responses of these two subgroups, we hoped to provide validity for a quantitative evaluation of flow, to complement the qualitative evaluations presented in the preceding chapters.

"Rock dance," the sort of dancing that people have done since the late 1960s at social gatherings such as parties and singles' bars, is generally danced to what is known as rock music. The term *rock dance* is not a universally held native name. In fact, no particular term for this sort of dancing is used today; many participants simply call it "dancing." An analysis of the distinctive features of rock dance provides the clearest path to its definition. First of all, rock dancing is purportedly participatory, as opposed to performance dancing. The people are not supposed to be dancing for an audience. (Often, however, the dancers are very cognizant of and affected by others watching them.) Second, rock dance is normally acted out by couples (usually male and female), not by groups. Third, rock dance is improvisational rather than choreographic. That is, dance movements are selected by the individual dancer in a relatively spontaneous manner; the dancer must create his own movements, his own sequences, and his own patterns. The improvisation may apply both to the smaller segments of individual movements and to the longer chains of movements. In other words, improvisational dance is composed of individually created segments or of more standard dance steps performed in random sequence; in contrast, choreographic dances consist of a relatively nonrandom, patterned set of movements. Fourth, rock dance is noncontactual rather than contactual. Finally, rock dance is usually done with fast rather than slow movements.

Rock Dance as Flow Activity

Rock dance is a rich and enjoyable activity for many people. Our interest lies in the fact that rock dance is structurally similar to other flow activities. Although its rules are not as defined as those of chess or climbing, rock dance does have rules, which the participants recognize, as well as clear limits. Within these limits and rules, the actor is confronted by a set of opportunities for action which are peculiar to the activity. He or she can move to the rhythm of the music, communicate and interact with partners, use the body in ways that are not done in ordinary life. Out of this match between opportunities and action develops the flow experience. Although some people are attracted to rock dancing by extrinsic rewards, such as getting physical exercise or meeting people and initiating sexual relationships with them, the primary motivation for rock dancing is usually autotelic. When asked to give the main reasons for their enjoyment of rock dancing, our subjects mentioned body movement, involvement with the music, involvement with a partner, and the feeling of togetherness. These are the primary opportunities for action offered by the activity. The dancer's attention is focused on a limited stimulus field, which includes his own body, the music, and often his partner's movements and messages. As one dancer sums it up, "I like the feeling of motion, the feeling of trying to coordinate motion with music, the social part of it." Several subjects commented on the kinesthetic feeling of body movement and the creative self-expression it allows.

> Once I get into it, then I just float along, having fun, just feeling myself move around.
>
> It's great physical activity. . . . I get sort of a physical high from it. . . . I get very sweaty, very feverish or sort of ecstatic when everything is going really well.
>
> The main thing about dancing is that it's an expressive medium. What do you do? . . . You move about and try to express yourself in terms of those motions. That's where it's at. It's a body language kind of communicative medium, in a way. . . . When it's going good, I'm really expressing myself well in terms of the music and in terms of the people that are out there.
>
> If I'm really into it, then it won't get boring; then I'll just be expressing and won't be thinking about movements at all.

> I don't necessarily think about my body and what my body's doing. And sometimes I discover things about my body. I discover things that my body can do that I didn't know it could do.

The music limits the stimulus field by focusing attention. A clear, consistent beat was frequently cited as the most important aspect of "good" rock dance music. Most subjects agreed with the subject who said: "That's why everyone likes the Rolling Stones—because they have this incredible beat in their music, and their music accentuates that beat so that you can't sit still."

The high volume of musical sound in a rock-dance situation serves to eliminate distractions and focus attention. Loudness also furthers the loss of self and a "merging with the music" which many subjects report.

> It has to be very loud to dance. . . . It's more overpowering when it's loud, and it gets you more into what's going on, concentrating entirely on the music.

> When you feel [the music] resonating through you, it really helps. 'Cause when it's loud, like when you're dancing to a rock group, you can really feel yourself vibrate almost. And also, the louder it is, the more it blocks out other noises, so it's more of a total immersion in the music, which is also a very good sensation and is also conducive to just dancing and being part of the music—almost incorporating it.

> I can get totally into the music and not get self-conscious about dancing. I know that when I first start or if there is some distraction, or I'm conscious of the way I'm dancing, I don't dance as well as when I'm really totally into the music. [I feel the music in my body] when dancing. That's the way it's expressed, the way I feel about it, the way I think about it—which is why it's hard to articulate, because it's something that just comes out in my body, 'cause I don't usually think about the steps I'm going to do consciously.

In addition to the body and the music, some dancers focus on interaction with their partners. The partner serves as a source of feedback to the subject's dancing and self-expression.

One of the main challenges perceived by some dancers is the coordination of the motion of the two partners: "I like doing something with another person, trying to coordinate with another person. . . . Usually the kind of dancing that I do is dependent upon feedback, because there is not a set sequence of events, not a set step, so you have to follow what the other person is doing to be compatible."

Opportunities for action of a "social" kind are much more salient in rock dancing than in any of the other activities we studied. The challenges perceived by the participants include not only involvement with movements, music, and partners but also their feeling of ease in the social situation. When asked what is rewarding about rock dance, one subject answered, "Spending pleasant times, especially with friends. A lot of people get together in a light, pleasant thing to do and nobody's usually too worried and everyone forgets about everything except just listening and moving. It's a good atmosphere, especially if there's lots of friends around." Another subject commented, "My behavior during a dance is directed mostly to enhancing this feeling of the group that I'm with."

In this sense an important element of rock dance is the joy of sociability that Durkheim has called "collective effervescence," the feeling of "communitas" that Turner (1974) has examined in ceremonials of status passage, in pilgrimages, and in other religious rituals. If the dancer feels "uncomfortable" or if he knows few people at the dance, he may become anxious and be unable to participate fully in the activity. As one subject said, "[One of] the . . . things that would distract me would be if there was a complicated social situation going on and [I was] trying to keep track of too many things and not paying attention to what I was doing." Distractions are minimized by dimming the lights, thereby reducing visual distractions. Alcohol, frequently cited by subjects as a prerequisite to enjoyable dancing, also limits the field of awareness, cuts out centers of critical thinking, and lowers self-consciousness.

Thus, rock dance allows for the elements of flow to be experienced by the participants. However, there are also aspects which detract from the possibility of the participants' experiencing flow. These consist in ambiguity of feedback, chance for self-consciousness, and the ease with which the action can be interrupted.

A typical element of flow activities is the presence of direct, unambiguous feedback. In rock dance, however, the rules are not clear enough to allow the dancer to determine precisely whether he or she is doing well or poorly. In addition, feedback from one's partner may be ambiguous; for instance, movements can be interpreted as a sexual advance or as merely a dance pattern. An articulate male subject states the situation well: "[In expressing your emotions,] you have ambiguity on your side. You can get away with a lot. You can pull something off and then the other person has to decide which level of meaning it had. Was it an advance? Was it a pass? Was it just 'dancing?' Was it meaningless? . . . It's a vocabulary that's not as clear as words, so you can get away with more that way. It's a little more elastic [than words] for most people. You can stretch it. . . . You can be very sexually aggressive and fall back on it as just dance. And you can watch for things that might not come up under a normal situation. Then you have to figure out whether they're just dance or whether they have content." A female informant describes the situation similarly: "Like being aggressive or flirting. Like there's a real back-out in a dance situation. You can always say you were dancing and not flirting. So you can do all kinds of things, and then act like, 'That was the way it went,' or if you get picked up, fine. Whereas you might hazard more of yourself if it was in a nondancing situation." This ambiguity about the meaning of action may be an asset to the skilled dancer, because it adds a whole new level of challenges. But people who are less sure about their ability to negotiate interactions are often confused and worried by it.

Self-consciousness is increased in rock dance because of the presence of bystanders, those people who are located around the dancing area and who watch the dancing. When asked whether she feels that people in the room are watching her, one subject replied, "That's part of what makes me self-conscious." A person who rarely gets deeply involved in dancing said, "Generally I tend to think about whether I'm [looking like] a fool . . . to everyone who is watching. . . . I tend to view them as threatening factors rather than anything else. . . . I feel embarrassed because I know there's a lot of people watching, and I feel that in their minds they're saying, 'Why is that idiot doing that?' and wishing perhaps they were in company where people wouldn't make an exhibition of themselves in that way."

The boundaries of rock dance are also much more permeable than those of some other flow activities. In chess, rock climbing, or surgery, once the action has begun, it must continue until its climax. In contrast, a rock dancer may stop at any point because every three or four minutes an exit is provided by the change of the music. It is also relatively easy for a dancer to stop the action even in the middle of a piece of music.

Thus, the structure of the rock-dance activity consists of aspects that both increase and decrease the probability of participants' experiencing flow. This combination might be used to classify dance as a "shallow-flow" activity, in contrast to deep-flow activities, in which fewer deterrents to flow are present.

Methods

Sample. This particular investigation deals with rock dance as practiced by white, middle-class Americans of varied ethnic backgrounds, at such occasions as parties, singles' bars, and college dances. The sample consisted of twelve subjects. All were white, middle-class Americans, and all were living in urban communities at the time of the study. The average age was 24.25 years, ranging from 19 to 29. The average educational level was 5.3 years of education beyond the high school level, ranging from completion of two years of undergraduate study to completion of three years of graduate study. No significant correlations were found between age or educational level and the frequency of involvement in rock dance. This sample was decided upon in order to maximize the possibility of observing the subjects in rock-dance situations. Because social dancing is a complex activity, highly different patterns from those presented here might be found if a different sample were selected. For example, social dancing in black American culture is a very different phenomenon from social dancing in white culture, as any comparison between *American Bandstand* and *Soul Train* (two television shows about young people dancing together—the first mostly white; the second, black) will verify. One might also expect variations to occur between the dancing experiences of high school and college students, and between populations of different colleges. For this reason, this analysis proposes to be accurate in detail only for the sample specified, though it is certainly relevant to similar activities among other groups.

The data were gathered from observations, casual discussions, interviews, and questionnaires. Of the twelve subjects selected, six were expected to experience flow when they dance, and six were not. However, we cannot say with certainty that any one of our subjects had *never* flowed in rock dance. Equal numbers of males and females were interviewed in each category, and all subjects seemed to be equally familiar with the activity.

Subjects were selected primarily by observation at parties and dances, supplemented by casual discussions. Before the desired subjects were selected, initial criteria had to be chosen for inclusion in the two groups; that is, people who experience flow in rock dance and people who do not. The following criteria were used in the selection of subjects: (1) Flow was assumed to occur if the subject verbally professed an enjoyment of rock dancing (saying, for instance, that he wished there would be more dancing parties) or if, in a potential dancing situation, the subject initiated the dancing and encouraged people to dance. Another way of determining the presence of flow was the appearance of the dancer while he was dancing. If he appeared to be "into" the dancing, he was assumed to be in flow. Being "into" the dancing—following the meaning of the contemporary vocabulary word *into*—means to be deeply involved in, interested in, and enjoying the elements of an activity. This was assumed to be happening when a dancer moved with energy and/or when the dancer's face conveyed that he was happy or that he was deeply engrossed in the activity. Obviously, these are very subjective judgments. But they proved to be useful as preliminary tools for gathering a balanced sample, and, as will be shown, they correlate with the self-ratings of the subjects. (2) Nonflow in rock dance was presumed to occur if the subject verbally professed a dislike of dancing, if he refused to dance when invited, or if he simply sat around at a dancing situation and never danced. (Note that the skill level of the dancer as perceived by the researcher was not a criterion for determining the presence or absence of flow.)

Interviews and questionnaires. After selection, each subject was interviewed. The interview schedule was based on the standard form used for other flow activities. As the study progressed, the interview schedule was modified. The interview schedule served as a framework; it was open-ended, and subjects were encouraged to ponder aloud. The average interview lasted three and a half hours, and a total of 330 pages of transcript was produced.

The emphasis with these interviews was on how rock dancing is experienced by the participants. Of great value, therefore, were phenomenological accounts of the dancing experience, of the motions and emotions involved in rock dancing. But such accounts are difficult to obtain. In *The Phenomenology of Dance,* Sheets (1966) introduces this problem by describing dance as a "form-in-the-making," a "dynamic image." Dancer and dance are one at the prereflective level. When the dancer reflects on the experience in order to describe it, the dynamism of the experience is gone and the dance is a different experience; that is, thinking about the dance is a different experience from dancing the dance. These difficulties limit the possibilities of any analysis based on phenomenological data, as we have pointed out in the preceding chapters. However, despite the problems, much useful information along these lines was gathered.

In addition to the interview, each subject filled out a questionnaire consisting of a list of challenges and a list of skills relevant to rock dancing. These challenges and skills involved body movement, music, and relationship with the partner. Challenges relating to the self and to the social situation in rock dance were also listed; however, at the time the questionnaire was developed, the skills involved in handling the self and the social situation were not known and therefore were not included in the list of skills.

The list of challenges included releasing energy, lacking self-consciousness, looking good, building up energy, dancing to songs that the subject has not heard before, feeling motion, feeling comfortable, losing the self, feeling in control of the social situation, relaxing, exercising, putting a lot of thought into the dancing, having people watch the subject's dancing, merging with the music, feeling in control of the relationship with the partner, controlling body movements, concentrating, having variety in body movements, feeling tired, attracting people sexually, repeating the same movement(s) many times, coordinating body motion with the music, being different from the way the subject usually is, communicating nonverbally, meeting people, seeing self as one with the universe, feeling high on drugs, communicating with the partner, and feeling drunk. The list of skills included communicating nonverbally, knowing a lot of dance steps, being able to follow the partner, being able to follow the beat, communicating with the partner, dancing to many kinds of music, repeating the same movement many times, being able to move the body a lot, being graceful, not repeating a movement many times, and enjoying the dancing.

Each subject was asked to indicate, by scores that were later ranked on a six-point scale, which challenges were important to him. In addition, on a similar scale, each subject was asked to rate his ability to do several particular things when he was dancing. The questionnaire also asked the subject to rate his general skill level.

Measurement of flow. After the interviews and questionnaires were completed, we began to use these two sources to determine which rock dancers were often in flow and which were not. Because the sample included subjects who were expected to be in flow and others who were not, an operational definition of flow became a crucial goal.

With the data at hand, the presence of flow could be determined in two ways: (1) If a subject were in flow, he or she would presumably experience a greater number of flow elements in the activity. So a checklist of the elements of flow derived from the model, and their appropriate degrees of intensity, was constructed. Each subject was then scored for the incidence of each element on the basis of his interview transcript. (2) If the perceived challenges were commensurate with perceived skills for a particular subject, that subject would presumably be in flow. If the ratio of challenges to skills significantly deviated from the one-to-one ratio, the subject would presumably not be in flow. The questionnaires which asked each subject to rate his perception of the challenges and skills involved in rock dancing were used as the basis for these calculations.

The basic hypothesis was the validation of the flow model. If the model was viable, then the six dancers with intense enjoyment of and involvement in the activity would differ from the remaining six in two respects: (1) They would mention more elements of the flow experience in their interviews. (2) They would list a more equal proportion of challenges to skills in the questionnaire describing the activity.

Results

Intensity of flow. The interviews were analyzed by two raters, to find out whether it was possible to identify flow from the respondents' answers. The raters used a checklist derived from the theoretical model; the elements in the checklist are listed in Table 6. For instance, if the reading of the interview suggested that the subject while dancing is never distracted, is unaware of his surroundings, knows clearly what to do, and feels in control of himself and in harmony with the environment, then he would be scored as having experienced these aspects of flow.

The intensity of each element of flow was differentiated on a scale of 4 to 0. The closer a person's answers came to the flow experience, the higher the numerical value assigned to them. For example, one predicate of the flow experience is that a person is rarely distracted from the activity. Each subject's interview was scored depending on whether he said that he is distracted during rock dance "always," "often," "sometimes," "rarely," or "never." "Never" was scored 4, "rarely" 3, and so forth; "always" was rated 0.

Table 6. Incidence of Elements of Flow in Involved and Uninvolved Rock Dancers

Element of Experience (rated from interviews)	Involved Dancers ($N = 6$) (in flow)		Uninvolved Dancers ($N = 6$) (not usually in flow)		t value of Differences*
	Mean	SD	Mean	SD	
Perception of surroundings (less)	3.0	1.67	2.7	1.03	.38
Thinking about other things (less)	2.3	.52	1.8	1.33	.85
Having to make an effort to keep mind on activity (less)	3.2	.75	2.3	1.51	1.32
Distractions (less)	3.2	.41	2.3	1.03	1.96[a]
Awareness of body (more)	4.0	.00	4.0	.00	.00
Awareness of problems (less)	4.0	.00	4.0	.00	.00
Passage of time (faster)	4.0	.00	3.0	1.20	2.04[a]
Clearly knowing right things to do	2.8	.75	0.3	.52	6.76[c]
Getting direct feedback (more)	3.7	.52	1.8	1.17	3.58[c]
Control of self (more)	2.7	.82	2.7	1.63	.00
Control of relationship with partner (more)	3.0	.00	2.5	1.05	1.16
Control of social situation (more)	3.2	.41	1.5	1.22	3.21[c]
Self-consciousness (less)	3.2	.75	1.0	.63	5.50[c]
Harmony with the environment (more)	4.0	.00	2.7	1.03	3.09[b]

*Numbers marked [a] are significant at the .05 level; those marked [b] are significant at the .01 level; and those marked [c] are significant at the .005 level.

Two independent raters without any training agreed completely on 50 percent of the scores; they disagreed by one point on 36 percent of the scores, by two points on 10 percent, and by three points on 4 percent of the scores. The three-point disagreements were resolved through consultation and compromise; otherwise, the senior author's judgment confirmed one of the scores. With more time it is clear that a completely reliable scoring system could be devised; the one adopted here was considered reliable enough for the exploratory goals of the study.

Table 6 reports mean scores based on the analysis of the twelve interviews. As the table shows, most of the expected elements of flow were usually experienced by all dancers in the activity, but the six subjects who were expected to flow more because they were more involved with dancing mentioned a more intense experience of the flow elements. The largest difference is in terms of "clearly knowing the right things to do" ($p < .005$). Uninvolved dancers, although they have just as much experience as the involved ones, almost never feel that they know the right thing to do when they dance. These subjects explained in their interviews that in rock dance there are never clear-cut actions to follow, either in dance movements or in social interaction.

> I don't know that there really would be any right or wrong things to do. Maybe some people might not think that you were quite as smooth a dancer as someone else, or were able to move quite as well along with the music. But I think just about anything you do is pretty much O.K.

> You see, when you're terribly self-conscious in social situations, the right thing to do is never clear. Something which should be perfectly routine to someone who is adept in dealing with social situations becomes very difficult, very problematic, to someone who is very self-conscious.

The lack of clearly knowing the right things to do may be attributed to the improvisational nature of rock-dance movements, in that there are no specific movements to be performed. The lack of clearly knowing the right things to do socially is probably inherent in any social situation.

The second-largest difference between involved and uninvolved dancers concerns self-consciousness. The uninvolved dancers are on the average "often" self-conscious, while the involved ones average a score of "rarely." Other elements that distinguish the two groups are clarity of feedback, control over the social situation, and the sense of self-transcendence that results in harmony with the environment. Seven of the fourteen elements show significant differences between the two groups—a quite impressive result considering the small samples involved. The results confirm that the involved dancers, who were selected with the expectation that they would experience flow more intensely, do in fact do so.

Table 6 also gives an indication of which elements of flow are most readily accessible in rock dancing and which can be experienced only with difficulty. It seems that every dancer feels more aware of his body but less aware of his personal problems while dancing. There is generally less awareness of the surroundings, a greater sense of control of self and of the relationship with the partner, and less chance to think about other things. On none of these dimensions was there a significant difference between the two groups. Perhaps these are more or less "constant" experiences that the activity offers to anyone who takes part in it. The remaining elements are presumably more complex experiences that are more difficult to obtain, and hence define the deep-flow state in rock dance.

An interesting aspect of control of self in rock dance is not shown by the table. It was assumed that people who flow in rock dance would feel greater control over themselves and their movements. However, when asked whether they feel more in control or less so during dancing, six subjects answered "Both." Here are some clues to the paradox:

> Yes and no. Yes in the sense that I'm not out of control, but no in the sense that it's also partially controlled by the music, and I wouldn't do that without the music, wouldn't move in the same way.

> I think I'm aware of myself, but I'm not using my awareness for the same thing that I usually use it for. I'm aware of myself, but when I'm dancing, I don't use my awareness

> of myself to control or direct my body. It seems to just exist. It's tuned in mostly to the music or the environment and less to controlling or directing my actions. . . . I think it's some kind of a paradox in a way, because I'm more conscious of my body because it's in action and doing things that it doesn't usually do and behaving in ways it doesn't usually behave, and it seems to take on a life of its own, kind of. And I'm so much a part of it, but I'm also separate from it in a way.

This feeling of being simultaneously in control and not in control may be a characteristic particular to rock dance, or it may indicate a general element of flow experiences.

Similarly, several subjects stated that time seems to pass both faster and slower than normal when they are dancing.

> It might go slower in terms of living the moment, that I would be more aware of it. But it would go faster in the sense of somebody says, "it's 12:00," and I feel like we've been there an hour, and we've been there three.

> Two things happen. One is that it seems to pass really fast in one sense. After it's passed, it seems to have passed really fast. I see that it's 1:00 in the morning, and I say, "Ah ha, just a few minutes ago it was 8:00." But then while I'm dancing . . . it seems like it's been much longer than maybe it really was.

Ratio of challenges and skills. In assessing the relationship between challenges and skills, we assumed that a one-to-one (1:1) ratio would indicate a flow state. Therefore, for each area of challenges and skills, we determined the optimum ratio—the ratio in which perceived challenges are commensurate with perceived skills—by dividing the number of challenge items by the number of skill items. For example, the total number of challenge items on the questionnaire was 29, and the total number of skill items was 11. Therefore, the optimum ratio of challenges to skills for the total activity is 29/11, or 2.64. By combining related challenge and skill items, we grouped the items into four sets: *total rock-dance activity, movement, music,* and *partner.* We then computed the ratio of challenges to skills in each of these four areas for each subject; finally, we calculated the distance of each subject's ratio from the optimum ratio. Those subjects who were closest to the optimum ratio were expected to experience flow in rock dance.

Table 7 shows the distance of each subject's challenges/skills ratio from the optimum ratio for the four areas mentioned above. As can readily be seen, the mean distance from the optimum ratio is always less for the subjects who were expected to experience flow in rock dance. The dancers who enjoy the activity and are involved in it find a more even match between their own skills and the opportunities offered by dancing than do dancers who are not involved. Most notably, people who enjoy dancing rate "moving well" as very important to dance, and

Table 7. Distance of Subjects' Challenges/Skills Ratios from Optimum Ratio

	Areas of Involvement with Rock Dance			
Subjects	Movement	Music	Partner	Total Rock Dance
Involved:				
901	.39	.64	.33	.08
903	.64	.40	1.40	.95
905	.51	.30	.50	.78
907	.07	.25	.50	.43
909	.29	.22	.00	.07
910	.07	.25	.50	.44
Mean	.33	.34	.54	.46
SD	.23	.16	.46	.36
Uninvolved:				
902	2.40	2.00	1.00	.98
904	1.20	.16	.00	.44
906	.74	.21	1.60	.81
908	2.20	3.00	2.50	2.61
911	.18	.00	1.00	.14
912	1.69	.50	.50	1.86
Mean	1.40	.98	1.10	1.14
SD	.86	1.23	.87	.93
t value of differences*	2.94[b]	1.26	1.39[a]	1.67[a]

*Numbers marked [a] are significant at the .1 level; the number marked [b] is significant at the .01 level.

they rate their skills high on this dimension. Those who do not enjoy dancing rate the importance of various forms of movement either higher or lower than their skills in that area—hence their significantly greater departure from the 1:1 ratio.

One might notice that subjects 904, 906, and 911, who were selected as uninvolved dancers, frequently fall within the range of those who flow. In the case of 904, a probable explanation is that this subject stressed (during her interview) that the pressures of the social situation were the main deterrent to her getting involved in rock dancing. She said, "I have to be really comfortable with people around here to dance with them, and I'm not very comfortable with most people around here in parties." But because the challenges and skills involving the social aspect of rock dance were not incorporated into the questionnaire on which the calculations in Table 7 are based, what might be her lowest skill is omitted from her profile. If social aspects had been included, this subject presumably would fall into the nonflow category. Subjects 906 and 911 present a different dilemma. During the preinterview selection process, both subjects professed a dislike of rock dancing, and at parties they were seen to refuse several insistent invitations to dance. However, during the interview, both subjects modified their positions, explaining that in fact they do enjoy rock dancing at times. Consequently, in their self-ratings of perceived challenges and skills, as shown in Table 7, the distance between their challenges/skills ratio and the optimum ratio is often very small. Thus, the preinterview selection of uninvolved subjects may have been in error in two, or possibly three, cases.

Table 8 shows the mean number of challenges and skills perceived by the two groups in the three areas and in the total activity. The results indicate that people who are expected to experience flow rate their skills higher in executing movements and responding to the music, but they do not see significantly more opportunities for action in these areas than those who are presumed not to flow. On the other hand, involved dancers perceive greater challenges in the "partner" area but attribute no greater skills to themselves in this area. As far as the total activity is concerned, the people who are supposed to flow see signif-

Table 8. Mean Challenge and Skill Ratings by Involved and Uninvolved Rock Dancers

Area of Activity		Involved Dancers $N = 6$		Uninvolved Dancers $N = 6$		t value of differences*	
		Challenges	Skills	Challenges	Skills	Challenges	Skills
Movement	Mean	24.50	18.17	21.83	9.33	1.04	3.46[b]
	SD	2.74	4.83	5.64	3.98		
Music	Mean	10.67	8.50	8.67	4.50	1.72	3.94[b]
	SD	2.66	1.22	1.03	2.17		
Partner	Mean	10.00	4.00	8.00	3.17	2.24[a]	1.53
	SD	1.26	.63	1.79	1.17		
Total Activity	Mean	89.67	41.17	79.67	25.83	2.12[a]	3.10[b]
	SD	11.00	7.50	3.50	9.56		

*Numbers marked [a] are significant at the .05 level; those marked [b] are significant at the .005 level.

icantly more challenges in rock dance, and they especially feel that they have greater skills in the activity.

It should be kept in mind that all subjects have been exposed to rock dance, and all seemed to have approximately equal familiarity with it. Hence, the differences are due not to greater or lesser experience with the activity but to the ability to derive enjoyment from it. This ability, in turn, seems to be based primarily on the level of skills a person perceives himself as possessing to meet the opportunities for action. The "skills" involved are not just physical, but include the ability to respond to music, to communicate with partners, and to negotiate complex interpersonal situations.

Conclusions

Rock dance shares the characteristics of other flow activities in that it presents specific demands and opportunities to the dancers, and the participants feel that they must exercise certain skills if they are going to enjoy rock dancing. However, unlike other flow activities which have been investigated, rock dancing is heavily a social activity in which challenges and skills are not as objective as they are in chess, rock climbing, or surgery. Nonobjectivity is compounded by the improvisational nature of rock dance; that is, since no specific steps and patterns are demanded by the activity, the skills of a rock dancer cannot be objectively measured.

Given these limitations, we developed two methods for determining the presence or absence of the flow state in rock dancers; each method led to different ramifications for the understanding of the activity under study. In the first method, scoring interview transcripts resulted in a significantly higher incidence of flow elements for subjects who get deeply involved in dancing than for subjects who do not. The scoring shed light on the nature of rock dance and suggested a useful way to compare other flow activities. In the future, this interview coding sheet could be given to subjects as a questionnaire in order to avoid translation from interview transcript to coding sheet. In the second method, the ratio of challenges to skills was significantly closer to the optimum ratio (a one-to-one ratio) for dancers who get deeply involved in dancing than for those who do not. The ratios for each subject showed that this method is useful for determining the presence or absence of flow in individual subjects. This method is also useful for clarifying the specific challenges and skills involved in an activity.

In future studies, a complete list of challenges and skills could be presented to each subject. The subject would then be asked to classify each element as a challenge or a skill and to rate the elements on the basis of their importance to him. With such data, a more complete picture of the flow activity could be assembled. These questionnaires could also be administered to groups of people who participate in different kinds of social dancing. This type of study might lead to insights about the differences between various groups—differences in their dancing and in more general characteristics.

Further investigations will be done with the data already at hand to determine the frequency of boredom and worry in subjects. Also, differentiating between female and male subjects may be found to be significant.

This study of rock dance has suggested viable methods for determining the presence or absence of the flow state in participants. A step has been taken to describe in concrete terms this intangible phenomenological experience. Despite the small number of respondents, statistically significant differences were found between people who were predicted to flow and those who were expected not to experience the flow state in rock dancing. The results showed that the former more often knew the right things to do, were less self-conscious, got clearer feedback, were more in control of the social situation, felt more in harmony with the environment, felt that time passed faster, and were less often distracted. In addition, people who were expected to flow perceived a significantly closer balance between their skills and the challenges of the activity. This match of actions and opportunities was in part due to their higher estimation of skills possessed.

These results confirm that the flow model developed in Chapter Four can be empirically verified, and they validate the hypothesis derived from that theory. It is now possible to use the methods presented here to continue testing the model in a variety of other settings, with larger samples, until a fair degree of confidence in its viability is achieved. When that point is reached, a number of other important questions will be opened up for investigation. We may then be able to determine, for example, why some people experience flow in one activity and others do not; how enjoyment can be intensified in a given setting; and whether different activities can be compared in terms of the enjoyment they make possible.

Chapter 8

Enjoying Work: Surgery

▲▲

That rock climbing and chess can be better understood in terms of a common model is perhaps not too surprising. They are both "leisure" activities, although one involves physical skills and the other relies on cognitive, symbolic performance. It is less obvious that dancing should fit the model, since dance is usually viewed as an expressive artistic form rather than a game or sport. But the real question is whether the flow model can be usefully applied to activities that are completely removed from the field of leisure and even artistic expression. If flow is experienced only in nonwork situations, it is hopeless to expect that work can be restructured into an intrinsically rewarding activity. Therefore, we need to show that jobs can also have some of

This chapter was written with Jean Hamilton Holcomb and Isabella Csikszentmihalyi.

the structural elements of flow activities, and hence that they are able to provide intrinsically rewarding experiences.

To illustrate the continuity between the worlds of play and work, we chose the profession of surgery. At first glance this choice may seem inappropriate. There appears to be little in common between the abstract combat of a chess player and the grim, life-and-death struggle of a surgeon. Yet surgery is an ideal example of a flow activity in an occupational setting. The surgeon's work consists of discrete episodes with clearly designated beginnings and ends. The surgical operation requires complete concentration, it provides immediate feedback, it has unambiguous criteria of right and wrong. Because of its structural characteristics, one expects that surgery will be experienced as enjoyable for the same reason that "leisure" activities are enjoyable.

The material in this chapter is based on a series of interviews with twenty-one surgeons. Nine are in private practice, twelve teach in training and research institutions; about half practice in the Middle West and half in the Southwest. A few are interns fresh out of medical school, and some are nationally known experts in very difficult specialties. The interviewer was a medical student with graduate psychology training.

Extrinsic Rewards in Surgery

Before turning to intrinsically rewarding qualities of the practice of surgery, one must account for the very substantial extrinsic rewards which are also available to surgeons. Medicine is at the very top of the status hierarchy in our society, and surgery is one of the most esteemed specialties within the profession. In addition, financial rewards are certainly not negligible. The layman might conclude that status and money are sufficient to explain why some people are motivated to be surgeons. But talking to them makes clear that the act of operating is a flow process with very strong intrinsic rewards. Practically all of the surgeons we interviewed describe surgery as "fun," "exciting," "feels great," "feels real good," "aesthetically pleasing," "dramatic and very satisfying," "like taking narcotics," and so on. Obviously, surgery is overdetermined by a host of extrinsic and intrinsic rewards. The task at hand is to find out how surgery can provide intrinsic rewards.

Researchers who have studied medical doctors usually postulate that the intrinsic rewards of the profession are mainly (a) the development of professional skills and (b) the opportunities for service to patients (Bloom, 1958; Nathanson and Becker, 1973, p. 270). Such rewards, however (which, according to the present model, are *extrinsic* in any case), sound suspiciously rationalized and high on social desirability. To the direct question "Why do you do surgery?" only about one third of the respondents mentioned as the primary reason the ability to effect a cure. Another third, while mentioning that helping patients is important, emphasized the challenge derived from their own efforts to arrest the disease. The others gave as their main reason for being in surgery the enjoyment of the activity: "It is fun," "I enjoy the entire process," "It is more exciting than anything else," "I like to work with my hands," and so forth. Even those most concerned with the patients' well-being stressed the importance of obtaining "specific answers," "a dramatic cure," "a clear resolution." These were some typical responses in this category:

> I like the direct results of my work. It's enjoyable to change the course of a disease, to effect a cure by direct action. You don't have to wait around for a pill or drug to take effect.

> Because of the joy it gives me to completely cure somebody by removing or repairing something once and for all. It's all or nothing, very direct.

In effect, curing the patient seems to be important as part of the feedback to the surgeon's activity, like a score in a tennis match, rather than an extrinsic goal. As one respondent phrased it, with perhaps a touch of exaggeration: "You get results right away, direct results which mean that the patient was either killed or cured." Surgeons surely would not enjoy operating if they did not heal a person in the process—just as climbers would not climb if they could not measure their progress by getting higher up on the rock, and chess players would stop playing if they never won. The point is that curing people is for surgeons a counter which proves that their skills were adequate to meet the challenges. Therefore, healing ceases to be an extrinsic reward and becomes the culminating event that gives closure to the activity.

When asked whether they had ever considered a different profession, all of our surgeons said that they had not; the academic surgeons would not consider being private practitioners or specialists in any other medical branch, and the private practitioners said that they would never practice any other specialty. All said that they would not want to be internists: "not for love or money," "not under any circumstance," "not if it paid twice as much." The internist's job, according to our respondents, is sedentary and does not allow for dramatic cures, direct intervention, clear-cut results. Only two out of the twenty-one surgeons admitted that financial considerations affected their experience of the activity. Most said that they would rather do surgery for low pay than anything else for any amount of money. All the academic surgeons argued quite convincingly that they could earn much more in private practice, but they preferred the challenges and the freedom of academic settings.

Even though these answers are probably strongly colored by ideology, their unanimity is impressive. Admittedly, the profession of surgery offers a variety of extrinsic rewards, ranging from social esteem to the gratification of restoring health to people. Yet it appears that our respondents perceive the activity of surgery as the strongest reward of their profession. Prestige and money are important in motivating people to become surgeons, and they do provide the baseline incentive that keeps people in the profession. But surgeons are almost totally involved with their work primarily because they enjoy the activity itself.

Intrinsic Rewards

Opportunities for action and enjoyment. Whether a surgeon experiences boredom, relaxation, flow, or anxiety in a given operation depends on the ratio between his or her skill and the complexity of the case. This ratio can be affected by three factors: the type of operation, the phase of the operation, and the surgeon's role during the operation. For example, surgeons admitted being bored in very routine (unchallenging) cases. Furthermore, the more mechanical aspects of surgery, such as opening and closing, are considered boring by some surgeons. Boredom is also common when the surgeon is an assistant rather than the main operator; that is, when he is not involved and responsible. In all three situations, surgeons are bored because their skills are not being used to the fullest possible extent. Although some of our respondents said that they are never bored while operating, nine specifically mentioned being bored during routine cases or when assisting. Another four reported problems with concentrating on the task and keeping their minds from wandering under various sets of circumstances. The more mechanical parts of surgery also lessen the amount of absorption and interest; fourteen of the twenty-one surgeons interviewed admitted that they frequently chat or daydream while they are sewing in the final stitches. Clearly, these situations do not require the intense involvement which produces intrinsically rewarding flow experiences. But at any moment a routine operation with few opportunities may change into a challenging situation that produces flow, or into an emergency that produces tension and anxiety, if a new problem is uncovered, a patient's body reacts in an unexpected way, or a member of the operating team fails to act appropriately. The variations inherent in each situation could, in fact, be endless were it not for the fact that good surgery involves minimizing the unexpected.

There seems to be a clear distinction between "very routine" cases, which are perceived as boring, and "routine" situations, which provide a relaxing if not completely absorbing involvement with the activity. Whether an operation is routine or very routine depends, of course, on the surgeon's skills. "Simple" cases that go well are found to be relaxing by many surgeons. An operation that is "easy and straightforward" is "satisfying," "pleasant," productive of a "great feeling." It is relaxing but not boring; as one surgeon puts it, that type is "a technical accomplishment and simply satisfying." Another finds that "it can be enjoyable to lapse into familiarity—everything clicks along. There is enjoyment of the craft—'symphony of motion.' " In this relaxed state one can think of other things, chat with the staff or with colleagues, or, more seriously, "explain academic points to residents." Surgeons usually also feel relaxed during scheduled surgery, "where you know what you are going to do." By the end of a complex operation, if it has gone well, even opening and closing are appreciated; since the operation itself has been more challenging, the mundane aspects are felt to be relaxing instead of boring. Operations that are relaxing can merge into the state of flow at certain points.

Flow is present in some routine cases but is more likely to exist when the surgeon is engaged in a "challenging" or "difficult" operation which is going successfully. The type of operation that produces flow, however, varies from surgeon to surgeon, depending on experience, specialty, type of practice, and the individual's skills. Skill means not only technical competence but emotional, managerial, and cognitive abilities required to structure the stimulus field of surgery into a flow activity and to operate within it. It is probable that "dropouts" from surgery are technically competent but unable to avoid anxiety or boredom.

Surgeons who are outstanding in their field avoid boredom by doing just one brief but exceedingly difficult portion of an operation and leaving the less challenging parts to others. One of our respondents, however, an ophthalmologist whose specialty is corneal transplants, enjoys his operations from beginning to end; he is "completely absorbed—never bored or distracted," because the task requires him to be compulsively meticulous: "Everything is important—if you don't close it the right way, the cornea will be twisted and vision will be impaired. . . . It all rests on how precisely and artistically you do the operation." A kidney-transplant specialist enjoys the fact that his specialty requires him to "put things together": whereas most surgeons cut and remove pieces, he implants a kidney and sees it work. He finds the process both "fun" and "artistic": "It's incredible to put in a kidney and have it start putting urine out before you're even closed." Others prefer the more dramatic, life-and-death kinds of surgery: "If you discover cancer early enough, you can cut it out and cure the patient. It's a life-and-death matter—very dramatic and very satisfying. That's the most satisfying sort of operation." Very specialized, expert surgeons feel most satisfaction when they are using new experimental techniques or creative procedures. In all cases, however, the satisfaction comes from successful involvement in a "difficult" or "challenging" case. One surgeon put it this way: "An unusual case is most satisfying—particularly when the patient does well." And others:

> The personal rewards are greatest in challenging cases where you extend the self and think more.
>
> I get intellectual enjoyment—like the chess player or the academic who studies . . . ancient Mesopotamian toothpicks. . . . The craft is enjoyable—like carpentry is in itself fun. . . . The gratification of taking an extremely difficult problem and making it go.
>
> I enjoy an economy of motion and try to make the operation as well planned and thought out as possible.
>
> It is very good, a lot of fun, and satisfying. It goes well when the stitches take properly, there is no excessive bleeding, and the group works together smoothly; . . . it works in an aesthetically pleasing way.
>
> It's enjoyable, challenging to diagnose illness and to operate. . . . I . . . do fairly mundane operations—I don't really care if it's routine or challenging—enjoy both, but it's fun to work up an unusual and challenging case.
>
> It's very satisfying and if it is somewhat difficult it is also exciting. It's very nice to make things work again, to put things in their right place so that it looks like it should, and fits neatly. This is very pleasant, particularly when the group works together in a smooth and efficient manner: then the aesthetics of the whole situation can be appreciated.

In trying to describe how it feels to be doing a complex operation, many surgeons used analogies involving active physical pursuits: skiing, water skiing, mountain climbing, driving a fast car, competitive softball, competitive sailing, and tennis. As one of them said: "Surgery is a body-contact sport, not a spectator sport." Thirty-seven percent said that working with their hands on crafts or carpentry gives a related experience. Three respondents found direct analogies in aesthetic or intellectual activities, such as photography or painting; and two people mentioned community work and church work as somewhat similar. But others claimed that the experience of flow in surgery is unique: "No other activity I do gives me the same sort of feeling."

The state of flow gives way to tenseness and then to anxiety if something goes wrong, if the operation changes from challenging to problematical. The cause of the shift may vary from an error in technique or judgment on the part of the surgeon or a member of the operating team, to an unexpected reaction by the patient, to a broken or dropped instrument. For example, the patient may start bleeding excessively or go into shock, or the tissues may not be rejoined properly and there will be blood-supply problems. The degree of tenseness, frustration, and anxiety depends on the seriousness of the problem. Some feel most frustrated and depressed when they run into things that they cannot cope with or that are beyond help; that is, in situations where challenges are in excess of skills. In such situations they describe themselves as "more keyed up, more tense," "terribly conscious of [my] actions," "upset," "[feeling] clumsy," and "worried and anxious," so that the "smoothness of the operation disappears."

The following statements further elaborate the surgeons' feelings and show their methods of coping with the problem:

> You become quite tense, pulse goes up, may be sweaty. The key to a good surgeon is one who is cool and can get out. Requires skill. He must keep calm and analyze the problem. Your reaction depends on how serious you think the problem is.

> I get mad at myself and think that I'm a stupid S.O.B., then I correct it, calmly.

> You get upset, but try to solve the problem. . . . You have to keep going because of the seriousness. Outside of the operating room you might scream and shout if something goes wrong—but not while operating.

> If things go wrong you may feel dreadful later, but at the time you just repair it. . . . It is a logical, technical problem —no reason to panic or lose one's temper.

But whatever the reactions, the result has been to do away with the state of flow; concentration has been broken, self-consciousness has returned, and satisfaction with the operation has disappeared.

Limitation of stimulus field. Like other flow activities, surgery is a world of its own, with a specified set of relevant stimuli, norms, and action. It has a special place—the "operating theater"—where the activity is performed, and a set of roles, uniforms, and rituals. To get from the everyday world into the circumscribed world of the activity, surgeons use a variety of transitional aids. Nearly all the surgeons interviewed said that they prepare for surgery by anticipating the event: they become "keyed up," tense, or "more alert."

> When you know an operation is coming, it's on your mind and occupying all your thoughts. You're "psyched up"—i.e., tense and worried. You anticipate all the little things that might go wrong.

> Before a difficult operation I have a certain mode or drama —a set routine. I put myself on automatic mode or pilot. I try to set up a pattern so I eat at the same time, drive to the hospital the same way, etc. Then I am free to think and prepare strategies for the important operations.

> To start with I am very anxious about the surgery and the patient's welfare. I want to do a good job and avoid complications. If troubles do come up it is very hard on the ego. One should have an idea as to what he can and cannot do and should be careful that he does not overextend himself.

During this transitional period, the surgeon has to adopt a neutral attitude toward the future patient's life. That is, although he must be committed to the success of the operation, he cannot become too concerned with the fate of the patient; for if he identifies too closely with the patient, he may become anxious under pressure and bungle the operation. Also during this transitional period, many surgeons review the knowledge and technique gained from previous operations. To shift into surgery, the setting and training are taken for granted: only three mentioned setting, only six training, as prerequisites for starting the operation. As one surgeon put it: "You are *trained* —you're already prepared. Your training makes you confident and you can 'shift automatically.' "

By the time the surgeon has dressed and scrubbed and entered the bustling operating room, the everyday world is practically forgotten and its stimuli have little opportunity to distract. Therefore, he is able to merge with the activity, to give full concentration to the task at hand. Thirteen surgeons specifically reported that concentration usually is no problem. Concentration does lapse, however, when the opportunities for action decrease; at these times the stimuli of the outside world return to awareness. Centering of attention is helped by the task and the setting. The rules of the craft define what the relevant stimuli will be. The surgeon deals with human lives, and the seriousness of the task is underscored by the surroundings: a quiet, appropriately equipped operating room, a patient with the area to be worked on prepared and exposed, assistants ready to provide the necessary instruments and to take care of the preliminary and subsidiary aspects of the operation. These leave the surgeon free to concentrate on what is most important: cutting into the patient's tissues toward a directed goal. As the surgeon proceeds with his job, his attention is so complete that he is likely to become unaware of the passage of time, of his own body, of the surroundings, and of other people. Seventeen of the surgeons interviewed said that they are either unaware of time or, more commonly, that it seems to pass much faster. Here are some typical comments: "I'd like to say it goes faster but I don't pay attention to time at all." "Fast, if difficult." "Time goes very fast; but afterwards, if it was a difficult operation, it may feel as if I had been working one hundred hours." "Like when you're doing anything pleasurable, time flits by." "Time is totally distorted—faster—seems like fifteen minutes, but it's been two hours." "It depends on the case but it usually goes much faster than I think. When I'm absorbed, it always goes very quickly." "It's faster when you're *really* operating."

This same centering of attention makes it possible for the

surgeon to ignore himself and his surroundings; fourteen of the twenty-one respondents mentioned this decrease in awareness of self and of others. For example: "You are not aware of the body except your hands. . . . Not aware of self or personal problems." "If involved, you are not aware of aching feet, not aware of self." "Much less aware of your self or your body or others. Just concentrate on what you're doing." "Totally enmeshed in what I am doing and I forget fatigue and forget the night before." "Less aware of things—so engrossed that I am not aware of the nurses going in and out; not aware of tired legs."

According to a perhaps legendary story that is widely repeated in the hospital, one of our respondents was performing a difficult operation when a section of the roof fell in and half of the room was covered with debris. Our surgeon was completely unaware of what had happened until after the operation was over and some of his assistants pointed out the fallen plaster behind him.

Clarity of goals and feedback. Concentration is further made possible by the constant feedback, which tells the surgeon how he is doing and thereby enables him to make instant corrections in his movements. As reported earlier, this aspect of surgery was listed as crucial to its enjoyment. In contrast to what happens in everyday life, nearly all (nineteen) respondents said that they *usually* know the right thing to do during an operation: "An experienced surgeon knows what to do most of the time. He rarely finds something he hasn't seen before." "In most cases it is [clear what is the right thing to do]; with elective surgery you know what you are going to do. Of course, judgment is always involved." "Usually very clear—training." "Almost always—90 percent of the time." "Clear on routine cases, but not always on all operations." The two subjects who felt least positive about being correct in their decisions were a fourth-year medical student and a surgery resident, whose lack of confidence in their own decisions can be explained by their lack of experience.

The possibility of contradictory demands and decisions is often eliminated by advance diagnosis or preparation, helping again to clarify the right steps to be taken: "If it is at all possible I will know what to do before I touch the patient. All diagnostic work will have been done." "Yes, we normally have a highly accurate diagnosis before we go in." "Yes—you have a clear plan to follow and it's unusual in our specialty to have changes—the unexpected is minimized in our type of surgery—you have choices outlined in advance just in case you need to change." "Some surgical problems require real organization—you prepare a checklist of possible sources of error in advance."

Each movement results in changes that are clear to interpret. This visual feedback can be judged either at a raw sensory level or at a very intellectual and technical one: "I know what is right not on an intellectual level but I sense the correctness by the way things look." "Thankfully, yes—it is usually clear what is the right thing to do. You get a feeling about it when things aren't going well. There will be supply problems and the tissues will not be rejoined properly." "You rely entirely on precise, immediate visual feedback. . . . When you look down the microscope to do an operation, it's like coming home. You have precise visual feedback."

Competence and control. Long and careful training go into the honing of a surgeon's skill. By the time he is ready to perform an operation, he will be ready to act successfully on the challenges he finds in the situation. Yet each time these challenges will be real and potentially dangerous. Hence, whenever a surgeon operates with success, he can experience a genuine sense of competence.

Eighty percent of the sample said that they feel very much in control during an operation. For example: "I'm more in control and feel more predictable. I enjoy being in control." "Completely; I need to be dominating; yes, I like the feeling of control and predictability." "Not more than usual—I am accustomed to feeling a great deal of control. I've always been in control and gotten my way." "Self-confident and in control so I can do things I couldn't otherwise do." "Yes—it's power." "Sure—that's what you know how to do best." One surgeon put it differently, but the meaning remains basically the same: "I do not feel that I am in control of everything but do try to be *aware* of everything going on. It bothers me if something happens without my knowledge."

Sometimes the control extends to other people: "If it is a routine operation, there is a conversation going on that will be directed by the primary surgeon. But if things get complicated everything quiets down and I concentrate only on the problem at hand." "You've got to be in control right from the very beginning to the end. You are also commanding the attention of the resident, and that's very challenging." "You're nicest to people when the operation is difficult; you need them to perform well. You ignore personal gripes—criticize later."

For some highly specialized surgeons time itself, which most surgeons are able to forget, becomes one of the action opportunities which must be brought under control: "I always know what time it is. . . . I know how long the clamps are on certain arteries, how long we've been in; I have to watch the anesthetic, etc. . . . I'm not just objectively aware. *I sense the time to the minute.* It doesn't seem faster or slower." "At first time was faster, but now I know what time it is subconsciously. I sense what time it is very closely to the minute." These are the exceptions that confirm the rule: the outstanding surgeons learn to manipulate time as one of the challenging elements of the activity. They are no longer slaves to time; instead, they structure it to their own purpose. Thus, they are able to take part in several concurrent operations by extremely precise scheduling of time.

Another form of control belongs to surgeons in teaching hospitals who are able to instill and insist upon style or certain levels of excellence: "Style or elegance is very important to me. I set a certain level of excellence for myself and my residents. I have a meticulous, fancy way of closing a wound so that there is little scarring—it's my trademark." The difficult details that must be carried out under time pressure provide almost infinite opportunities for the surgeon to use his skills and demonstrate his personal style:

> Plastic surgery [skin grafts] are not "complicated"—but they are very gratifying from an aesthetic point of view. I like neatness in operations, having things just right.
>
> I'm particular about how the needle is held, where the stitches are placed, the type of suture, etc.—things should look their best and seem easy.

> [In ophthalmology] you use fine and precise instruments. It is an exercise in art. You operate by yourself, not in a team with assistants. It's a one-to-one situation. It all rests on how precisely and artistically you do the operation.
>
> It is important to watch for details, to be neat and technically efficient. I don't like to waste motion and so try to make the operation as well planned and thought out as possible.

Transcendence of ego boundaries. Like most other flow activities, surgery does seem to be conducive to "loss of ego"; but the other flow activities often lead to a sense of transcendence and merging with the environment, and surgery usually does not. Although he may be completely absorbed in the activity, and forget his body, identity, and personal problems, the awesome responsibility placed on the surgeon tends to make him self-conscious, if not somewhat self-centered, when he is not immersed in the operation. Yet, in surgery also the actor is led to identify with the operating team and with the aesthetic rhythm of the activity: "Surgery is a team effort. But it's like basketball: you don't have to stop and look around to see where the ball is; you know how things are by the way the motion is going. You fade out of the awareness of the team only in the most difficult times." A major or minor error by anyone on the team brings out the ego and ends whatever feeling of identification with the group had been achieved:

> In good surgery everything you do is essential, every move is excellent and necessary; there is elegance, little blood loss, and a minimum of trauma. . . . This is very pleasant, particularly when the group works together in a smooth and efficient manner. . . . But if a problem comes up, the smoothness of the operation can disappear.
>
> Most things that go wrong are frustrations—an instrument breaks or drops and has to be sterilized and it makes me angry.
>
> If there is a disaster, then you are terribly conscious of your actions—if you panic it could destroy the team. You compromise by being casual and yet authoritarian. Keep the team moving.

Conclusions

The interviews with surgeons suggest that the experience of flow, which we found in leisure activities, can also be found in work. Therefore, since the dichotomy between work and leisure is not necessary, we should be able to structure or restructure activities to make them challenging and enjoyable. Games, sport, and various art forms have developed spontaneously along those structural lines. But work and education, two institutions that occupy most of our time, are not built to provide optimal intrinsic motivation—partly because of the engrained cultural distinction between work and play, or study and play. People tend to suspect that if work is enjoyable, it cannot be productive. Yet, as we have seen, surgery, which is one of the most skilled and responsible professions, is eminently enjoyable. In fact, many—perhaps most—occupations can be made to provide intrinsic rewards if the activity is restructured, either from above or by the person himself, so that it can produce a flow experience. For instance, the supermarket checker interviewed by Terkel (1974) has discovered a number of unique action opportunities on her job, from keeping in rhythm with the cash register ("It's like playin' a piano") to learning to know each customer, until she feels as engrossed in her work as a surgeon is.

Surgery is admittedly a very special activity. The highly selective nature of the profession and the long training involved make it inaccessible to all but a few people. In addition, it takes a certain type of personality to withstand the endless hours and constant emergencies of the surgical routine, and the periodic crises that failed operations entail. To derive intrinsic rewards from surgery, a person must like to work with his hands; he must be concerned with immediate results and all-or-nothing solutions; and he must have a large dose of self-confidence. Without these attributes it is questionable that anyone could enjoy performing surgical operations.

The point is, however, that the structure found in this particular activity seems to be present in every other pattern of stimuli which produce intrinsic rewards. Games, artistic and scientific creativity, and religious ritual and ecstasy also provide an organized set of opportunities for action, a limited stimulus field, clear goals and feedback, a chance to be in control of the activity, and a feeling of transcendence of self.

One of the most stubborn distinctions made between play and work is the assumption that the former has no real-life consequences; mistakes in play carry no penalty. That is why Piaget (1951) believes that play is "pure assimilation." If this were a true distinction, the flow model could not be applied to surgery, since performance within that activity carries life-and-death consequences. But it is simply not true that "play" is an isolated sphere in which nothing can go wrong. We have seen that rock climbers expose themselves to constant dangers as they "play." A dancer's mistake on stage or a chess player's loss in a tournament results in severe threats to the player's self-esteem. Gamblers can lose all they own in a game. Racing drivers, sky divers, and many other athletes risk life and limb routinely. In all of these cases, including surgery, the dangers serve as a means to focus attention on the activity and to provide feedback to the actor's skills. Rather than being a hindrance to enjoyment, they are part of the challenges that provide the flow experience.

The interviews also point to a peculiar danger of intense flow activities. The experience can be so enjoyable that one becomes overdependent on it. Everyday life begins to seem drab by comparison. One surgeon mentioned that operating is "like taking narcotics"; another, that it is like "taking heroin." A seasoned practitioner described a vacation in Mexico—the first vacation that he and his wife had taken in several years. After two days of sightseeing, he became so restless that he volunteered his services to a local hospital and spent the rest of the holiday operating, leaving his wife to fend for herself. Another one confessed that the worst tension he feels is during family vacations in the Bahamas. He tries to "dull his brain" with detective novels, but that only works for a few days.

Dependence on the flow of surgery can become a real problem if for some reason the surgeon is permanently deprived of the experience. A man who has made a few mistakes may become permanently anxious. Or at the other extreme, the job can turn into a boring routine for a variety of reasons. In either case, the activity will no longer provide flow. All too often the consequences may include alcoholism, family disruption, and even suicide.

Any kind of flow activity can become habit forming. Many chess champions have been known to suddenly go to pieces once they reached the top and were deprived of the accustomed challenges (Fine, 1956). One hears the same about practically every activity of this kind. Even while a participant is still fully involved in flow, he may become dependent on a narrow set of challenges, and anything else will not be enjoyable. It does not seem very adaptive for a person to feel alive only when playing chess or climbing rocks (Csikszentmihalyi, 1969). Such a preoccupation is analogous to adaptation to a very specialized ecological niche: a slight change in the environment can be fatal. Therefore, one probably should develop skills in several different areas, so that one can experience flow in a variety of circumstances.

The addictive properties of flow and its potential for offering a metasocial critique are two sides of the same coin. We have seen in connection with rock climbing that a rich flow activity provides a perspective from which people evaluate everyday life and from which they gain impetus for social change. But the simple beauty of the deep-flow world is so seductive for some that they relinquish their foothold in everyday life and retreat into the self-contained universe of the activity. When this happens, the constructive potential of flow is lost. The flow activity is still enjoyable, but it becomes a rigid, isolating system instead of a growing, integrative one. The fragile dialectical tension between the flow sphere and the rest of experience is indispensable if the former is to enrich the latter.

These dangers, however, only confirm the power of intrinsic motivation. Just as one can become power crazy or money hungry, it is possible to be hooked on flow in its many manifestations. Like all forms of motivation, flow is a dangerous resource. But given its advantages over extrinsic rewards, it is a resource which one cannot afford to neglect.

Chapter 9

Flow Patterns in Everyday Life

The chapters in Part II have shown the extent to which various formal leisure and occupational activities conform to the flow model. Enjoyment of an activity seems to depend on whether its structure allows a person to match his skills with demands in the environment, to center his attention, to receive clear feedback, to be in control of his actions, and to lose self-consciousness. These structural characteristics produce a sense of elation, a feeling of creative achievement which, although typical of games, can be provided in any structured activity, including work.

The identification of flow activities suggested a further question: Is the experience of flow limited to structured activities, such as games, artistic performances, or occupations; or

This chapter was written with Ronald Graef.

does it occur also in everyday life? In everyday life, people use a variety of devices to give pattern to their experience, to center their attention, to get feedback, and so on. We all engage in small, almost automatic behavior patterns which are not extrinsically rewarded yet appear to have a necessary function. These patterns may include idiosyncratic movements, daydreaming, smoking, talking to people without an expressed purpose, or more clearly defined activities like listening to music, watching television, or reading a book. To extend the definition of flow to such "trivial" activities may seem to be stretching the concept beyond its proper meaning. After all, one rarely gets involved with them to the extent that is typical of the flow activities we have just reviewed. Yet trivial, sometimes automatic behaviors in a person's everyday life appear to be important not only because they are enjoyable in themselves but also because they sometimes facilitate involvement with more structured activities. For instance, one may doodle to help maintain interest during a boring lecture, smoke a cigarette to help achieve concentration in writing a letter or a paper, or daydream to help focus attention on the reading of a difficult book.

Because these trivial activities appear to fit the flow model, although at a lower level of complexity, we will refer to them as microflow activities. Rules govern microflow activities just as they do games or surgery, although they are of a more simple and idiosyncratic kind. A daydreaming episode, for example, has limits on the course of fantasy; some images follow sequentially, and others are excluded (Singer, 1966). Because the rules are less demanding, most trivial activities require lower levels of skill; therefore, their complexity is lower than that of so-called deep-flow activities. Yet microflow activities may be as intrinsically rewarding as deep-flow activities, depending on a person's life situation. In fact, the flow model suggests that flow exists on a continuum from extremely low to extremely high complexity. It is appropriate, therefore, to study these less structured automatic activities in the context of the flow model.

The concept of microflow is similar to what John Dewey

(1934, p. 35) calls a completed experience: "We have *an* experience when the material experienced runs its course to fulfillment. Then and then only is it integrated within and demarcated in the general stream of experience from other experiences. A piece of work is finished in a way that is satisfactory; a problem receives its solution; a game is played through; a situation, whether that of eating a meal, playing a game of chess, carrying on a conversation, writing a book, or taking part in a political campaign, is so rounded out that its close is a consummation and not a cessation. Such an experience is a whole and carries with it its own individualizing quality and self-sufficiency. It is *an* experience." In Dewey's view, there is a continuum from the most ordinary experience, like an informal conversation, to the most unusual experiences, like artistic creativity or scientific discovery. What they have in common, although to different degrees, is structure, pattern, goal, challenges, feedback, and a feeling of control. In the same sense one may look at everyday microflow patterns as the weakly structured, low-challenge counterparts to the fully developed flow activities reviewed in the past chapters.

In our study of microflow activities, we hoped to answer three main questions: (1) What are the kinds and the frequencies of "unnecessary" behavior that people report performing during an average day? The answer to this question would allow us to obtain a baseline map of the various microflow activities in which people engage. We would also know whether all people engage in similar activities or whether there are characteristic patterns for different people. The same data would also enable us to find out whether certain kinds of microflow are related to each other or whether some are mutually exclusive. (2) How are various kinds of microflow patterns related to other characteristics of a person? Specifically, do men and women differ in what they do to structure their everyday experiences; does age affect intrinsically rewarding activity patterns; are there any cognitive and personality correlates to microflow patterns? (3) What happens if people stop doing these unnecessary, simple behaviors and just go on doing what is required by their social roles and what is necessary for physical survival? Chapter Ten describes the flow-deprivation experiment which provided some preliminary answers to the third question. The remainder of this chapter deals with a description of microflow patterns, their interrelationships, and their relationship to other variables, such as sex, age, and cognitive and personality traits.

Method: Sample and Design

The design of this part of the study was simple. We obtained twenty subjects, mostly students at the University of Chicago, and asked them to keep a detailed record of all playful, noninstrumental but rewarding behavior that they did during a forty-eight-hour period. Before and after this forty-eight-hour observation/recording period, each subject took a battery of tests: four personality measures and six cognitive measures. A week later, each subject was to stop all enjoyable, noninstrumental behavior for a forty-eight-hour period. At the end of flow deprivation, the battery of tests was given a third time. Each of the three testing sessions lasted approximately ninety minutes. Besides this repeated core of tests, subjects filled out an attitude inventory (an alienation scale) during the first session; and at the end of the third session they filled out a questionnaire and answered an interview about their reactions to the deprivation experience (see Appendix 2-D and Appendix 3). Each subject was tested individually in a small office with only an examiner present. From this material we constructed a preliminary picture of microflow patterns and their function. (See Appendix 1 for order of procedures.)

A poster describing the experiment was displayed on bulletin boards in an effort to elicit subjects for the study. Twenty-eight people volunteered. Three dropped out between the first and second testing sessions, and five were not asked to participate because the sample was complete. Subjects who finished the experiment were paid $15.

The sample contained eleven males and nine females with an age range from 17 to 28 years. The mean age was 22.2 years —21.7 years for the males and 23.1 years for the females. Each subject was tested at the same time of day for his/her three testing sessions, although each subject was given the choice of morning, afternoon, or evening testing sessions. The time of day tested did not significantly affect the subjects' reported activities or their responses to the personality and cognitive tests. (Those tested in the morning and afternoon started their forty-eight-hour observation/recording and deprivation periods immediately after the testing sessions. Those tested in the evening started theirs when they woke up in the morning.)

Three checklists were included in the testing sessions (see Appendix 2-A, 2-B, and 2-C). The first is a physical-feeling inventory designed to assess the subject's level of concentration, tiredness, hunger, and so on; the second is a somatic inventory to measure the presence of headache, muscular tension, and so on; the third is a twenty-item semantic-differential-type mood inventory with choices between *hostile* and *friendly, creative* and *dull,* and so forth. These checklists were to give a well-rounded self-description of the respondents' perceived state during the different testing sessions.

A projective test developed by Gottschalk and Gleser (Gottschalk, Winget, and Gleser, 1969) was also included (see Appendix 7). Subjects were asked to write about a significant personal experience for ten minutes. The resulting protocols were scored for anxiety by the developers of the test and one of our research assistants, with an *r* of 92.

An attitude inventory developed by Maddi and based on his theoretical work (Maddi, 1970) was included to measure alienation. In this test alienation is broken down into four different dimensions (powerlessness, vegetativeness, nihilism, adventurousness), and five different sources of alienation are measured (work, social institutions, interpersonal relations, family, and self). It was our intent to find out how being alienated from work or self might affect the pattern of unstructured flow activities.

Four cognitive tasks were included to measure various convergent intellectual abilities, and two divergent cognitive tasks to measure creative abilities. The convergent tasks are (a) a memory test adopted from the Wechsler-Bellevue IQ battery (requiring correct recall of various sets of digits), (b) estimating the sizes of three geometric shapes cut from construction paper, (c) estimating a short and a long time span while talking to the examiner, and (d) Raven's "matrices" test of intelligence. The divergent tasks are (e) the "unusual uses" test, designed to measure spontaneous semantic fluency and flexibility (Guilford, 1967, p. 145), and (f) the "matches" test, which measures adaptive flexibility in solving visual problems (Guilford, 1967, p. 152). In addition, performance on a tilt board was used to measure coordination; for various reasons, however, this technique did not prove useful, and hence it will not be discussed further. (The digit-recall task is reproduced in Appendix 4; the "matches" task in Appendix 5; the "unusual uses" task in Appendix 6.) The cognitive tasks were assembled in three comparable sets. For instance, Raven's thirty-six matrices were divided into three groups of twelve items, each set of approximately equal difficulty. The three forms for each of these tasks were designated A, B, and C, and their sequence was selected randomly for each subject.

At the end of the first testing session, the following instructions were given for the forty-eight-hour observation/recording period: "For the next two days . . . live as you normally live but be aware of your actions as much as possible, and take note of *everything* that you do for pleasure, especially those things that you would normally do absentmindedly, as well as the obvious. Record your behavior" (see Appendix 8). The subjects were given notebooks for keeping their records. If there were questions about what to record, the examiner stressed that any thought or behavior which was not necessary, or required, or expected—anything done for its own sake—should be reported. After the records were returned, the examiner went over them with the subject to make sure they conformed to instructions and in order to get a more accurate idea of the frequency of occurrence and importance of the activities for each subject.

After all the records had been collected, an examiner and a person not connected with the study categorized the reported activities in as few groups as possible without distorting the meaning of the activity. They grouped the 762 events reported by the twenty subjects over the forty-eight-hour period into forty categories. These included activities like "talking to self," "talking to plants," "talking to pets," or "reading books," "reading newspapers," and "reading magazines." Two raters then agreed 94 percent of the time in placing the activities into these same forty categories. The two other examiners subsequently reduced the forty categories to eighteen on the basis of similarity and reported frequency. For example, playing a musical instrument, painting a picture, sewing a dress, and writing a letter were combined into a single category because each of these activities was reported very infrequently, and because they have in common a "creative" dimension, relative to the other microflow events. Snacking, smoking, and chewing gum, also reported infrequently, were placed in a single category because they have a common "oral" dimension. Finally, the eighteen activity categories were further grouped into six general activity areas–imagining, attending, oral, kinesthetic, creative, and social (see Table 9).

Patterns of Microflow Activities

Of the activities reported by the respondents, the most frequently mentioned area is the one we call "social" (Table 9). It accounts for 28.6 percent of all activities reported. It includes unnecessary talking and joking with other people (21 percent); social events like parties and dinners (5 percent); browsing, shopping, and visiting galleries (2 percent); and (presumably underreported) sexual activity–hugging, kissing, and making love (1 percent). However, the frequency of social events is not evenly distributed across people. Some subjects reported that only 6 percent of their microflow activities involved other people; others claimed that as much as 82 percent of their noninstrumental behavior was in this category. This wide range suggests that there are diverging patterns of microflow characteristics for different persons.

The second-largest activity area, the one labeled "kincsthetic," accounts for about one fourth of all the events reported, and includes all those activities that involve primarily

Table 9. Frequency and Percentage of Noninstrumental Activities Reported During Forty-Eight-Hour Period ($N = 20$)

Activities	Total No. of Activities	Mean No. of Activities	% of Total	Range: Lowest % for a Subject	Range: Highest % for a Subject
Imagining	144	6.8	18.9	0	32.1
Daydreaming, music in head	53	2.6	6.9	0	28.6
Talking to self, plants, or pets	32	1.3	4.2	0	13.6
Humming, whistling, or singing	59	2.9	7.7	0	18.5
Attending	124	6.2	16.2	7.6	29.4
Watching people or things	20	1.0	2.6	0	10.8
Watching TV	20	1.0	2.6	0	11.8
Listening to radio or records	32	1.6	4.2	0	17.6
Reading books, magazines, or paper	52	2.6	6.8	0	19.0
Oral	57	2.9	7.5	0	26.7
Snacking, smoking, or chewing	38	1.9	5.0	0	23.3
Chewing on objects	19	1.0	2.5	0	13.6
Kinesthetic	194	9.7	25.5	0	60.6
Walking, pacing, or running	26	1.3	3.4	0	10.8
Small muscle movements	63	3.2	8.3	0	18.5
Touching, rubbing, fiddling with objects	99	4.9	13.0	0	42.4
Playing games or sports alone	6	0.3	0.8	0	5.4
Creative	25	1.3	3.3	0	20.0
Doing art work, playing a musical instrument, working, sewing, writing a letter, or doodling					
Social	218	10.9	28.6	5.9	81.8
Browsing, shopping, or galleries	17	0.9	2.2	0	22.7
Talking or joking with others	157	7.8	20.6	0	57.1
Social events, eating, parties	36	1.8	4.7	0	27.8
Sexual activity	8	0.4	1.1	0	11.5

body movements: touching, rubbing, fiddling with objects (13 percent); small muscle movements (8 percent); walking, pacing, or running (3 percent); and any games or physical activities that a respondent engaged in alone (0.8 percent). Again, the range is very large, suggesting that people develop strong personal styles in the use of microflow activities. Some respondents did not report any kinesthetic events, while one placed as much as 61 percent of his events in this category.

The next-largest group involves activities like daydreaming; talking aloud without other people around; humming, singing, whistling, and playing music in one's head. We called this area "imagining" because all the events are primarily intrapsychic in nature. They account for a little less than one fifth of all microflow activities listed.

"Attending" is the next area, and it accounts for about 16 percent of all activities. Here we have combined all the passive forms of spectatorship, from reading a book to watching people walk down the street, from listening to the radio to watching television. The remaining two areas, which together account for a little over one tenth of all activities, are the "oral" and the "creative" ones.

These six areas seem to exhaust the things which people spontaneously do during a normal day for intrinsic reasons. Of course, the sample we used was small, young, and highly educated. The frequencies reported in Table 9, therefore, probably are not representative of populations that are older and from different cultural or socioeconomic backgrounds. Yet the six activity areas and the eighteen categories obtained from this sample are probably sufficient to map microflow patterns in other groups as well. The relative frequencies may vary, but the total range ought to remain essentially the same.

One limitation of our method for obtaining the data was that each respondent was free to report as many or as few events as he or she chose. During the forty-eight-hour period one person reported as many as 159 events, and another as few as 11. This could mean that the first person indeed had about fifteen times as many microflow experiences as the second, but it may also mean that he was simply more observant or more conscientious in filling out his report. In the future, we shall clearly need to use a better method to tell whether a large number of reports is evidence of a higher frequency of microflow, or whether it is due to a reporting artifact. In the meantime, in order to avoid the possibly misleading effect of using absolute frequency counts, we shall use the *percentage of activities reported in various categories and activity areas* as our main data.

Table 9 shows the patterns of behavior that people in this sample use to give structure to otherwise patternless experience. Chatting with acquaintances, pacing a room, whistling to oneself, reading a novel, biting on a pen, or baking bread are things people do not because they expect to obtain something at the end of the activity but presumably because while they are doing it the structure of the activity, however tenuous, provides a respite from worry and boredom and an opportunity to merge action and awareness in a limited stimulus field.

The results also suggest that people pattern their everyday lives differently: some rely on interaction with others, some depend heavily on fantasy, and some use mainly physical movements. It is therefore important to know the relationships between the various activities and activity areas. Are some microflow patterns exclusive of others? We can answer this question by examining correlations between the eighteen activity categories and the six activity areas. One of the first things we found is that the two largest activity areas, social and kinesthetic, are internally homogeneous and mutually exclusive. In other words, a person who does a lot of walking and pacing will also report the other kinesthetic categories but will be significantly less likely to report social interaction ($r = -.58, p < .01$). Perhaps these two main forms of patterning experience correspond to some basic difference among persons. (We will discuss this possibility below.) The remaining activity areas are not as clearly separable. The three items in the imagining group, for instance, are unrelated to each other, and so are the items within the attending and the oral clusters. The justification for leaving them in the respective areas is that the individual items are related on a commonsense basis, and the lack of correlation could be due to the complementarity of the activities. In other words, watching television and listening to records may be similar activities, but a person will tend either to watch or to listen, but not both; hence, the two activities will not be correlated.

In any case, since the activity areas are somewhat ambiguous, the correlational pattern of the eighteen separate variables is more immediately meaningful. The person who reports talking to himself or to nonhuman objects is less likely to report talking to other people ($r = -.50, p < .05$) and watching television ($r = -.41, p < .05$). Inner talk seems to be a substitute for (or complementary to) social interaction and entertainment provided by the mass media. People who report spending time reading books and magazines are more sedentary—they use kinesthetic patterns less—but seem to be more sociable. The correlation between reading and talking is .51 ($p < .05$). In contrast, those who report more kinesthetic and oral activities tend to be more asocial. The tendency to be engaged in creative, or at least productive, activities for fun is related to the attending area, especially to watching television. Many of these activities tend to be also more sedentary and are negatively related to kinesthetic activities.

There are more trends that could be traced among the interactivity correlations. For the time being, however, we will concentrate on the two largest areas: the kinesthetic and the social. These two are mutually exclusive in our sample; when an activity correlates positively with one of the two, it tends to correlate negatively with the other.

Age and Sex

If one looks at the effects of age on what people enjoy doing during an average day, one of the keys to the kinesthetic/social antithesis becomes clear. Older respondents (23-28 years) reported fewer kinesthetic activities in general ($r = -.54, p < .01$), especially less touching, rubbing, and fiddling with objects ($r = -.58, p < .01$). On the other hand, they reported more social activities ($r = .54, p < .01$), especially talking and joking with others ($r = .42, p < .05$). This evidence suggests a developmental trend in the patterning of experience: the younger respondents (17-22 years) rely more on idiosyncratic, private body movements to give shape to their experience; the older ones rely more on interpersonal relations. Another strong age difference is that older people spend a lesser proportion of their time listening to radio or records ($r = -.57, p < .01$). In general, one can say that with age all forms of microflow except the interpersonal ones tend to decrease. This is true in terms of absolute frequencies as well as in terms of proportions.

The sex differences that emerged in this study are few and rather stereotypic. Females reported talking significantly more often to themselves, pets, and plants. They also reported spending more time browsing, shopping, visiting galleries, and going to parties and other social events. It should be noted that our respondents were probably as free of sex-role limitations as one can be in our society. They were all students in a sophisticated urban university. One may expect, therefore, that in the general population sex will have a more pronounced effect on microflow patterns.

Because age and sex roles are so homogeneous within this sample, the results can only begin to show some of the parameters affecting microflow. It is possible that younger adolescents structure experience quite differently and that the patterns of people in middle and old age are not represented in this limited sample. In any case, it is clear that intrinsically rewarding behavior is not random. Sex and age are systematically related to the way people use microflow activities.

Alienation

A possibility to be investigated was that the use of flow patterns in everyday life might be a sign of alienation. Perhaps people who report many instances of intrinsically rewarding behavior find life without meaning and engage in microflow because they feel powerless and alienated from work, or from other people, or from themselves. But none of the alienation scores correlated significantly with the *amount* of microflow reported. Even the correlation between the total alienation score and the total number of microflow activities reported was only .12 (NS). Therefore, it appears that flow activities are not simply compensations for an alienated life.

Several interesting patterns emerge, however, when one turns to the relationship between alienation and the *proportion* of different activities people engage in (see Table 10). For instance, people who talk to themselves or to plants or pets relatively more than others tend also to be more alienated. So do people who structure their day with oral activities like eating snacks, chewing gum, or drinking. Those who report kinesthetic activities also feel alienated, especially from work. People who pace and walk a lot, and those who engage in sports and games, score high on the "adventurousness" dimension of alienation. Adventurousness refers to a tendency to find socially expected life patterns meaningless. Life for these people appears worth living only when and where it offers extraordinary challenge and adventure. Thus, it is fitting that those who structure experience through the more active kinesthetic forms—pacing, sports—should be the ones who score higher on this form of alienation.

The social cluster shows an opposite pattern. People who depend more on interpersonal activities for instrinsic rewards tend to be less alienated. This is especially true of those who frequently talk and joke with other people. The largest correlation is between this variable and alienation from interpersonal relations ($r = -.69, p < .01$).

It appears that one's microflow pattern is related to the degree of one's alienation. People who are alienated derive enjoyment from talking to themselves, from having snacks, and from kinesthetic activities but not from talking to other people. Of course, we do not know whether this alienation indicates a preference for solitary enjoyment or a lack of opportunity for social interaction. Neither do we know whether there is a causal relationship between solitary flow and alienation, and, if there is, which is the cause and which is the effect. Does one become alienated because one cannot develop enjoyable interactions with people, or vice versa?

Although we cannot specify causal relationships between microflow activities and alienation, the correlations show that

Table 10. Significant Correlations Between Percentages of Selected Microflow Activities and Dimensions of Alienation

Selected Microflow Activities	Kinds of Alienation*					Objects of Alienation*				
	Powerlessness	Vegetativeness	Nihilism	Adventurousness	Total Alienation Score	Work	Social Institutions	Interpersonal Relations	Family	Self
Talking to self, plants, or pets	.41[b]	.42[b]	.53[c]	.19	.48[b]	.49[b]	.40[b]	.52[b]	.20	.44[b]
Snacking, smoking, or chewing	.60[c]	.22	.35[a]	.37[b]	.47[b]	.56[c]	.43[b]	.27	.51[c]	.34[a]
Walking, pacing, or running	.37[b]	.00	.20	.58[c]	.34[a]	.40[b]	.27	.13	.43[b]	.28
Playing games or sports alone	.21	-.05	.17	.45[b]	.23	.47[b]	.20	.06	.23	.05
Talking or joking with others	-.54[c]	-.65[c]	-.69[c]	-.37[a]	-.68[c]	-.65[c]	-.64[c]	-.69[c]	-.37[a]	-.56[b]

*Numbers marked [a] are significant at the .1 level; those marked [b] are significant at the .05 level; and those marked [c] are significant at the .01 level.

adopting a particular flow pattern is not a random process. The way a person structures his daily life to make it enjoyable constitutes a trait which is related to the rest of his characterological traits. It should be noted here that alienation was measured by a test, while the flow channels were reported by the respondents over a period of forty-eight hours after the test was taken. Hence, it is unlikely that congruence between the variables is a result of situational artifacts.

Self-Perception

In the testing sessions participants were asked to rate their "present mood" on a checklist containing twenty adjective pairs, such as *hostile-friendly, creative-dull, sad-happy* (see Appendix 2-C). It was expected that if choice of flow activity is a stable personal trait, the percentage of involvement in various flow activities would relate meaningfully with the self-descriptive items. We used correlations between these two sets of variables to verify this expectation.

The findings are intriguing on several counts. In the first place, 25 percent of the correlations between the eighteen activities and the twenty mood variables are significant at less than the .1 level of probability, and 15 percent are significant at the .05 level or less. What is more, the patterns are consistent. Surprisingly, however, the implications of the findings appear to contradict those of the previous section.

People who use more social microflow had been found to be less alienated; when they described themselves, however, they consistently chose more negative traits. On the other hand, those who rely on kinesthetic activities were more alienated; yet they invariably chose more positive terms to describe their mood. One could easily explain this result if alienation were positively related to self-perception. But the opposite is the case. People high on alienation tended to describe themselves in more negative terms; all the correlations between the total alienation score and mood are negative, three at a significant level. Thus, people who use social interaction to get intrinsic rewards are less alienated but appear to have a more negative view of themselves, even though alienation and positive self-image are negatively related. Clearly, we are dealing here with a complex interaction between flow patterns and more general personality traits.

Table 11 gives a clear picture of how the choice of microflow channels relate to self-perception. As the table shows, subjects who reported a strong fantasy life described themselves as

Table 11. Self-Descriptive Traits Associated with Proportion of Flow Reported in Various Activity Areas

Activity Areas	Positive Traits*	Negative Traits*
Imagining	Elated[c] Cheerful[b]	Passive[a]
Attending	Believing[b] Satisfied[a]	Dopey[c]
Oral	Strong[b]	Bored[b] Suspicious[a] Isolated[a]
Kinesthetic	Good[b] Happy[b] Satisfied[b] Free[b] In control[b] Relaxed[a] Strong[a] Worthy[a]	
Creative	Excited[c] Trusting[b] Believing[b] Fast[b] Creative[a] Satisfied[a]	Out of control[b]
Social		Sad[c] Resentful[c] Constrained[a] Unworthy[a] Out of control[a]

*Correlations marked [a] are significant at the .1 level; those marked [b] are significant at the .05 level; and those marked [c] are significant at the .01 level.

relatively more elated and cheerful but, quite appropriately, also more passive than others. Those who said that they spend much time listening to records, watching television, and reading described themselves as more believing and satisfied but also more dopey. People with marked oral patterns described themselves as stronger but also as more bored, suspicious, and isolated.

Subjects who reported predominantly kinesthetic activities were consistently more positive in their self-perception. To a greater extent than other respondents, they described themselves as good, happy, satisfied, free, in control, relaxed, strong, and worthy—possibly because they are more autonomous in getting enjoyable experiences. While social flow requires other persons, kinesthetic flow can be experienced any time and any place. Perhaps that is why frequency of kinesthetic flow is related to traits like *happy, satisfied, free,* and *in control,* while frequency of social flow is related to exactly the opposite traits: *sad, resentful, constrained,* and *out of control.* Enjoyment of body movement, as opposed to social interaction, tends to be alienating, but at the same time it makes one independent of others. Enjoyment of social contact is antithetical to alienation, but it is based on a dependency which results in a less positive self-perception.

Finally, the frequency of creative activities also has a strong positive association with self-perception. Those who do more of this type of flow described their mood as more excited, trusting, believing, fast, creative, and satisfied. They also rated themselves as more out of control—perhaps because, like those who use social flow, they depend on relatively structured activities to experience intrinsic rewards.

The trend of these results again confirms that the way one patterns experience is an important trait, related systematically to other aspects of a person's functioning. In fact, a "flow profile" may become a useful means for characterizing people. Knowing what a person is likely to do in order to derive enjoyment would be as valuable a piece of information as, for instance, knowing his or her pathological symptoms or typical defensive strategies.

Cognitive Performance

It is possible, however, that our measures of microflow are actually just an artifact due to differences in intelligence. Perhaps people with greater verbal fluency or higher intelligence report more flow events because their records are more detailed and complete—not because they engage in microflow more often. Therefore, we needed to examine the relationship between cognition and the various forms of flow, to determine to what extent the two sets of variables were independent. Once again, correlations were used. The main result is that the sheer amount of microflow reported is not related to memory (digits task), to semantic fluency or flexibility (unusual uses task), or to general intelligence (Raven matrices). There is only a slight relationship between the amount of flow reported and adaptive flexibility as measured by the matches task. (See Appendices 4 to 7 for tests.)

A closer look at the correlation results indicates that adaptive flexibility is related to the proportion of kinesthetic activities people engage in, but inversely related to the percentage of social flow that people report. Spontaneous flexibility represents the ability to change strategies when confronted with problems, a habit-breaking disposition. It is the opposite of a rigid approach to problems (Frick and others, 1959; Guilford, 1967, p. 326). Therefore, it appears that people who structure their experience along kinesthetic lines are more open in their intellectual approach, while people who rely on social interaction to give pattern to experience are more rigid in problem solving.

These results are in line with the findings reported in Table 11, where people high on kinesthetic activities described themselves as more free and in control, while people high on social activities saw themselves as more constrained and out of control. Again, these data may mean that the dependency on people which results from structuring experience around interaction also affects one's flexibility in approaching intellectual problems. In any case, the main implication of these correlations is that the amount and kind of flow reported is not a function of a better memory, a greater fluency with words, or a higher intelligence. The way one structures experience appears to be a process which is orthogonal to cognitive abilities.

Conclusions

The normal waking state is potentially full of problems. An almost infinite number of opportunities for action clamor for our attention. Hence, we need rules to pattern the information input, our attention, and our actions. Without such patterns life would turn into a paralyzing cacophony of stimuli.

There are different kinds of "rules" that help to structure experience. When physiological needs (such as hunger and sex) are operative, they help restrict the field of stimuli that one is aware of, and they set one's actions along a predictable course toward predetermined goals. Acquired needs, such as desire for wealth or status, also impose clear patterns on perception and behavior. To play a social role means paying selective attention to the environment and performing structured actions. In the same situation, a mother will be aware of a different range of opportunities for action than a policeman or an artist.

But physiological needs and social expectations are not enough. There are periods of time in everyone's life, in everyone's day, when neither visceral nor social pressures are forcing us to pay attention or to act with total involvement. During these periods we are "free." But we can also be anxious or bored–anxious because there seems to be so much that could be done, bored because there is nothing one can do. It is then that flow comes into play. Flow activities are arbitrary patterns that people use to give shape to their experience. They are arbitrary because physiological needs or social constraints do not dictate their form. Flow is potentially the most creative, the most fulfilling kind of experience, because it is free of phylogenetic and historical constraints and hence allows people to experiment with new actions and new challenges. Deep-flow activities like chess, climbing, composing, surgery, and religious rituals provide structure to perception and action for long periods of time. Such activities produce vivid experiences which can transform and give meaning to a person's whole life.

The microflow activities explored in this chapter seem to serve a similar but much more reduced function. They are the activities that fill the gaps in daily routine. They give structure to experience in the interstices between the action patterns dictated by need and social role. When a person reads, and the book does not absorb all his attention, part of the body needs to be occupied—perhaps he will tug at a lock of hair, chew a pencil, or rock in the chair. When someone is bored, he still needs to give some order to experience—through fantasy, or watching people, or doodling. Some coherent, patterned form of experience appears to be necessary to keep the mind from being overwhelmed by randomness.

When people are asked to report the enjoyable but not necessary things that they do during a normal day, a relatively limited set of activities emerge. Two types account for over half of the events reported. The first includes patterns of body movements, both large and small, like pacing in a room or fiddling with a pen. The second includes forms of social interaction, from conversation to sexual intercourse. The findings suggest that these two main types of microflow correspond to drastically different approaches to experience. A person who reports frequent kinesthetic activities reports few social ones, and vice versa. Relative frequency of kinesthetic activities correlates with alienation, while the opposite is true for frequency of social activities. Yet people who report kinesthetic microflow have a more positive self-perception and are intellectually more flexible than those who rely on social flow.

It is tempting to identify the kinesthetic-social dichotomy with the classical introverted-extroverted distinction often made in personality theory. For the moment, it seems premature to do so. It does seem clear, however, that there are two basic ways a person can give structure to everyday experience. One is by using one's own body, or parts of it, as an instrument with which to act and produce feedback in the environment. The other involves patterned interaction with other people, which again sets limits to action and produces feedback. The choice of either of these has far-ranging consequences, because depending on which one is used different patterns of experiences follow. Reliance on one's body leads to alienation, independence, and flexibility; reliance on others leads to belongingness, dependence, and relative rigidity.

The remaining microflow patterns are quantitatively less important in the psychic economy. These patterns include various forms of fantasy and inner dialog, passive forms of entertainment, a number of oral activities, and productive, "creative" activities. Along with the kinesthetic and social areas, these activity areas appear to exhaust the possibilities for organizing experience, at least in this sample.

It is quite likely that further investigations of microflow patterns will contribute important knowledge about human behavior. We may learn more, for instance, about the consequences of using one kind of flow over another. What is perhaps more important, we might learn how to produce environments in which the organization of experience is easier to achieve. If microflow in fact helps to make reality manageable, its educational and clinical implications cannot be ignored.

Up to now, however, we have had to take the importance of microflow more or less on faith. The assumption has been that the noninstrumental activities people report are functional; yet no evidence has been presented to prove that in fact they do have a purpose. In the following chapter we present our findings concerning the function of everyday flow patterns. A good way to find out whether a thing serves a purpose is to take it away and note the consequences. If nothing happens after a while, chances are that it was not important. So we asked our twenty subjects to try to do without the noninstrumental activities they had listed. Any changes in their experience and behavior would, we believed, help us to understand the function of microflow activities.

Chapter *10*

Effects of Flow Deprivation

▲▲

People who have studied play generally agree that playful behavior confers many advantages, both on the individual and on the species that practice it, in primates as well as man. According to investigators (see, for instance, Ellis, 1973), play provides mental and physical stimulation, results in feelings of competence, satisfies psychic needs not met by working, and allows for learning new roles. None of these claims has been proved, however, for the simple reason that to find out the function of play one would have to observe an organism that is perfectly normal in every respect except that it does not play. As Bekoff (1972, p. 422) has noted: "It appears virtually impossible to verify experimentally the existence of a play drive, because methodological insufficiencies do not allow an

This chapter was written with Ronald Graef.

experimental manipulation that deprives an organism solely of play experience."

This problem is especially salient in research with nonhuman subjects, where it is almost impossible to restrain an animal from playing without at the same time impairing its motor functions, its feeding and social habits, and so on. The methodological problem is less insurmountable if one does research with people, because it is possible to explain to human subjects that they should function in normal ways in all respects except they should stop playful behavior. Thus, one could, in principle, observe the effects of play deprivation without the contaminating influence of motor, social, or stimulus deprivation.

That is what we did with our twenty subjects. After they had turned in the forty-eight-hour self-observation record (discussed in the previous chapter), they were asked to wait five days and then: "Beginning [morning of target date], when you wake up and until 9:00 P.M., we would like you to act in a normal way, doing all the things you have to do, but not doing anything that is 'play' or noninstrumental" (see Appendix 9). For instance, during deprivation a person was allowed to talk to others but only to exchange necessary information or to answer when addressed by another person. One subject who reported that she enjoyed washing dishes several times a day because it gave her a purposeful task, during which she could fantasize without feeling guilty about it, was asked not to wash dishes except when absolutely necessary. Others who enjoyed shopping or cooking were asked to do these activities in as instrumental a way as possible, without indulging in whatever intrinsic rewards the activity offered. Subjects who were employed and enjoyed aspects of their work were asked to avoid such noninstrumentally rewarding situations on the job as talking to coworkers. In short, all noninstrumental activities—fantasizing, reading for pleasure, watching television, chewing gum, pacing, stretching, playing tennis, chatting with friends—were to be avoided.

For each subject we had a variety of psychological measures taken seven days and five days prior to the beginning of deprivation. If we matched the scores they got immediately after deprivation with the two sets of comparable scores obtained prior to it, we could find out to what extent, if any, flow deprivation affects people's psychological functioning. Before reporting the findings, however, we should point out some issues that may have confounded the results.

First of all, the small number of subjects, and their relative similarity in age, background, education, and intelligence, somewhat restricts the generalizability of the findings. Although we had measures of cognitive performance, somatic and mood self-ratings, and open-ended interview questions, a number of dimensions that could be affected by flow deprivation were not tested.

A second possibly limiting factor was the duration of the experiment. That is, since flow deprivation might impair normal functioning in those participating in the experiment, we limited the deprivation to a forty-eight-hour maximum and decided on the following additional instruction. Each participant was told to notify us if he or she needed to terminate the experiment, for whatever reason, before the forty-eight-hour period ended. None of the participants appeared to become unduly stressed, however, and each completed the deprivation period without early termination.

A third confounding issue is the possibility of deception. The design of the experiment was based on self-monitoring. Whether a person did in fact deprive himself of flow was known only to him or her—and sometimes not even that, since some microflow activities are so automatic that even the most conscientious subject may not notice that he is doing them. During the debriefing interview (Appendix 3), all the subjects admitted to minor lapses—most of them unintentional. In general, however, we believe that each subject tried to be as responsible as he or she could. Lapses were to be expected, and any form of outside supervision would have been too intrusive to justify the gains in added deprivation. Moreover, we felt that cheating was not a major methodological problem in this study. If, despite the possibility of cheating, we still found effects due to flow deprivation, it would mean that even imperfect deprivation affects behavior. In fact, lapses or deception in this case would act as safeguards against overstating the effects of deprivation.

The three issues listed above are similar to "Type 1" errors in statistics; they tend to mask the existence of a real effect. There are also possibilities for "Type 2" errors, which might lead one to believe that there were real effects due to deprivation when there were none. The two main sources for this kind of error are (1) that subjects had to continuously monitor their own behavior, to make sure they did not engage in microflow, and (2) that subjects had to stop themselves when they inadvertently started a microflow activity. Thus, changes in test performance after deprivation could be due to these two confounding variables rather than to the deprivation itself. The lack of freedom produced by unusual self-consciousness and by inhibition of action may have effects on the participants independent of the deprivation of microflow experiences.

The experiment was designed to control for the first of these two confounding variables. The second testing session took place after the forty-eight-hour self-observation period, during which subjects had to continually monitor and record their noninstrumental activities. Hence, tests administered during the second session are affected by the increased self-consciousness due to monitoring of behavior. Therefore, any differences in performance between the first and second sessions should be due to self-consciousness and not deprivation. The effects of interrupting one's behavior were not controlled for. This is a weakness which may be eliminated in future research on this topic.

In any case, in spite of these limitations on the study, it still appears that much useful information can be obtained from it. Both the concepts and the methods used are new, and as such are in need of refinement and improvement. The importance of the topic is such that even tentative, preliminary findings ought to be stimulating and of seminal heuristic value.

General Effects

Physical states. What effect, if any, did flow deprivation have on the self-reported physical states of the respondents?

Table 12 indicates changes on eight dimensions of physical well-being. There were no significant differences between session 1 (prior to the forty-eight-hour observation period) and session 2 (after the observation period); eleven subjects improved or reported no change, and nine subjects got worse. One could expect such results simply by asking people to make physical self-ratings on two occasions with no experimental design. In other words, the self-awareness engendered by the forty-eight-hour observation period produced no measurable shifts in physical state. But after deprivation (session 3) several indices show significant deterioration. Moreover, the changes reported are meaningful because they show that respondents were selective in assessing their feelings: not all scores changed similarly over the testing sessions. Ability to concentrate, hunger, and sensitivity to heat, sound, or light were not affected by flow deprivation. But subjects reported being more tired, more sleepy, and having more headaches after session 3 than after either sessions 1 or 2. In addition, they rated themselves as less relaxed and less healthy after the deprivation than after session 1; the differences between sessions 2 and 3 on these variables were almost significant ($p < .06$).

When all the physical-state variables for each subject are totaled, we can see (Table 12) that only one subject reported feeling better after deprivation than at time 1, three remained the same, and sixteen reported feeling worse ($p < .005$). It should be noted that the sign test used in computing the significance of these differences actually underestimates the change. When a t test is applied to the mean differences in scores at the three testing sessions, the deterioration shows up in an even more drastic light. The sign test is more conservative but was retained because of its greater clarity and simplicity. Thus, it appears that when people stop using the habitual forms of experience patterning through microflow, they notice an increased sluggishness about their behavior. They report feeling more sleepy and tired, less healthy and relaxed, and having more headaches. They do not lose their ability to concentrate, nor is their appetite or their sensitivity to stimuli affected. Thus, the main somatic effect of flow deprivation is lessened alertness. This pattern seems to be in line with the theories of Hebb

Table 12. Effects of Deprivation on Physical Symptoms

	Difference Between Sessions 1 and 2		Difference Between Sessions 1 and 3		Difference Between Sessions 2 and 3	
Physical Symptoms	Subjects who improved	Subjects who got worse	Subjects who improved	Subjects who got worse*	Subjects who improved	Subjects who got worse*
Ability to concentrate	5	6	7	9	5	10
Tiredness	3	8	2	11[b]	3	10[a]
Hunger	5	4	5	6	4	8
Sleepiness	7	7	2	11[b]	2	9[a]
Relaxation	4	6	2	14[b]	4	11
Sensitivity	3	5	4	8	2	5
Health	1	5	0	8[c]	1	6
Headaches	3	3	3	11[a]	1	8[a]
Total (overall change)	7	9	1	16[c]	3	17[c]

*Numbers marked [a] are significant at the .05 level; those marked [b] are significant at the .01 level; and those marked [c] are significant at the .005 level. Significance was determined by sign test.

(1955) and Berlyne (1960), who suggest that "play" fulfills the function of maintaining stimulation at an optimal level. If microflow serves to compensate for insufficient stimulation, then its absence may result in a slackening of the organism. Or perhaps the energy expended when one stops himself from engaging in certain behaviors is responsible for the tiredness. The "tiredness" variable (Table 12) did show the greatest increase between sessions 1 and 2, although it was not significant. Further research on flow deprivation should include a control group which deprives itself of behaviors other than flow experiences.

Self-perception. The subjects' reported self-perceptions were negatively affected by the experiment. But in this case it is not clear what caused the changes, because many had already occurred between sessions 1 and 2. These changes are probably not due to the deprivation. They may be due either to anticipation of deprivation or to the increased self-consciousness required by the experiment. The former reason, however, is not likely to be affecting the results because of the five-day interval between the end of the self-observation period and the beginning of the deprivation period. On the whole, eight of the twenty adjectives showed significant deterioration between sessions 1 and 2, eleven between sessions 1 and 3; only two adjectives became significantly more negative between sessions 2 and 3.

During the self-observation period the respondents were shocked by the extent of noninstrumental behaviors they observed themselves doing, and this negatively affected their self-perceptions; or else the additional energy output needed to monitor behavior made them feel less positive about themselves. The physical symptom *tiredness* did change considerably between sessions 1 and 2 (eight people rated themselves more tired), and this increase in tiredness could produce more negative self-perceptions. Thus, we have some indications of what happens to people's self-perceptions when they must observe their behaviors and stop engaging in flow experiences for a time. It appears that self-perception is affected not by the deprivation itself but by other confounding factors.

Two of the twenty dimensions, however, show what seem

to be pure experimental effects. These are the adjective pairs *creative-dull* and *reasonable-unreasonable.* Neither one of these changed significantly between sessions 1 and 2, but both had deteriorated significantly by session 3. Fifteen subjects felt as creative and twelve felt as reasonable at session 2 as they had felt at session 1; but fifteen subjects felt less creative and twelve felt less reasonable at session 3 (after deprivation). Flow deprivation apparently makes people feel dull and unreasonable. These findings, as we shall see later, were confirmed independently by other results. Creativity-test scores *do* drop after deprivation, and in the open-ended interviews people reported being more irritable, angry, hostile, guarded, and abrupt, and less reasonable than they usually are. The loss of creativity and increased feelings of unreasonableness at session 3 could be the result of an increase in negative physical ratings, especially tiredness and tenseness. However, this relationship is less clear because *creative* and *reasonable* show much less of a decrease at session 2 than most of the physical symptoms rated. It seems much easier here to make the argument for deprivation effects because fewer confounding variables seem to be present.

It is worth noting the self-perception dimensions which were *not* significantly affected by the experiment. Six of the twenty adjective pairs did not change enough to make a significant difference by the sign test. Subjects did not report becoming appreciably more suspicious, passive, cynical, slow, or constrained as a result of the experiment. And, surprisingly, they did not report an increase in boredom, whereas one would expect people to feel more bored when deprived of playful behavior. Perhaps the stress of the experiment provided excitement of its own, and that is why boredom failed to increase. This appears to be supported in the discussions below.

In general, one can say that while physical symptoms did not change significantly before the experiment (Table 12), the mood of the subjects deteriorated significantly even before deprivation had a chance to be felt. The two clear effects of deprivation on mood are that people feel much less creative and less reasonable when they cannot engage in their usual microflow activities.

Cognitive performance. It was perhaps too much to expect that a brief forty-eight-hour period of flow deprivation would appreciably change people's scores on cognitive tests. After all, longer periods of much more severe sensory deprivation usually fail to affect mental performance (Bexton, Heron, and Scott, 1954). Yet, on at least one of the four tests used, mental performance did decrease significantly. As one might expect, memory and intelligence *improved* (although not significantly), probably due to practice effects. The same is true of performance on the "matches" test, which is supposed to measure creative thinking in a structured, visual situation. But performance on the "unusual uses" test, which is supposed to measure creative thinking applied to spontaneous verbal problems, declined severely between sessions 2 and 3. Between sessions 1 and 2, there was no decline. Nine subjects were as fluent and eleven as flexible at session 2, while sixteen subjects decreased in verbal fluency ($p < .005$) and fourteen in flexibility ($p < .05$) by session 3. This finding suggests that the impairment is due purely to deprivation effects.

Since decline in creativity—as measured by the subjects' own reports and by actual scores on tests of spontaneous creativity—is a major effect of deprivation, we can probably conclude that microflow is a form of microcreativity; choosing how to pattern experience could be the most simple and most basic manifestation of the creative process. It will be recalled that when people describe deep-flow experiences like climbing, dancing, composing, or chess, the one thing they rate as most similar is the experience of "designing or discovering something new." Apparently, microflow activities also promote creative feelings similar to those available in the more structured flow patterns.

Self-reported changes. After the third testing session, the subjects were asked about the general effects of the experiment. Their reports were in general overwhelmingly negative. Most subjects felt that the experimental condition had been extremely debilitating. Typical descriptions of their feelings during deprivation included the following:

Tense, more hostile, angry and irritated

More tense toward people
Head going in circles, infuriated
Slept badly, listless, more nervous, more guarded
Hungry for people, everything became more of a chore, felt weaker, it was harder to cope
More irritable, restless, shorter concentration
Colder, less decisive
More angry with problems, reading less effectively
Furtive, more like a machine
More impatient, abrupt, reading more difficult
More depressed, unfriendly, couldn't concentrate
Less vital, less active
Felt weaker, less able to concentrate on reading
Oppressed, grim, apathetic
Listless, worthless, less energetic, lost interest

Some subjects felt that they were going to have a "nervous breakdown," and only the thought of the experiment's terminating in a few hours kept them going. One subject attributed three minor accidents—a burned wrist, a skinned knee, and a bruised arm—to the conditions of the experiment. Another subject was so dazed by the second day that he walked into a door and broke his glasses. These reports are in some ways frighteningly similar to reports of acute schizophrenic patients. For example: "My thoughts wander round in circles without getting anywhere. I try to read even a paragraph in a book but it takes me ages" (McGhie and Chapman, 1961, p. 109). Although such reports were initially associated only with acute schizophrenia, they have now been associated with other psychopathologies as well (Harrow, Tucker, and Shield, 1972; Shield and others, 1974). Since experiences similar to those reported during flow deprivation seem to occur in various pathological states, there may be a relationship between lack of flow and severe life disruptions.

Another intriguing aspect of this experiment is that several people managed to go through the two days of deprivation by setting some necessary and long-delayed task as their goal—for instance, cleaning the apartment or reading a boring textbook; at the same time, under flow-depriving conditions many people found it almost impossible to go on reading. When a person cannot let his mind wander at will and fantasize, he apparently has great difficulty in absorbing what is written on the page. In attempting to overcontrol his thoughts, he apparently experiences a loss of control similar to what some clinicians have called "overinclusion": "perceptual experiences characterized by the individual's difficulty in attending selectively to relevant stimuli, or by the person's tendency to be distracted by or to focus unnecessarily on irrelevant stimuli" (Shield and others, 1974, p. 110). As mentioned, this disordering of attention has been associated with a wide range of psychopathologies.

It must be added that four subjects (20 percent) reported generally positive changes. These exceptions are important, and their existence suggests that future research should focus on trying to establish which people in what situations may profit from flow deprivation. The four subjects who felt better during this experiment had been feeling guilty about devoting too much time to noninstrumental activities in normal life; because the experiment gave them a chance to avoid guilt-producing behavior, they felt relieved. These respondents also appeared to enjoy their instrumental activities more than the others did. For instance, one subject reported that during deprivation she was more disciplined, spent less time thinking about herself, and did not have to be "social" with other people; therefore, she was able to reduce "wasted" activities, could deal with work-related problems more easily, and could think more sustainedly about future plans. The exceptions suggest that task-oriented people who experience flow in their *instrumental* activities may resent noninstrumental microflow as a distraction. For them noninstrumental microflow deprivation is actually a relief, because it legitimizes total absorption in instrumental flow-producing activities. In the present sample such people were in a distinct minority, but they could be proportionately more numerous in the general population.

We tried to find out from the subjects' reports precisely what about the deprivation produced the strongest effects.

They were asked to rate, on a five-point scale, eight of the most salient aspects of deprivation (see Appendix 2-D). Most subjects rated "decreased contact with other people" the worst thing about the experimental condition, followed by "the act of stopping yourself from doing what you wanted to do." This second factor indicates once again the importance of monitoring effects. The least important effects were due to "decreased ability to engage in fantasy" and "lack of self-given rewards" such as snacking or resting after work. Here again we see that casual interaction with others, or "socializing," is one of the most prevalent forms of microflow, and one of the most difficult to do without. This particular hierarchy of effects, however, may be an artifact of the forty-eight-hour deprivation period. In so short a period many people may be able to tolerate lack of certain activities which after more extended deprivation would be severely missed.

Secondary Effects

Age and sex differences. Males and females had somewhat different reactions to the experimental conditions, as did younger people and older people. Specifically, females were more affected physically and cognitively than males were; and older people were more affected than younger people. At the same time, the older subjects did not change their self-perceptions after deprivation, while the younger ones changed theirs drastically. Apparently, an older person is objectively more vulnerable to the lack of flow, but his self-concept is more sturdy; consequently, his moods are less affected by the relatively greater hardship.

On the questionnaire administered at session 3, after the deprivation period (see Appendix 2-D), females reported more severe effects as a result of deprivation than males did. On four of the eight items in the questionnaire they rated the effects of deprivation significantly higher than males did. The largest difference is in self-given rewards ($p < .001$); apparently, women rely more on setting up a reinforcement schedule to get them through the day. They also listed greater losses due to kinesthetic and social microflow.

Figure 4 shows some of the patterns of change on the cognitive tests. On the short-term memory test, which involves repeating a series of digits, men and women had essentially identical scores, and both slowly improved over the three testing sessions (Figure 4-A). By contrast, the spontaneous fluency and flexibility scores, which measure creative thinking (Figure 4-B), dropped considerably over the experiment, for both sexes. The curve for spontaneous fluency was identical for males and females, although the women performed at a higher level at each stage.

On the match problems, which measure adaptive flexibility, males scored higher than females; moreover, the males improved their performance, whereas the women remained essentially the same (Figure 4-C). By the end of the deprivation, the men were significantly better at coping with these problems

Figure 4. Changes in Cognitive Performance Scores by Sex. Numbers marked [a] are significant at the .01 level; those marked [b] are significant at the .005 level.

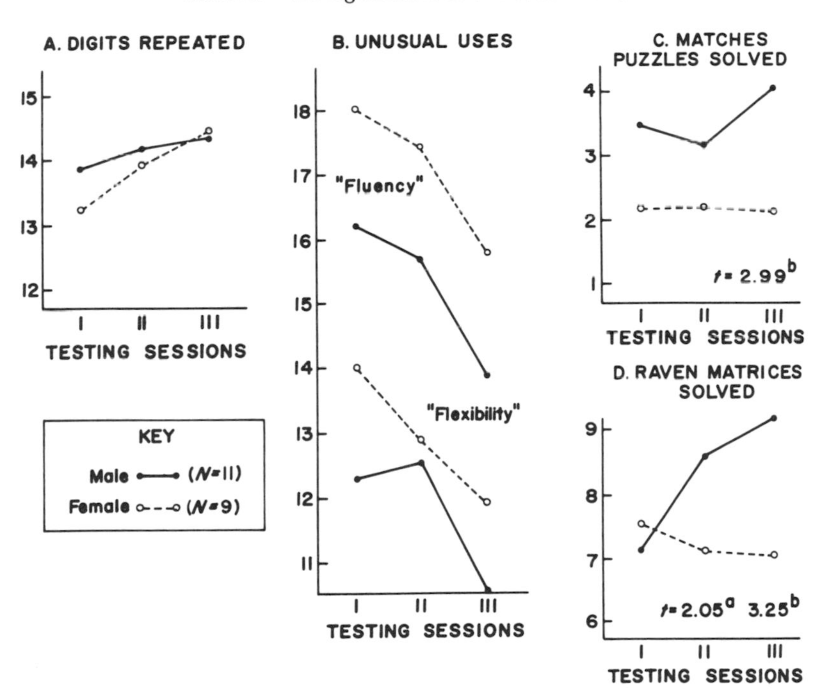

($p < .005$). The same pattern holds, even more dramatically, for the Raven matrices, measuring intelligence (Figure 4-D). At session 1, women scored slightly better than males on this test. But by session 2 and especially by session 3, men had improved their performance by about 30 percent, while women were doing worse than at the beginning. The difference between the two sexes after deprivation was very significant ($p < .005$).

Despite a restricted age range and the flexibility in sex roles prevalent in this sample, both age and sex interact with the effects of deprivation. These two variables will have to be researched further in connection with flow. Perhaps the sex differences are explained by the fact that women have fewer opportunities to enjoy their instrumental roles and hence depend more heavily on microflow activities. Men may find enjoyment more readily in their jobs or their studies, so that lack of noninstrumental microflow affects them less. These findings may also indicate that females are more sensitive to environmental changes and became more disturbed by the deprivation (see Biase and Mitchell, 1969).

Alienation. The correlations between alienation scores and changes between sessions 1, 2, and 3 show that alienated people are more affected by deprivation. Cognitive scores are least affected; the only drop in performance was on the memory test ($p < .05$). Physical symptoms are more variable; alienated subjects feel less able to concentrate, less hungry, more sleepy, and more sensitive than nonalienated ones ($p < .05$ in each case). Even more consistent results appear when changes in self-perception are considered. The "alienation from self" subscore shows eleven correlations with negative changes between sessions 2 and 3 ($p < .1$), and no positive changes. The more significant effects are that self-alienated people rated themselves as more bad ($p < .01$) and more hostile, suspicious, weak, and out of control ($p < .05$) after the deprivation.

Alienated people rated themselves more positively at session 1, possibly due to the novelty of engaging in the experimental situation (see Chapter Nine). This inflated self-perception is probably more susceptible to deprivation effects than are the self-perceptions of less alienated participants. Also, since alienation, as here defined, involves estrangement from self and social roles, alienated people should find less enjoyment in normal academic or occupational activities; thus, they compensate by depending more on noninstrumental microflow experiences. When deprived of these experiences, they suffer more negative effects than people who could find some enjoyment in their instrumental activities. In other words, because of the initially inflated self-perception and the increased dependence on noninstrumental flow, alienated subjects reported the most negative changes as a result of the experiment.

Microflow patterns. The tendency to pattern microflow in one area instead of another also affects deprivation. For instance, people who fantasize a lot—especially those who talk to themselves, plants, or pets—dropped significantly in performance on three of the four cognitive tests after deprivation. Conversely, people who do a lot of "attending," especially those who read books, improved significantly on three of the same tests. Thus, it seems that deprivation of spontaneous imagination and inner dialog causes cognitive disruption, while deprivation of more vicarious imagination—derived from watching television, reading books, or listening to records—actually results in a relative improvement of cognitive performance.

A similar picture appears when one looks at changes in self-perception. People who reported proportionally more microflow activity in the "Imagining" areas saw themselves in more negative terms after the deprivation. They became more tense ($p < .001$); more suspicious, cynical, and resentful ($p < .05$); and more depressed, weak, dull, and unreasonable ($p < .1$) than people who use other microflow channels. Nineteen out of the twenty possible correlations were negative, 40 percent at a significant level. By contrast, subjects who use the "Attending" channels rated themselves as significantly more free and relaxed; sixteen of the twenty correlations were positive.

Perhaps the most convincing explanation for these findings is that fantasy and imagination are more adaptive forms of patterning experience (Singer, 1966, 1973). When they are blocked, people feel their loss acutely. In contrast, people may consider watching television, reading books that are not required, and listening to records a waste of time; when these activities are blocked, therefore, they may feel relieved rather than depressed.

Subjects who use social flow more than the other activity areas reported relatively small negative change in self-perception. Before deprivation, frequency of social flow was related to the least positive self-perception; after the deprivation, those who spend much time in casual encounters with others saw themselves in more positive terms. They became relatively more friendly, good, excited ($p < .01$); and more elated, in control, and gregarious ($p < .05$). Again, perhaps people who do a lot of socializing sometimes feel guilty about it, especially in an academic setting; and when they are forced to stop it, their self-perception does not suffer from it as much as that of people who use other forms of flow.

Conclusions

The many inconspicuous little things that we do during a normal day, the seemingly useless bits of behavior interspersed with our serious instrumental activities, are indeed very useful, perhaps essential to normal functioning. Even a brief, imperfectly monitored deprivation produces negative changes in physical feelings, cognitive functioning, and self-perception, and brings about a general disruption of behavior. Changes occurred in the participants' behaviors that appear in some ways similar to the "overinclusion" or disordered-attention phenomenon associated with schizophrenia.

The subjects in this experiment were not confined in isolation booths; their sensory input was not reduced. Contact with people was not excluded, as it is in studies of social deprivation (for example, Gewirtz and Baer, 1958a, 1958b; Rankin, 1969). They were free to continue their daily life with no change in the external environment. The one change which constituted the experimental condition was that they desist from initiating intrinsically rewarding behavior. As a result, the function of this type of behavior has become more clear.

When people stop noninstrumental behavior, they feel

more tired and sleepy and less healthy and relaxed. They report more headaches. They judge themselves in more negative terms, and they especially feel less creative and reasonable. Spontaneous creative performance decreases. Normal daily activities become more of a chore, and they are accompanied by irritability, loss of concentration, depression, and the feeling of having turned into a machine. Subjects report experiences similar in many respects to the disruption found in people who suffer acute psychotic breaks (Payne and Hewlett, 1960; McGhie and Chapman, 1961; Freedman, 1974). This leads us to suspect some relationship between flow deprivation and thought disruptions, which can be serious enough to result in hospitalization.

By reversing these symptoms, one may infer that the function of microflow experiences is to keep a person alert, relaxed, with a positive feeling about himself, a feeling of being spontaneously creative. To be able to do things that may not appear necessary to a person's survival gives one a feeling of effectance (White, 1959), of being in control of one's actions rather than a pawn in the hands of deterministic fate (De Charms, 1968). In addition, this kind of behavior probably regulates the amount of stimulation available to the organism, by supplying novelty in a barren environment or reducing input when the stimulation is excessive (Berlyne, 1960). Obviously, when such behavior is not available to people, for whatever reason, the attention process is disrupted, the control of stimulus input breaks down, and serious consequences may result. At the least, people deprived even for a short time show significant negative effects.

In terms of the flow model, one could say that a person tends to maintain himself in a situation where his skills match the opportunities for action in the environment. But everyday life often does not provide such opportunities. Hence, people are constantly busy structuring their interaction with the environment, creating patterns where none would exist otherwise. Some of these are elaborate, complex patterns—the ones that provide deep flow. Others—for instance, an episode of daydreaming, a pattern of walking, and informal conversation—are organized at a barely perceptible level and involve minimal skills. Yet these apparently trivial activities seem to have an important role in the psychic economy. Without them a person falls out of the balanced state of interaction with the environment; he is no longer coping as an active agent in control of his own experience but is a cog being moved by forces outside his control. This is most strikingly reported by schizophrenics in their acute phases (Freedman, 1974).

The findings of this chapter also suggest exceptions and refinements to the general effects. The exceptions are the kind that confirm the rule. They suggest, for instance, that people who can experience flow in productive, instrumental activities —who are in control on their jobs or in their social roles—may depend less on noninstrumental microflow activities. That alienated people, women, and young subjects are more affected by deprivation points toward the same conclusion. They depend more on noninstrumental activities because they enjoy the instrumental ones less. In the same vein, it seems that when a person has learned to structure his experience through activities that our culture defines as being more wasteful—like passive entertainment or casual socializing—then he will be less affected by deprivation, presumably because he feels relieved at having broken a guilt-producing habit. How long such relief may last is of course questionable.

Are these findings replicable? Do they point in the right directions? These are rhetorical questions that only further research will resolve. At this point, the strength and relative clarity of the findings suggest that we take them seriously, especially if they may relate to overinclusion, which is present in many psychopathologies. If we do, everyday behavior will never look the same. Acts that were previously seen as useless and insignificant should assume an important role in mental health. And a number of new questions will become crucial: How much enjoyment is and should be available to different people? Can enjoyment in life be substantially increased? Can people be taught to make experience more enjoyable—to engage more frequently in flow experiences?

Chapter *11*

Politics of Enjoyment

▲▲

The cumulative effect of the studies reported in this volume is to suggest a new theoretical emphasis for the understanding of human motivation. The more general implications of these findings, which have been presented in a sometimes disjointed fashion, are explored more fully in this chapter. But before we proceed to unravel the deeper significance of the empirical results, it might be convenient to recapitulate them with a brief summary of the questions that were asked and the evidence that was found.

The study began with this question: Do activities for which extrinsic rewards are minimal provide a set of intrinsic rewards of their own; if so, what are these intrinsic rewards? For an answer we looked at groups of people deeply involved in activities which required much time, effort, and skill yet produced little or no financial or status compensation. In general, the responses of such people indicated that what sustained their dedication was some experience inherent in doing the activity, rather than some goal beyond the activity itself. On a questionnaire, "enjoyment of the experience and the use of skills" and "the activity itself: the pattern, the action, the world it provides" were the items most often marked to indicate the sources of rewards obtained from the activity; by contrast, such items as "prestige, glamor" and "competition, measuring self against others" were ranked invariably lower. These results suggested that many patterns of action, superficially very different from each other (activities such as composing music, playing chess, climbing rocks), share a common "autotelic" function; that is, they provide an experience which is intrinsically rewarding.

At the same time, while a strong base of intrinsic rewards was present in all activities, this was more true of some than of others. For instance, dancers and composers were the ones for whom autotelic reasons provided the strongest motivation. Basketball players, on the other hand, appeared to be motivated more by competition and by the chance to develop their physical skills. This finding suggested that playful activities vary in the amount of intrinsic rewards they are able to provide, and that therefore they can be arranged on an "autotelic" scale from low to high. Whether or not an activity is enjoyable, however, does not depend only on the fact that one is a game and the other an occupation. Writing music was a job for the composers and basketball a game for the players; yet composers seemed to find more enjoyment in what they were doing than basketball players did. Apparently, something besides the activity itself must be analyzed to decide whether it is intrinsically rewarding; specifically, one must consider the structure of external rewards that ties the activity to other social institutions. If for a disadvantaged young man basketball offers one of the few opportunities to experience competence and one of the few hopes for economic advancement, then these considerations will provide a stronger motivation to play than the enjoyment he can get from the game.

Therefore, while there seems to be a general class of action patterns which we may call "autotelic," there is a large variation within that class. In addition, the data suggested that individuals may also be differentiated as more or less autotelic. That is, just as activities vary in the degree to which they make enjoyment possible, persons within each activity vary in the extent to which they respond to intrinsic rewards. In our study, for instance, older people, more educated people, people from higher socioeconomic backgrounds, and females all derived more enjoyment from the activity itself than their counterparts did.

All this, of course, still tells us very little about the roots of enjoyment. Our next question, therefore, concerned the nature of intrinsic rewards operating in autotelic activities: What exactly makes some action patterns worth pursuing for their own sake, even without any rational compensation? If the reward is in the experience of doing the thing, what is this experience like, and is it the same in rock climbing and chess, in composing music and playing basketball? The questionnaire responses suggested some strong commonalities in the underlying experience. Autotelic activities were rated by participants as being most similar to the experiences of "designing or discovering something new," "exploring a strange place," and "solving a mathematical problem." Despite anticipated differences between the activities, these three items were rated consistently high by all groups. Apparently, something that is enjoyable to do gives a feeling of creative discovery, a challenge overcome, a difficulty resolved. People who see what they are doing in these terms tend to enjoy the activity more for its own sake.

Beyond these basic similarities, each activity also showed an expected pattern of unique differences. In chess challenge and discovery relate to intellectual processes; in dance they involve kinesthetic movement. In some activities the experience is strong on feelings of camaraderie; in others it involves a sense of competition; in still others, a solitary coping with some aspect of the inanimate environment. Common to all these forms of autotelic involvement is a matching of personal skills against a range of physical or symbolic opportunities for action that represent meaningful challenges to the individual.

The activities we studied were in general "elite" or at least middle-class cultural forms, the result of leisure and particular socialization processes. It may be hazardous, therefore, to generalize from them to forms of enjoyment prevalent among people with a life style more characteristic of lower socioeconomic classes. Fishing, bowling, or gambling, for instance, may not provide the kind of experience typical of the autotelic activities studied here. Yet the scant evidence we did collect, consisting of only a few interviews, suggests that people who enjoy bowling or gambling enjoy it for the same reasons that a composer enjoys writing music or a chess player enjoys a tournament. The challenges may have a narrower range, the sense of discovery may be less overwhelming, but these elements are definitely present and relatively salient.

After examining our interview and questionnaire results, we concluded that people who enjoy what they are doing enter a state of "flow": they concentrate their attention on a limited stimulus field, forget personal problems, lose their sense of time and of themselves, feel competent and in control, and have a sense of harmony and union with their surroundings. To the extent that these elements of experience are present, a person enjoys what he or she is doing and ceases to worry about whether the activity will be productive and whether it will be rewarded. Conversely, a "flow activity" is an activity that makes flow experiences possible. Such an activity provides opportunities for action which match a person's skill, limits the perceptual field, excludes irrelevant stimuli, contains clear goals and adequate means for reaching them, and gives clear and consistent feedback to the actor. If high school basketball is not as flow-producing as composing music, for instance, that is at least partly because its competitive structure fails to isolate the activity from everyday life, making concentration and the loss of ego relatively more difficult.

A closer look at four such activities provided a more concrete view of how this model of enjoyment works. Chess, for instance, turns out to be a game that offers opportunities for action at several independent levels. The main challenge seems to consist in matching one's skills in reasoning against those of another person. The rules of the game, the organized tournaments, the system of ratings—all are designed to provide clear goals and feedback to a battle of wits. Most players respond to these opportunities and enjoy the activity because of them. But there are other challenges in chess. Some people find in it a chance to study a complex game and to solve its problems at their own leisure; others find in the social organization of chess clubs an opportunity to make friends; still others use the game as a repetitive activity that affords a direct escape from worry or boredom. Each of these dimensions has its own set of challenges; one could say, in fact, that chess is not a single activity but at least six games in one. Although objectively all people who play chess are doing the same thing, subjectively it makes quite a difference whether one is responding primarily to the competitive elements or to the opportunity to solve problems, to find companionship, to enhance status, to study past championships, or simply to relax. Each is a possibility within the complex structure of the game, and each can provide the experience of flow. Because chess is presumably not unique in this respect, one might conclude that any reasonably complex activity presents challenges along various dimensions and can be acted out at different levels. Therefore, a close analysis of any such activity may reveal possibilities for enjoyment that are not obvious at a first glance.

The same pattern emerges from a closer look at rock dancing. Popular dance also provides diverse opportunities for involvement. Some people emphasize the movement of their bodies; others try to maximize emotional communication; still others respond to the social dimensions of the activity. By specifying the challenges that people find in the dance, and the skills they bring to it, we were able to show that a close match between the two is responsible for the involvement and the enjoyment derived from the activity. Although still tentative, the methods used in this section of the book point toward an objective assessment of the flow potential of activities and persons. By refining these methods we may learn how to make everyday-life situations more enjoyable.

The analysis of rock climbing highlights a different set of issues, which are also relevant to other flow activities. Here we are looking at a "game" which involves the risk of life with no apparent justification. The "irrational" behavior of the climber, however, turns out to be vindicated by the depth of flow the activity provides. As in similar situations, one is so entranced by the inner order of the experience that the "real" world appears irrational by comparison. Climbing becomes a microcosm that makes more sense than the everyday reality ruled by selfishness, expediency, and chance. We get here a glimpse of the liberating power of play, its potential for creating new social forms.

Turning to the profession of surgery, we tried to show that flow is not confined to games or dangerous sports but can be experienced in any other setting that conforms to the conditions described by the theoretical model. Surgery is a good example because it is a pattern of action with well-defined goals, clear limits, trainable skills, and instant feedback. Surgeons accordingly tend to enjoy what they are doing, and they describe their experiences in terms almost identical with those used by climbers or chess players. Although they get prestige and financial rewards from the job, surgeons become intrinsically motivated by it—especially those who can maximize the flow conditions, instead of being tied down to routine operations. In the right circumstances, operating becomes exhilarating, "addictive like a narcotic." From this example, one may draw added support for the expectation that enjoyment need not be confined to games—that with enough knowledge everyday life could be made more rewarding.

Finally, we turned our attention to the routine, unstructured events of everyday life itself. We wanted to find out what people do during an average day to make its experience more enjoyable. The activities reported were often trivial, like chewing gum, stretching one's fingers, or pursuing a daydream; yet they seemed to consist of behaviors which are rudimentary forms of the more structured activities we had studied earlier. Each was a form of action that, although often requiring only infinitesimal skills, helped concentration on a limited stimulus field, set some goals and procedures, and provided feedback. Even when these processes took place automatically, at a preconscious level, their effect had an embryonic similarity to flow. They seemed to bring a certain order into the random flux of a person's life, and they appeared to give a basic feeling of control or effectance; hence, we called them "microflow" activities. That they are important in the psychic economy of everyday life is shown by the results of our flow-deprivation study, in which we asked a group of subjects deliberately to stop all such activities for forty-eight hours. Almost unanimously, our subjects reported being less relaxed, more tired, more sleepy, and less healthy after being deprived of microflow than they had been before the deprivation. Performance on creativity tests dropped sharply. Subjects rated themselves as more dull and in general perceived themselves in more negative terms. After just two days of deprivation, several had unusual minor accidents, and the general deterioration in mood was so advanced that prolonging the experiment would have been unadvisable.

What we have found out about the culturally structured flow activities, and the more idiosyncratically structured microflow, points to the possibility of making enjoyment a measurable entity. This fact has some consequences, both for our understanding of human behavior and for practical social action.

Reflection on what we have learned so far suggests two major changes in the way human behavior may be understood. The first reassessment concerns the deeply entrenched dichotomy between work and play. That "work" and "play" describe two separate and even opposite conditions seems to be so obvious as not to require any further proof. Even social scientists simply assume that the distinction is real, and use it as a given. When psychologists or sociologists write about play, they deal with it as a process that is only tangentially related to the rest of life. Yet all the evidence from our investigations suggests that the essential difference is not between "play" and "work" as culturally defined activities but between the "flow" experience (which typically occurs in play activities but may be present in work as well) and the experience of anxiety or boredom (which may occur at any time and any place but is more likely in activities that provide either too few or too many opportunities for action).

By downplaying the structural distinction and emphasizing the experiential one, we are better able to deal with the *esprit de jeu* that Huizinga, Callois, and many others have held to be the central issue of the phenomenon of play. Yet the same scholars have been unable to study this "spirit of play," because they fell back on the obvious structural distinction and looked at games instead of at the experience of playfulness. Playfulness, or flow, is not limited by the form of the activity, although it is affected by it.

The significance of eliminating the distinction between play and work becomes evident when one applies the new concept to a complex historical problem—for instance, Weber's explanation of the emergence of the Puritan work ethic. Weber's point is that modern, rational capitalism was made possible by a change in attitude toward work on the part of large segments of the population in Western Europe and later in the United States. Whereas work had traditionally been considered a painful but necessary task, necessary for survival and for reaping the fruits of leisure, the Protestant Reformation slowly redefined work as the main purpose of life. It did so because it made a convincing symbolic connection between hard work and the proof of eternal salvation. Before the Reformation, men were pursuing two major unrelated goals: the first was to achieve material comfort; the second was to reach the ultimate contentment of knowing that everlasting peace was waiting for them in the afterlife. But work and salvation were independent and unrelated activities. After Calvin, however, it became possible to redefine the two activities as mutually supportive: success in worldly affairs became a sign of election to eternal life.

As a result of this reformulation, the early capitalist and industrial worker felt justified in working much harder than he had before, since work was now a means not only to material comfort but to an eternity of happiness as well. The man who pursued the new work ethic did not, however, enjoy greater material rewards; in fact, he had fewer pleasures and less leisure. "He [got] nothing out of his wealth for himself, except the irrational sense of having done his job well" (Weber, 1930, p. 71). Like a chess player, rock climber, or surgeon, the worker at the dawn of modern capitalism apparently was motivated by rewards intrinsic to the activity itself. But, one might object, the ultimate goal in this case was salvation of the soul; hence, the main reward was extrinsic. From Weber's analysis, however, it appears that the hope for eternal life was a plausible excuse for reorienting people's energies, rather than the literal end of their activities. Salvation served as a goal in the same sense that the top of a mountain is a goal that helps to focus a climber's actions, or that curing a patient provides closure to a surgeon. The real contribution of the Protestant ethic was to offer a consistent set of rules, with clear means and clear feedback, by which the believer could order his life and avoid boredom and anxiety. In Weber's words: "To attain . . . self-confidence intense worldly activity is recommended as the most suitable means. It and it alone disperses religious doubts and gives the certainty of grace." And again: "The moral conduct of the average man was thus deprived of its planless and unsystematic character and subjected to a consistent method for conduct as a whole" (Weber, 1930, pp. 112, 117). According to Richard Baxter, the early Puritan writer, the modern specialized worker "will carry out his work in order while another remains in constant confusion, and his business knows neither time nor place" (quoted in Weber, 1930, p. 161).

In other words, we may see the Protestant work ethic as a new "game," or flow activity, which comes into existence when work is redefined with a logical set of goals and means. It is ironic that the followers of this doctrine should have condemned all forms of enjoyment, whereas—at least according to our interpretation—they must have been enjoying the very rigors of their ascetic way of life. Even now, many hard-working, dedicated people frown on the activities subsumed under the concept of flow; they look upon these activities as hedonistic and decadent. Enjoyment is suspect; work is godly. It is very difficult for these people to realize, let alone admit, that the serious work they do is more enjoyable for them than any form of leisure could be. Weber himself—probably because he also accepted the play-pleasure versus work-unpleasure dichotomy—never saw clearly that the ascetic withdrawal from all pleasure can in itself be enjoyable. But at several points he came very close to seeing how arbitrary the work-play distinction really is. For instance, in discussing the development of the capitalist system, he says: "Where the imagination of a whole people has once been turned toward purely quantitative bigness, as in the United States, this romanticism of numbers exercises an irresistible appeal to the poets among businessmen." And again: "In the field of its highest development, in the United States, the pursuit of wealth, stripped of its religious and ethical meanings, tends to become associated with purely mundane passions, *which often actually give it the character of sport*" (Weber, 1930, pp. 71, 182; italics added).

Weber, then, has described two different ways in which work can be structured so as to provide a flow experience. In the early days of capitalism, the goal consisted in the proof of election, and the means involved the practice of worldly asceticism. The whole of a person's life was thereby turned into an ordered, unified activity with manageable challenges: in other words, into a flow activity. With the passage of time, capitalism developed its own rules, its own "irrational" rewards: the "irresistible appeal" of quantification, the possibility of lawful competition and of getting immediate feedback to one's decisions through the ticker tape, the dramatic combination of skill and chance that is involved in business decisions. These rewards have made the former sacred goals unnecessary and have turned the businessman's work into a self-contained flow activity. The reasons that legitimize the activity have changed, but presumably the flow experience has remained essentially the same.

A similar transition from sacred to profane justifications has affected a number of other activities. Most games of chance were originally forms of religious divination (Csikszentmihalyi and Bennett, 1971); athletic contests, legal trials, and the origins of science and art were also inseparable from their religious contexts (Huizinga, [1939] 1950). Perhaps a supernatural, eschatological goal was necessary at the beginning of history to motivate people to engage in "superfluous" activities which were not directly related to survival or prompted by urgent needs. But once these activities acquired their own inner logic, by defining new opportunities for action and skills needed to cope with them, they became more or less autonomous from the original sacred justifications. At that point they turned into truly autotelic activities, for which the main motivation was the flow experience itself.

Of course, the two types of capitalist game structure that Weber describes are not the only ways in which work can be made enjoyable. Many anthropologists have described the life activity of hunting, nomadic, or farming cultures as one well-ordered flow experience (see, for instance, Carpenter, 1973, on the Eskimos; Turnbull, 1962, on the pygmies of the Ituri forest; Mead, 1935, on the Arapesh). In certain rare historical moments, a few fortunate primitive cultures apparently were able to achieve a delicate balance between environmental challenges and their own skills in coping. Whether the balance is achieved through technological or symbolic means does not seem to matter; the important thing is that the people in such cultures feel at one with their actions and their surroundings. A similar state conducive to flow experience appears to have been the lot of many craftsmen before the Industrial Revolution. For them the opportunities for action were specified by the standards of the trade, and their skills were honed through long apprenticeship. The English master weavers prior to the nineteenth century and the various artisans of that time were proud, independent people who seemed to enjoy their work as much as any flow activity can be enjoyed (Thompson, 1963).

But for each example of a successful structuring of work as a flow activity, the historical record contains many contrary examples. There are preliterate cultures that are so overwhelmed by their physical environment, or by the social obstacles that they themselves have created, that life in them is pervaded by anxiety and strife. The all-encompassing fear of magic of the Dobuans (Fortune, 1963) or the Tiv (Bowen, 1964); the suspicious hostility of the Mundugumor (Mead, 1935); the helpless apathy of the Ik of Uganda (Turnbull, 1972): these are examples of what happens when whole communities lose their ability to face life as a unified, manageable, rule-bound task. And, of course, Western history provides ample evidence of the drudgery that work meant to millions under various forms of conscious or inadvertent social and political exploitation. The capitalist process of production, originally a creative and voluntary activity of many "players," has become, in Weber's words, an "iron cage" in which only a few privileged actors can find opportunities for enjoyment.

The concept of flow makes it possible to see work, and cultural definitions of life style in general, as much more flexible than they are usually thought to be. It allows us to question the necessity of drudgery and anxiety, and it suggests ways in which everyday life can be made more free. There is no reason to believe any longer that only irrelevant "play" can be enjoyed, while the serious business of life must be borne as a burdensome cross. Once we realize that the boundaries between work and play are artificial, we can take matters in hand and begin the difficult task of making life more livable. That is what Marcuse (1967, p. 12) must have meant when he wrote: "I believe that one of the new possibilities of demonstrating the qualitative difference between a free and an unfree society lies precisely in our ability to discover the realm of freedom *in* labor and not merely *beyond* it."

The second theoretical contribution of this research concerns the function of playful behavior. On this issue, our study has brought to light the subjectively salient, immediately experienced rewards of the activity. Earlier theories of play have focused on the long-range survival advantages to be gained from play: preparation for adult tasks, compensation for routine behavior, outlet for unexpressed needs. More recent theories have assumed that play provides stimulation needed to satisfy a physiological need for optimal arousal (Ellis, 1973). Both of these approaches have much to offer. But the explanations they provide are based on a different level of abstraction from the one used here. Classical theories emphasize adaptation of the species, or of the individual, to a changing environment. Arousal theories focus on the relationship between the cerebral cortex and the reticular system of the brain. The flow model, on the other hand, takes for its datum the person's subjective experience when he is involved in various activities. These three levels of explanation are not conflicting but complementary accounts of a complex phenomenon with physiological, experiential, and cultural components. The present study attempts to show that explanations of playful behavior based on subjective reports can be collected and analyzed rigorously and systematically. When one looks at play from this perspective, one is led to conclude that its function is to provide a specific state of experience, which we have called "flow." Perhaps this experience has been selected through evolution because of its survival value. Perhaps it is caused by a set of neurological events. All we know at this point is what people say about how it affects them; and for the time being this knowledge is adequate to shed light on many questions. At the most general level, it can be said that flow is a state of experience that is autotelic or intrinsically rewarding; hence, it provides its own motivation.

Perhaps the most salient element of the flow state is a sense of control over the environment. A person has to feel that his ability to act is adequate to meet the opportunities for action available. "Inner" skills and "outer" challenges must be in balance before the flow state can be experienced. But on closer reflection this simple prerequisite of flow turns out to be a very complex matter indeed. In the first place, it becomes evident that "skills" and "challenges" are not objective entities but flexible quanta dependent on cultural convention and open to individual interpretation and change. Chess, rock climbing, musical composition, and surgery all offer real enough challenges—but only because our culture has defined these activities as challenging, and the definition has been accepted by some people. In a culture where illness is cured through magic, through the use of herbs, or through hypnosis, there are no opportunities for action comparable to what we know of as surgery. In all cultures up to the nineteenth century, and in most cultures even now, mountains or rocks are not considered challenging. People living at the foot of mountain ranges think of the high hills as a world apart where man has no business to be. To feel in control of the environment, therefore, one must be able to define what the environment *is*. Noone can feel in control of the total environment, the totality of forces and processes that may impinge on the state of human beings. Hence, one has to begin selecting stimuli from the surroundings, restrict one's attention to a manageable pattern of items *about which one can do something.* Ultimate control is impossible, but a temporary sense of mastery based on a selective structuring of the world can be accomplished. Flow activities are the prime example of how a person can manipulate the potential input to awareness so that he or she can manage within its limits.

Chess, rock climbing, music composition, basketball, dance, surgery—all define narrow aspects of reality as important. Because of the narrowness of the definition, one can develop a set of skills to tame the challenges lurking within the confines of each subworld. At the same time, each of these activities is "deep" enough to present ever more difficult opportunities for action, so that the level of skills one can attain is in principle inexhaustible, and a person who takes advantage of the opportunities can feel that his control is increasing all the time.

But again it would be wrong to presume that one can achieve such a structuring of reality only through play, or flow activities in general. In a recent summary of the various uses of the concept of "culture," Nelson (1965) lists four main classes. The first category includes perspectives on culture which treat it as *dramatic design.* Seen from this perspective, culture gives form to experience; it makes a likely story out of what otherwise would be "a tale told by an idiot." The second way to look at culture is as a *defensive system,* or the array of beliefs that help man to allay his anxieties. It can also be seen as a *directive system* which prescribes how one should see the world, how one should feel, think, and act within it. The fourth conception of culture is as a *symbol economy,* which determines how various social systems legitimize social inequalities by the differential allocation of scarce resources through symbolic means.

These are the same characteristics that one finds in flow activities. Chess, for instance, provides a coherent structure or dramatic design; a symbolic battle between two armies, it has a well-defined beginning and end. It constitutes a defensive system in that it removes doubts about what needs to be done, and for the duration of the activity it effectively screens out any other concern. It is a directive system because it prescribes exactly how one should go about reaching the goal of the activity. And it is a symbolic economy since one's standing in the world of chess is affected by the outcome of each game.

Therefore, we can see again that flow activities are continuous with the rest of culture; they are simply more restricted, more clearly articulated examples of the same forms that culture writ large consists of. This conclusion is reminiscent of Huizinga's argument that culture develops out of earlier play forms. What this investigation adds to that insight is a more specific operational analysis of the structures that produce playfulness, and hence of the ways in which optimal cultural forms can be created.

And just as culture itself is man-made, flow activities are also the result of human decisions. Emphasis on the culturally structured aspects should not conceal the fact that people can turn any situation into a flow activity. We have seen that surgical operations can be tremendously enjoyable as long as the surgeon is able to maintain the flow-producing conditions of the activity. Even in concentration camps, prisoners who are able to superimpose a symbolic world, with its own goals and rules, on the grim "reality" of their condition seem to survive better and sometimes even to enjoy their experience. Some poets, for instance, are able to continue experiencing flow in the most dismal captivity (Tollas Tibor, personal communication); in fact, this appears to be true of many specialized intellectuals, especially mathematicians (Weissberg, 1951).

But one need not be highly trained in the manipulation of symbols—as intellectuals are—to change everyday life into a flow experience. The ethnographic record contains many examples of entire societies that look as if flow had been built into their warp and woof. History and personal experience are similarly full of individual instances that stand out as curious exceptions: people who have no objective reason to enjoy what they are doing, yet manifestly do so. It is, of course, much easier to enjoy an activity which is already structured to produce flow. Yet the fact that almost any situation can be turned into an enjoyable one raises some important issues. We need to find out how some people learn to impose limits on the flux of experience, how they create goals for their actions and means to reach those goals; how they learn to recognize and manipulate feedback until they are completely absorbed by what they are doing and afterward can say: "That was worth it."

The ability to control the environment—by limiting the stimulus field, finding clear goals and norms, and developing appropriate skills—is one side of the flow experience. The other side, paradoxically, is a feeling which seems to make the sense of control irrelevant. Many of the people we interviewed, especially those who most enjoy whatever they are doing, mentioned that at the height of their involvement with the activity they lose a sense of themselves as separate entities, and feel harmony and even a merging of identity with the environment. In some ways, this finding ought not to be unexpected. The great Eastern traditions of physical and "spiritual" control, for instance, are clearly built around this same paradox. The Hindu Yogi perfects his control over physiological processes with the ultimate aim of abolishing all distinctions between self and other. The Zen archer develops his skills to the point that the desire to hit the target becomes extinguished, and man, arrow, and target are discrete aspects of the same process. A similar pattern seems to hold in the Yaqui tradition represented by the sorcerer Don Juan, whose great efforts to achieve power and control over the self and the environment are subordinated to the ultimate goal of "seeing," or a desireless flowing along with cosmic forces (Castaneda, 1971, 1974).

From what we have seen, it appears that people achieve a state of harmonious participation with the environment only when they are to some extent able to affect their surroundings. In a sense they have to be "equal partners" with the forces impinging on their lives before they can identify with anything outside the self. A person who feels carried along by powers beyond his control resists these alien forces and experiences them as inimical. This simple rule has long been recognized in politics and in business. Participatory democracy is based on the idea that people who have some measure of control over public policy will identify with the body politic and forgo disruptive selfishness. "No taxation without representation" is a slogan which embodies the same concept: we are willing to give to a system that we can control. Profit sharing and participation in management decisions assume that people who have such options will identify more closely with company goals. These are examples of limited amounts of control in limited areas of experience. Religions attempt to provide unlimited control for the totality of experience. The flow activities we have studied offer high degrees of control in rather narrowly defined areas of experience.

The importance of this relationship between control and a broadening of the boundaries of the self cannot be overstated. If true, it would mean that the way to cope with problems of personal and societal disintegration is by increasing people's control over their own lives. Alienation, as Marx pointed out long ago, occurs when a person feels that he has lost the ability to direct the part of his life that is invested in work. Similarly, it would seem that people become alienated from each other, from political institutions, or from life itself to the extent that they cease to feel in control of these realms of experience. Flow activities provide a means of mastering a limited area of reality and thereby eliminate alienation, at least temporarily. Our respondents, whether they play chess, or dance, or climb rocks, or perform surgery, reported an exhilarating feeling of power while involved in the activity; at the same time, they spoke of the soothing sense of being part of something larger than themselves. It would be wrong, however, to conclude that one can eliminate personal and social alienation by providing more "games" or more flow activities isolated from the rest of experience. The Lydians' attempts to cure hunger with playful contests, or the Roman emperors' attempts to avoid popular restlessness by providing circus games, did not solve any problems in the long run. Instead, the whole of life must be restructured along the lines exemplified by these specialized forms of flow. For as long as people experience control and participation only in these isolated activities, the split between "work" and "play" will continue to exist in practice. A few fortunate people, like the composers and the surgeons in our sample, will be able to experience flow in their work. Others will do so briefly, in special settings that allow limited control over aspects of reality that do not seem to matter much in the general scheme of things. And for many people flow may be confined to those exceedingly trivial forms of control which we have called microflow: the patterning of everyday experience through idiosyncratic habits of thought, movement, perception, and social interaction.

The task of building deep flow into everyone's everyday life is clearly an immense project. Social, political, and economic differences all form barriers to people's ability to control their environment, and hence to their ability to experience flow. Therefore, any attempt to make life more enjoyable to a majority of people will have to contend with these deeply engrained and powerfully defended differences. There is strange poetic justice in the fact that a study of playful behavior should lead to sober economic and political issues. Yet this outcome is not so surprising after all. Early in our history, the framers of the Declaration of Independence believed that the pursuit of happiness is an unalienable human right. If in the succeeding two centuries we have made little progress in finding out what happiness is and how it can be pursued, that is a loss for which social scientists must bear part of the blame.

Too often in the past it has been assumed that mental health or happiness means simply a passive adaptation to social demands, a normative adjustment to the status quo. Consequently, psychologists and sociologists have tried to find ways to make the worker more productive, without caring whether in the process he became alienated; or they have tried to make the student learn what schools have to teach, without paying attention to whether he lost his personal autonomy along the way.

This approach has reinforced a political and economic trend which is already widespread in our culture. By recognizing only *what is* instead of *what could be,* the social scientist is not being "objective"; he is simply taking the course of least resistance by supporting existing values and institutions. It has been often said that the task of the social sciences is to be critical as well as normative (Smith, 1969; Habermas and Luhman, 1971;

Radnitzky, 1973). Karl Jaspers (1969, p. 128) states the essential point: "Tacitly present in all human psychology is an interest in possibilities and an appeal for further self-development." Unfortunately, since this tacit dimension of psychology is seldom made explicit, changes in the way men live occur in spite of, rather than because of, our formal knowledge of human behavior.

If we continue to ignore what makes us happy, what makes our life enjoyable, we shall actively help perpetrate the dehumanizing forces which are gaining momentum day by day. Because we can compute material costs, increase production, rationalize institutions, and control behavior, we go ahead and do these things. They are controllable; they are feasible. They offer opportunities for action to our skills, and hence we may enjoy doing them even though we destroy the possibility of enjoyment in the process. To build an assembly line is fun; it is a fascinating problem to solve, and the cost/production ratio provides concrete feedback to the engineer. It cannot be helped, it seems, that as a result the workers are deprived of opportunities to enjoy their own work. Enjoyment is left out of the equations for production, rationalization, and behavior control, partly because it has remained for so long a vague concept. Something that cannot be defined can safely be ignored. Instead of enjoyment, leisure is used as an indicator. Leisure, as defined in the various official documents that measure society's collective well-being (see, for instance, Executive Office of the President, 1973), reflects patterns of *consumption* and has nothing to say about personal satisfaction. The number of outboard motors or snowmobiles owned, the quantity of tennis players or theatergoers, does not tell us anything about whether people enjoy their lives.

If the trend toward increased mechanization of life is to be reversed—and social alienation and individual meaninglessness thereby reduced—the first step must be the recognition that there is such a thing as positive enjoyment. Once this concept is defined and made operational, we can deal with it as we deal with the other "real" dimensions of life, like the GNP, the IQ, physical health, and caloric intake. It will be possible then to find out how enjoyment relates to other variables, how it is distributed across social classes, how it is affected by selective changes in the environment. Inevitably one will be led to face decisions of a political nature: Is this increase in production worth the loss of potential enjoyment to the worker? Does this plan for urban development offer enough chances for enjoyment to potential tenants? Is the way schools are currently run conducive to enjoyment for teachers and students? Such questions cannot be answered on a rational basis until we know the laws of enjoyment, and we cannot learn these until we begin defining and measuring enjoyment itself.

It is of course paradoxical, and perhaps self-defeating, to define, measure, and analyze enjoyment. It may sound, in fact, like a recipe for perverting enjoyment, one more blow against freedom and spontaneity. Just as the process of adaptive intelligence is distorted when we embalm its creative potential in an IQ score, enjoyment could also be tamed and corrupted if more were known about it. This danger is real. But it is also true that one can destroy something by knowing too little about it. Enjoyment is already stamped out of the lives of millions. The longer this dimension of experience is ignored, the more likely it is to diminish, sacrificed to the measurable, hence "real," pseudo-advantages that can be squeezed out of the environment.

The contribution of this study is to provide a stimulus to understanding enjoyment. It is a first step in making that reality "real" in the sociological sense: by labeling it and adding it to the store of operational constructs. More specifically, we have tried to provide a perspective and a vocabulary for dealing with the phenomenon of intrinsic motivation, and we have started to develop some methods for assessing the amount and kind of intrinsic rewards present in different activities.

The view of enjoyment proposed here is in many respects different from the main lines of interpretation that have been used before. Our investigations have led us to emphasize the elements of freedom, skill, growth, and self-transcendence that appear so conspicuously in autotelic experience. Enjoyment is not synonymous with pleasure. The satisfaction of basic needs may be a prerequisite for experiencing enjoyment, but by itself it is not enough to give a sense of fulfillment. One needs to grow, to develop new skills, to take on new challenges to maintain a self-concept as a fully functioning human being. When skills are stunted or when opportunities for action are reduced, people will turn to pleasure as the only meaningful experience available. Or they will work harder for extrinsic rewards, to accumulate some tangible feedback for their existence. Status, power, and money are signs that one is competent, that one is acquiring control. But these are secondary rewards that matter only when the primary enjoyment that could be had from action itself is not available.

In this society, where the opportunity to satisfy pleasure and to obtain material comforts is unprecedented, the statistics on crime, mental disease, alcoholism, venereal disease, gambling, dissatisfaction with work, drug abuse, and general discontent keep steadily worsening. The rates of these indices of alienation are increasing more sharply in the affluent suburbs. It is not the bottling up of instinctual needs that is responsible for this trend, nor the lack of external rewards. Its cause appears to be the dearth of experiences which prove that one is competent, in a system that is geared for the efficient transformation of physical energy. The lack of intrinsic rewards is like an undiscovered virus we carry in our bodies; it maims slowly but surely.

Anyone who stops to watch children at play will see how intrinsically rewarding action can be. What children do is "play" only by the conventional wisdom of adult perspective. One could say just as well that what they do is work. But both labels are confusing: what children do most of the time is interact with the environment on a level at which their skills match opportunities. Left to themselves, children seek out flow with the inevitability of a natural law. They act without interruption if they can use their bodies, their hands, or their brain to produce feedback which proves that they can control the environment. They stop only when the challenges are exhausted, or when their skills are.

Already in childhood, however, the forces that tend to exclude intrinsic rewards are at work. Much has been written in developmental psychology about environments that deprive children of stimulation (see, for example, Spitz, 1949; Bronfenbrenner, 1970). More important from our point of view is the fact that the typical environment in which children grow up is not designed to offer opportunities for action. Action deprivation, and therefore flow deprivation, must be the consequence of growth settings which exclude room for free imagination, room for free movement, room to explore and manipulate real objects. At the same time, societal values begin to affect the child's interpretation of his actions. Efforts that bring no concrete results are branded a waste of time, and the child is encouraged to work only at tasks which will bring extrinsic rewards. Little-league baseball and piano lessons are organized not to give a child confidence in his or her skills but to show off these skills to an audience. Because of our general ignorance about enjoyment, we do not spend nearly enough time making sure that children meet opportunities for action which will sustain their growth. Most parents are content believing that the challenges of the school system and a television set will make an autonomous person out of their child. When they can afford to enrich the child's environment, by enrolling him in summer courses, ballet school, or a riding academy, it is usually in terms of status criteria that the choice is made, rather than the child's own needs and skills.

It is indeed paradoxical, as many observers have noted, that childhood may have been more enjoyable in less affluent times. The physical and human environment to which a child had access in a simpler society was often more varied and less structured than it is now. Children can exercise more freedom in such a setting; they can find a better match between their skills and the stimuli available. They have more resources at hand to build a growing, competent self. There is some irony in the fact that when urban planners in highly technological societies like Britain, Germany, or Sweden attempt to build an ideal environment for children, they produce replicas of the jungle or the disappearing slums with their loose timber, old tires, and decaying walls (Bengtsson, 1970). Such attempts are on the right track in that they do go some way toward compensating for the sterility of urban or suburban settings in which most children live. Yet there is also something artificial about them; they are a little like zoos or museums. They perpetrate the division between enjoyment and "real" life. Instead, we should try to make the total environment in which we live—from bedrooms to lobbies, from streets to offices and schools—one that is geared to growth. The playground as a special enclave for enjoyment will be abandoned, as the child grows up, for the poolroom, the tavern, the rock festival, or the golf course—all perfectly legitimate areas for enjoyment but separate from the rest of life and hence not likely to heal the basic split between "what needs to be done" and "what is enjoyable to do."

The adolescent's situation in technological societies is even worse than the child's. The skills of a child are still low enough to be met, here and there, by appropriate challenges; but there are not that many things for a teenager to do. In most cultures other than our own, a fifteen-year-old youth is actively involved in coping with the important challenges of life—work, marriage, decisions, and responsibility. He knows that he has to use all of his skills to meet the opportunities that any adult in his society must face. Very few adolescents have that feeling in our society. They may fly to Switzerland to ski, they may own racing cars, they may live in the most luxurious surroundings; but they know that, relative to adults around them, their actions have no real consequence.

This sheltered period of disengagement from serious issues, which Erikson and others have called a "moratorium" in the life cycle (Erikson, 1959, 1965), is one that in theory should offer excellent opportunities for experiencing intrinsic rewards. And in fact it is from the subculture of youth that much of the ideology for enjoying life and rejecting material possessions gains its support (Roszak, 1969; Csikszentmihalyi, 1971). Young people know what they are lacking, but they are not equipped to help themselves. Deprived of meaningful skills and of opportunities to use what they do have, they are starved for the experience of flow. As a consequence, they develop a social system of their own, in which drugs and a leisure technology focused on cars, skis, and surfboards provides dreams and action. In some ways these systems constitute a protostructure, a "liminoid" situation (Turner, 1974) that could act as a critical antithesis to mainstream culture. But because of its profound alienation from the rest of society, the solutions attempted by the counterculture probably cannot be integrated into adulthood. The usual pattern seems to be for adolescent activities to assume the character of escape. These activities are then exchanged for more "mature" forms of escape as the individual grows older. The identity that emerges from participating in such activities is not the assured, expanding self of a person who is doing his best to cope with real challenges, but a self which is unsure of its ability to function outside the artificial confines of the world it has created.

It is not that the world the adolescent builds is any less real than the one in which the rest of us live. To the extent that reality is socially constructed (Berger and Luckmann, 1967), a way of life based on play could be just as normal, or fulfilling, as one based on work and achievement. The problem arises when the dichotomy of "play" and "work" is set against itself, each of its terms repressing the possibilities for enjoyment present in the other. This artificial dualism creates a schizophrenic split which makes responsible workers fear enjoyment as a dangerous opiate, and makes those who have tasted flow in countercultural settings reject the work ethic. Neither side is whole within itself: the first cannot help yearning for the experience it has banished; the second feels secretly guilty for refusing to face the challenges it has rejected.

One way to reconcile this split is to realize that work is not necessarily more important than play and that play is not necessarily more enjoyable than work. What is both important and enjoyable is that a person act with the fullness of his or her abilities in a setting where the challenges stimulate growth of new abilities. Whether the setting is work or play, productive or recreational, does not matter. Both are equally productive if they make a person experience flow.

There are two ways in which this study can contribute to changes in the present state of affairs. In the first place, some of the directions explored here could stimulate further research and thereby increase our knowledge about intrinsic rewards and enjoyment. As has been said earlier, labeling and defining has its own magic and can make things that have been concealed suddenly obvious. And that in itself may start a process of change. More specifically, the methods barely outlined in this study need to be improved and refined. In Chapter Seven, we presented a way to analyze the challenges and skills available in rock dancing as an example of how the flow potential of an activity and the skills of a person involved in it can be assessed. This is one direction to be developed. A whole range of other deep-flow patterns could be analyzed, with increasingly improved techniques, until we know how much challenge and what kinds of challenges they are able to convey. At the same time, an inventory of individual skills can be perfected. The two combined would then allow us to know how different people can best find a match for their potential. In addition, the flow model could be extended to work situations and other "non-leisure" settings. Although neither management nor labor is terribly eager to face up to the deeper human questions of the workplace, there is much that ought to be learned about the costs of doing various jobs. The same analytic categories developed for deep-flow activities should be applied to occupations. We ought to find out how many of a person's skills are actually utilized by any given job, and hence how much flow can be expected to be produced by the task, and for how long. A job in which people cannot experience flow should receive a high social-cost rating, in that it contributes to human stagnation and a consequently heightened need for external rewards, or for "cheap thrills" that stifle the growth of skills.

An entire book could be written about the implications of this study for redesigning schools, urban environments, and homes. Some of these books have already been written, because many of the critics of existing institutions have come independently to conclusions that could be derived from the flow model (Henredon, 1965; Holt, 1967; Goodman, 1969; Bronfenbrenner, 1970; Illich, 1971; Dreitzel, 1973). But it is important to find out piecemeal and experimentally what combination of challenges and skills can be accommodated in a schoolroom, a neighborhood, or a home, so that it can maximize flow involvement in as many people as possible.

We need to know what activities are most enjoyable for

different people, at different ages. Chapters Nine and Ten suggest that the forms by which experience is patterned to make it enjoyable vary across people. Some rely more on imagination, others on bodily movement, still others on social interaction. There is much yet that needs to be found out about how widespread these patterns are, and how they are distributed in the general population. It is especially important to learn about flow opportunities for the elderly, who in our society are deprived, as adolescents are, of instrumental outlets for their skills.

The severe effects caused by flow deprivation open up a whole realm of investigations. The results need to be replicated with larger and more diverse samples. If they are upheld, they will point very clearly to the fact that some people suffer a subtle form of torture when they are unable to use their limbs freely or to have casual interactions with others. This finding then would have direct implications for redesigning many of the settings in which we live and work.

But the implications of this study are not for the professional researcher alone. There are very real opportunities for each individual to experiment in his or her daily life, to see whether its enjoyment can be increased. The findings suggest that one of the most basic things to be taught to children is to recognize opportunities for action in their environment. This is the skill on which all other skills are based. It is striking to see children—and adults—complaining that "there is nothing to do" when they are surrounded by innumerable stimuli. In the first place, one's own body is capable of the most incredible feats. Yoga disciplines aim at control of one's physiology as the central challenge. A sound education would begin by showing children what they can do with their bodies—through scaled-down Yoga, the martial arts, tumbling, juggling, isometrics, dance. Next a child may be introduced to the specific functions of discrete parts of his body. He would be shown the many things he can do with his breath: sing, shout, recite poetry. What the fingers can do: build with clay, smear paint, do a cat's cradle, use tools. And the most important thing: what the mind can do. We are accustomed to the idea that education begins with training children's minds to solve problems, to learn letters and numbers. But the groundwork for a real education consists in showing the child how his mind can make order in the environment through images, analogies, puns, and definitions. These are skills he already has, and so he can experience flow while building his self-confidence. To test the limits of the mind, the first education should be an artistic one—not in the sense of learning about art or even learning to do art, but in the deeper sense of acquiring an artistic vision. It is important for children to learn that clouds can be made into pictures in the mind. It is important that they learn to hear patterns in the sounds around them. They need to learn to play with words, to construct wild phrases and atrocious puns until they develop a sense of confident mastery over verbal tools. A child trained to develop all the skills of his body and his mind need never feel bored or helpless and therefore alienated from his surroundings. Utopian planners from Plato to Auguste Comte and Aldous Huxley have insisted that the use of the body in physical exercise and artistic discipline should precede book learning in the schools. Has any school system ever taken them seriously?

It is not only *what* should be taught to children that is important, but also *how* it should be taught. The studies of flow activities suggest that anything can be made enjoyable as long as certain structural conditions are preserved. If educators were to start with the question "How can learning be made more enjoyable?" the students' gains in performance should increase tremendously. It is crucial to remember, however, that one does not make learning more enjoyable by trivializing it—by making it easy, or pleasant, or "fun." The hardships and dangers of rock climbing are probably a better model for enjoyment in learning than the gussied-up educational techniques based on a hedonistic escapist notion of what enjoyment is.

In theory, it is simple enough to make any learning task enjoyable: find out what the student's skills are and what their level is—not only in the three Rs but in the other modalities of human action; then devise limited but gradually increasing opportunities for the expression of those skills. The learning then will become intrinsically motivated. Of course, any good teacher or textbook writer already knows this. The problem is that mass education is too impersonal and rigid to allow the application of this simple recipe. But the more we know about the mechanism of enjoyment, the easier it should become to build it into our institutions.

A person who has reached the point of being able to resonate his abilities with the surroundings, whatever they are, is in harmony with the world. He can be in solitary confinement or in a boring job; but as long as he knows how to respond to the few stimuli around—through fantasy, scientific analysis, or intervention—he will still be enjoying himself. The meshing of highly developed personal skills with the nonself creates that harmony and transcendence of self on which further social evolution depends. A person who learns to flow with confidence wherever he or she is becomes both truly autonomous and truly connected with the world. Extrinsic rewards will be less needed to motivate him to put up with the hardships of existence. A constant ability to "design or discover something new," "to explore a strange place"—the rewards that people experience in deep flow—will be enough to motivate action. Only with such a shift in perspective will we avoid "devouring the world" (Arendt, 1958). We must "deliberately choose a life of action over a life of consumption" (Illich, 1971), or the human and physical resources of our environment will be depleted.

The task is not easy. In the past, enjoyment of the few has always been achieved at the expense of drudgery for the masses. This we cannot afford any longer—not just ethically, but practically as well. The power of the disadvantaged is great enough to destroy the world, if not to heal it. Therefore, we must find solutions that will lift as many people as possible into a pattern of growth. Alienated children in the suburbs and bored housewives in the homes need to experience flow just as much as anyone else. If they cannot get it, they will find substitutes in the form of escape or consumption. The task is awesome, bristling with the oldest problems of economic and social justice. Fortunately, there are many ways that work toward a solution can proceed. There is research for researchers, thought for thinkers, and action for people of good will. The impetus for change is coming from many directions. One way or another, if human evolution is to go on, we shall have to learn to enjoy life more thoroughly.

Appendix

Tests and Procedures Used in Microflow Experiments

1. Order of Procedures

*Session 1**	*Session 2**	*Session 3**
Sign release sheet	—	—
Questionnaires	*Q*	*Q*
A	A	A
B	B	B
C	C	C
Tests	*Tests*	*Tests*
Digit spans	(same as 1)	(same as 1)
Size estimation		
Time est. (1)		
Unusual uses		
Matches		
Time est. (2)		
Tiltboard		
Raven matrices		
Gottschalk-Gleser		
Alienation scale	Collect records	Collect records
Instructions for Recording Noninstrumental Behavior	Instructions for Flow-Deprivation Period	Questionnaire D
		Debriefing Interview
		Pay subject

*Session 1 occurred prior to subjects' 48-hour recording of noninstrumental behavior; session 2, after recording of noninstrumental behavior; session 3, after 48-hour period of flow deprivation.

2. Questionnaires

A. Compared with an average day, during the last 48 hours did you feel:

1. Much better ability to concentrate	Better	About Normal	Less	Much less ability to concentrate
1	2	3	4	5
2. Much more tired	More	About Normal	Less	Much less tired
1	2	3	4	5
3. Much more hungry	More	About Normal	Less	Much less hungry
1	2	3	4	5
4. Much more sleepy	More	About Normal	Less	Much less sleepy
1	2	3	4	5
5. Much more relaxed	More	About Normal	Less	Much less relaxed
1	2	3	4	5
6. Much more sensitive to heat, light, sound, etc.	More	About Normal	Less	Much less sensitive
1	2	3	4	5
7. Much less healthy physically	Less	About Normal	More	Much more healthy physically
1	2	3	4	5

B. During the past 48 hours, did you experience (circle one):

1. Headache	a) none	b) slight	c) bothersome	d) severe	e) intolerable
2. Body aches	a)	b)	c)	d)	e)
3. Itching	a)	b)	c)	d)	e)
4. Toothache	a)	b)	c)	d)	e)
5. Muscular tension	a)	b)	c)	d)	e)
6. Hallucinatory symptoms	a)	b)	c)	d)	e)
7. Other physical symptoms (specify) ____________	a)	b)	c)	d)	e)

C. How would you describe your present mood? Please circle appropriate answer.

	Very	Quite	Some-what	Some-what	Quite	Very	
Hostile	0	o	.	.	o	0	Friendly
Alert	0	o	.	.	o	0	Dopey
Elated	0	o	.	.	o	0	Depressed
Tense	0	o	.	.	o	0	Relaxed
Good	0	o	.	.	o	0	Bad
Suspicious	0	o	.	.	o	0	Trusting
Irritable	0	o	.	.	o	0	Cheerful
Sad	0	o	.	.	o	0	Happy
Strong	0	o	.	.	o	0	Weak
Active	0	o	.	.	o	0	Passive
Cynical	0	o	.	.	o	0	Believing
Creative	0	o	.	.	o	0	Dull
Resentful	0	o	.	.	o	0	Satisfied
Fast	0	o	.	.	o	0	Slow
Free	0	o	.	.	o	0	Constrained
Excited	0	o	.	.	o	0	Bored
Unworthy	0	o	.	.	o	0	Worthy
In control	0	o	.	.	o	0	Out of control
Gregarious	0	o	.	.	o	0	Isolated
Unreasonable	0	o	.	.	o	0	Reasonable

D [administered at end of Session 3]. Would you say that, compared with an average day, in the past 48 hours your general psychological state was (circle one):

Very normal	Somewhat different	Different	Very different
1	2	3	4

If you circled 2, 3, or 4 above, do you think this was due to (circle one).

1. Decreased ability to engage in fantasy, daydreaming, etc.

Had no effect	Had little effect	Had some effect	Had much effect	Had very much effect
1	2	3	4	5

2. Decrease in entertainment—listening to music; watching TV, movies; reading for fun; etc.

Had no effect	Had little effect	Had some effect	Had much effect	Had very much effect
1	2	3	4	5

3. Decrease in free body movement—tapping; moving arms and legs; playing with objects; feeling body; doodling; etc.

Had no effect	Had little effect	Had some effect	Had much effect	Had very much effect
1	2	3	4	5

4. Decreased contact with other people—e.g., talking with friends.

Had no effect	Had little effect	Had some effect	Had much effect	Had very much effect
1	2	3	4	5

5. Inability to move freely; being "rooted to a chair."

Had no effect	Had little effect	Had some effect	Had much effect	Had very much effect
1	2	3	4	5

6. Lack of self-given "rewards"—having snacks, drinks, etc.

Had no effect	Had little effect	Had some effect	Had much effect	Had very much effect
1	2	3	4	5

7. The constant self-consciousness about your actions.

Had no effect	Had little effect	Had some effect	Had much effect	Had very much effect
1	2	3	4	5

8. The act of stopping yourself from doing what you wanted to do.

Had no effect	Had little effect	Had some effect	Had much effect	Had very much effect
1	2	3	4	5

Of the eight reasons that might have affected your psychological state,
which had the most effect? No. ________
which had the least effect? No. ________

3. Debriefing Interview

1. How long did deprivation last? ________________
2. Why did you quit? (couldn't do it any longer, didn't want to . . .)
____
3. What was the most difficult thing about the experience? ________________
4. Did you feel angry or irritable? Why? ________________
5. Did you feel deprived? How? ________________
6. How did you get yourself to do it? (pay, interest, etc.) ________________
7. Did your daily routine change? ________________
8. Did you notice any change in the way you
   a. acted? ________________
   b. thought about things in general? ________________
   c. thought about yourself? ________________
   d. coped with problems? ________________
   e. read books? ________________
   f. made decisions? ________________
9. Did you at any time purposely ignore the instruction and engage in play behavior, and then continue with the experiment? If so, what caused you to do this?
____

10. Did you ever inadvertently engage in such behavior? How many times, and in what context?

____

11. Could you have extended your participation to:

a. 2 days ________	If you were paid: a. $20 ________
b. 3 days ________	b. $50 ________
c. 4 days ________	c. $100 ________
d. One week ________	d. $250 ________
e. More	e. More? ________

12. What are your feelings about the experiment?

4. Remembering Digits Task*

DIGITS FORWARD

I am going to say some numbers. Listen carefully, and when I am through say them right after me.

	I	II	III
3)	5-8-2	6-9-4	8-9-5
4)	6-4-3-9	7-2-8-6	4-3-6-3
5)	4-2-7-3-1	7-5-8-3-6	1-9-3-8-7
6)	6-1-9-4-7-3	3-9-2-4-8-7	4-5-2-1-2-9
7)	5-9-1-7-4-2-8	4-1-7-9-3-8-6	2-4-6-5-2-6-4
8)	5-8-1-9-2-6-4-7	3-8-2-9-5-1-7-4	2-6-7-9-8-1-3-6
9)	2-7-5-8-6-2-5-8-4	7-1-3-9-4-2-5-6-8	2-8-6-7-2-1-4-8-1

DIGITS BACKWARD

Now I am going to say some more numbers, but this time when I stop I want you to say them backward. For example, If I say "7-1-9" what would you say? (If correct, say: "Here are some others.")

	I	II	III
2)	2-4	5-8	6-4
3)	6-2-9	4-1-5	6-1-7
4)	3-2-7-9	4-9-6-8	8-3-2-6
5)	1-5-2-8-6	6-1-8-4-3	2-1-8-6-7
6)	5-3-9-4-1-8	7-2-4-8-5-6	4-1-5-3-9-2
7)	8-1-2-9-3-6-5	4-7-3-9-1-2-8	8-6-1-5-4-7-2
8)	9-4-3-7-6-2-5-8	7-2-8-1-9-6-5-3	4-5-2-1-7-8-3-9

*Adapted from the Wechsler-Bellevue Intelligence Test.

5. Matches Cognitive Task* (Form A)

In this test, groups of matches will be laid out to form patterns of squares or triangles. Your task will be to take away a certain number of matches so that a certain number of squares or triangles remain. They must come out even with no extra matches left over.

For example:

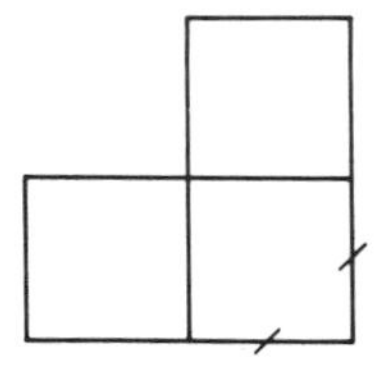

Take away 2 matches
and leave 2 squares.

You are to indicate the correct matches to be taken away by crossing out with short heavy marks as has been done in the figure above. Notice that if you take away any other two matches you will have an extra match left over, in addition to the two squares.

If you have any questions, please ask them now, since no questions will be answered once the test is begun. This test is a speed test, so work as rapidly as you can. If you have difficulty with an item, go on and come back if you have time.

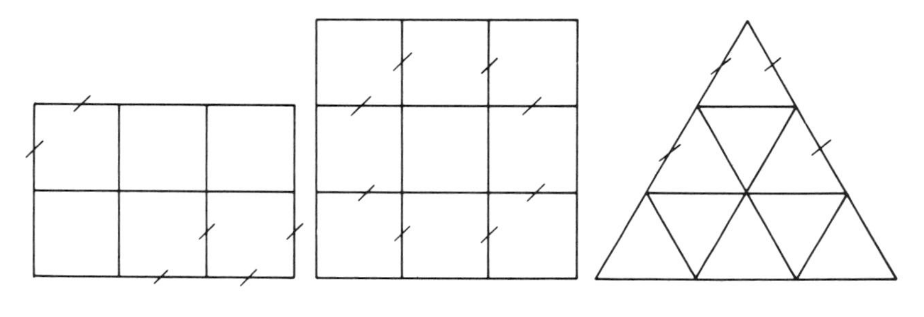

Take away 6 matches and leave 3 squares. | Take away 8 matches and leave 2 squares. | Take away 4 matches and leave 6 triangles.

*Adapted from Guilford, 1967, p. 152.

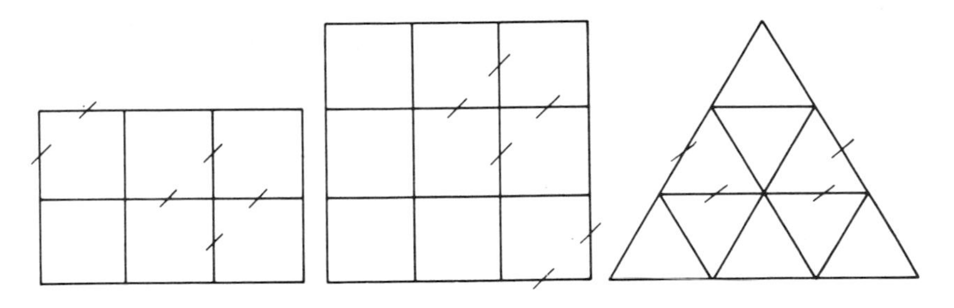

Take away 6 matches and leave 2 squares.

Take away 6 matches and leave 5 squares.

Take away 4 matches and leave 5 triangles.

6. Unusual Uses Cognitive Task (Form A)*

Listed below are two objects. Your task is to write down as many different *uses* as you can for each object. For instance, the object "pair of eyeglasses" could be used to start a fire, to send messages, to disguise oneself, and so on. You will have approximately six minutes. Be sure to write down some uses for both objects. Write down anything that comes to mind, no matter how strange it may seem.

Wooden pencil

Auto tire

*Adapted from Guilford, 1967, p. 145.

7. Gottschalk-Gleser Projective Task*

Upon a signal from me I would like you to write for ten minutes about any interesting or personal life experiences you have had. Once you have started I would prefer not to reply to any questions you may feel like asking me until the ten-minute period is over. Do you have any questions you would like to ask me now before we start?

*Adapted from Gottschalk, Winget, and Gleser, 1969.

8. Instructions for Recording Noninstrumental Behavior

Code: Year in school:
Age: Major:
Sex: Field of interest:

The purpose of this part of the experiment is to determine the types of "play" behavior (i.e., behavior which is noninstrumental but rewarding in some way) in which you specifically indulge. Aside from obvious recreational practices (games, hobbies, etc.), we are interested in more subtle modes of play behavior. For instance, we would define reading for pleasure as "play" but reading for a course as instrumental; exchanging information with a friend would be instrumental, but talking to him merely for the sake of interaction would be "play."

For the next two days, beginning ____________ morning when you wake up until 9:00 P.M. ____________ evening, live as you would normally live but be aware of your actions as much as possible, and take note of *everything* that you do for pleasure, especially those things that you would normally do absentmindedly, as well as the obvious. Record your behavior as follows:

1. Divide the day using specific, natural landmarks (e.g., mealtimes, class-times, etc.) *or* into three-hour segments (9:00-12:00, etc.). Report at least every three hours on the behavior of the previous three hours, beginning at 12:00 noon, but feel free to jot things down at any time. If possible, indicate also how important the behavior is to you. Note the time of each report.

2. Report contingencies of common or characteristic behavior (e.g., talking to self *while* washing dishes, chewing gum *whenever* reading, etc.).

3. *Be aware* of yourself as much as possible. Subtle, unconscious behavior may go unnoticed. Don't be afraid to report what you may think is insignificant or trivial (or weird).

4. Try not to be tense or strained, but merely observant.

9. Instructions for Flow-Deprivation Period

1. Show records made previous week. Make sure that all entries are clear and conform to definition of "play."

2. Instruct S as follows:

Beginning ____________ [tomorrow morning] when you wake up and until 9:00 P.M., we would like you to act in a normal way, doing all the things you have to do, but not doing anything that is "play" or noninstrumental.

In other words, you have to avoid the sort of things listed here [refer to record], and anything like them.

Please keep a record of things you wanted to do but stopped yourself from doing, just as last time. We are counting on you to report honestly and accurately.

You should try to keep this up for at least two days.

If for any reason you feel you have to terminate this experiment, please contact immediately:

There is no penalty for stopping the experiment, but if you fail to notify us right away, the results will be useless.

References

Abrahams, G. *The Chess Mind.* London: Penguin, 1960.

Arendt, H. *The Human Condition.* Chicago: University of Chicago Press, 1958.

Avedon, E. M., and Sutton-Smith, B. *The Study of Games.* New York: Wiley, 1971.

Beach, F. A. "Current Concepts of Play in Animals." *American Naturalist,* 1945, *79,* 523-541.

Bekoff, M. "The Development of Social Interaction, Play, and Metacommunication in Mammals: An Ethological Perspective." *Quarterly Review of Biology,* 1972, *47* (4), 412-434.

Bekoff, M. "Social Play and Play-Soliciting by Infant Canids." *American Zoologist,* 1974, *14,* 323-340.

Bengtsson, A. *Environmental Planning for Children's Play.* New York: Praeger, 1970.

Berger, P. L. "Some General Observations on the Problem of Work." In P. L. Berger (Ed.), *The Human Shape of Work.* New York: Macmillan, 1964. Pp. 211-241.

Berger, P. L., and Luckmann, T. *The Social Construction of Reality*. Garden City, N.Y.: Doubleday, 1967.

Bergler, E. *The Psychology of Gambling*. New York: International Universities Press, 1970.

Berlyne, D. E. *Conflict, Arousal, and Curiosity*. New York: McGraw-Hill, 1960.

Berlyne, D. E., and Madsen, K. B. (Eds.) *Pleasure, Reward, Preference*. New York: Academic Press, 1973.

Bexton, W. H., Heron, W., and Scott, T. H. "Effects of Decreased Variation in the Sensory Environment." *Canadian Journal of Psychology*, 1954, *8*, 70-76.

Biase, D. V., and Mitchell, J. "Anticipated Responses to Short-Term Sensory Deprivation." *Psychological Reports*, 1969, *24*, 351-354.

Binet, A. *Psychologie des Grands Calculateurs et Joueurs d'Echecs*. Paris: Hachette, 1894.

Bloom, S. W. "Some Implications of Studies in the Professionalization of Physicians." In E. G. Jaco (Ed.), *Patients, Physicians, and Illness*. New York: Free Press, 1958.

Bowen, E. S. *Return to Laughter*. Garden City, N.Y.: Doubleday, 1964.

Bronfenbrenner, U. *Two Worlds of Childhood*. New York: Basic Books, 1970.

Brown, N. O. *Life Against Death*. Middletown, Conn.: Wesleyan University Press, 1959.

Bühler, K. *Die geistige Entwicklung des Kindes*. Jena: G. Fischer, 1930.

Callois, R. *Les Jeux et les Hommes*. Paris: Gallimard, 1958.

Carpenter, E. *They Became What They Beheld*. New York: Ballantine, 1970.

Carpenter, E. *Eskimo Realities*. New York: Holt, 1973.

Castaneda, C. *A Separate Reality*. New York: Simon and Schuster, 1971.

Castaneda, C. *Tales Of Power*. New York: Simon and Schuster, 1974.

Chase, W. G., and Simon, H. A. "Perception in Chess." *Cognitive Psychology*, 1973, *4*, 55-81.

Chepko, B. D. "A Preliminary Study of the Effects of Play Deprivation on Young Goats." *Zeitschrift zur Tierpsychologie,* 1971, *28,* 517-526.

Chinoy, E. *Automobile Workers and the American Dream.* Garden City, N.Y.: Doubleday, 1955.

Csikszentmihalyi, M. "The Americanization of Rock Climbing." *University of Chicago Magazine,* 1969, *61* (6), 20-27.

Csikszentmihalyi, M. "The Hippie as a Revolutionary." In R. J. Havighurst, B. Neugarten, and J. Falk (Eds.), *Society and Education.* Boston: Allyn and Bacon, 1971. Pp. 189-193.

Csikszentmihalyi, M., and Bennett, S. "An Exploratory Model of Play." *American Anthropologist,* 1971, *73* (1), 45-58.

Csikszentmihalyi, M., and Getzels, J. W. "The Personality of Young Artists: An Empirical and Theoretical Exploration." *British Journal of Psychology,* 1973, *64* (1), 91-104.

Csikszentmihalyi, M., and Gruenberg, P. "Extrinsic and Intrinsic Reward Patterns in Sports." Unpublished manuscript, 1970.

Day, H. I., Berlyne, D. E., and Hunt, D. E. (Eds.) *Intrinsic Motivation: A New Direction in Education.* New York: Holt, 1971.

De Charms, R. *Personal Causation.* New York: Academic Press, 1968.

Deci, E. L. "Effects of Externally Mediated Rewards on Intrinsic Motivation." *Journal of Personality and Social Psychology,* 1971, *18,* 105-115.

Deci, E. L. *Intrinsic Motivation.* Rochester, N.Y.: University of Rochester, Management Research Center, Technical Report 62, 1973.

De Groot, A. *Thought and Choice in Chess.* The Hague: Mouton, 1965.

Dember, W. N. *The Psychology of Perception.* New York: Holt, 1960.

Deren, M. *Divine Horseman.* London: Thomas and Hudson, 1953.

Dewey, J. *Art as Experience.* New York: Putnam, 1934.

Dillon, J. T. "Approaches to the Study of Problem-Finding Behavior." Unpublished manuscript, University of Chicago, 1972.

Dreitzel, H. P. (Ed.) *Childhood and Socialization.* New York: Macmillan, 1973.

Eberl, D. "Matterhorn." *Ascent,* 1969, *9,* 11-15.

Eibl-Eibesfeldt, L. *Ethology: The Biology of Behavior.* New York: Holt, 1970.

Eliade, M. *Yoga: Immortality and Freedom.* Princeton, N.J.: Princeton University Press, 1969.

Ellis, M. J. *Why People Play.* Englewood Cliffs, N.J.: Prentice-Hall, 1973.

Erikson, E. *Identity and the Life Cycle.* New York: International Universities Press, 1959.

Erikson, E. (Ed.) *The Challenge of Youth.* Garden City, N.Y.: Doubleday, 1965.

Executive Office of the President. *Social Indicators, 1973.* Washington, D.C.: Office of Management and Budget, 1973.

Fagen, R. "Selective and Evolutionary Aspects of Animal Play." *American Naturalist,* 1974, *108* (964), 850-858.

Fine, R. "Chess and Chess Masters." *Psychoanalysis,* 1956, *3,* 7-77.

Fine, R. *The Psychology of the Chess Player.* New York: Dover, 1967.

Ford, R. *Motivation Through the Work Itself.* New York: American Management Association, 1969.

Fortune, R. F. *Sorcerers of Dobu.* New York: Dutton, 1963.

Freedman, B. J. "The Subjective Experience of Perceptual and Cognitive Disturbances in Schizophrenia." *Archives of General Psychiatry,* 1974, *30,* 333-340.

Freud, S. *The Ego and the Id.* London: Allen and Unwin, 1927.

Freud, S. "Dostoevsky and Parricide." In E. Jones (Ed.), *Collected Papers of Sigmund Freud,* vol. 5. New York: Basic Books, 1959.

Frick, J. W., Guilford, J. P., Christensen, P. R., and Merrifield, P. R. "A Factor-Analytic Study of Flexibility in Thinking." *Educational Psychological Measurements,* 1959, *19,* 469-496.

Garai, J., and Scheinfeld, A. "Sex Differences in Mental and Behavioral Traits." *Genetic Psychological Monographs,* 1968, *77,* 253.

Geertz, C. *The Interpretation of Culture.* New York: Basic Books, 1973.

Getzels, J. W., and Csikszentmihalyi, M. "Creative Problem-Finding: A Longitudinal Study with Artists." Unpublished manuscript, University of Chicago, 1975.

Gewirtz, J. L., and Baer, D. M. "The Effect of Brief Social Deprivation on Behaviors for a Social Reinforcer." *Journal of Abnormal and Social Psychology,* 1958a, *56,* 49-56.

Gewirtz, J. L., and Baer, D. M. "Deprivation and Satiation of Social Reinforcers as Drive Conditioners." *Journal of Abnormal and Social Psychology,* 1958b, *57,* 165-172.

Ghiselin, B. (Ed.) *The Creative Process.* New York: Mentor, 1952.

Ginzberg. "Work: The Eye of the Hurricane." *Humanitas,* 1971, *7* (2), 227-243.

Goffman, E. *Frame Analysis.* Cambridge, Mass.: Harvard University Press, 1975.

Gooding, J. *The Job Revolution.* New York: Walker and Co., 1972.

Goodman, P. "The Present Moment in Education." *New York Review of Books,* April 10, 1969, pp. 18-24.

Gottschalk, L. A., Winget, C. N., and Gleser, G. C. *Manual of Instruction for Using the Gottschalk-Gleser Content Analysis Scales.* Berkeley: University of California Press, 1969.

Groos, K. *The Play of Man.* New York: Appleton, 1901.

Guilford, J. P. *The Nature of Human Intelligence.* New York: McGraw-Hill, 1967.

Habermas, J., and Luhman, N. *Theorie der Gesellschaft oder Sozialtechnologie.* Frankfurt: Suhrkamp, 1971.

Harrow, M., Tucker, G. J., and Shield, P. "Stimulus Overinclusion in Schizophrenic Disorders." *Archives of General Psychiatry,* 1972, *27,* 40-45.

Hebb, D. O. "Drives and the CNS." *Psychological Review,* 1955, *62,* 243-254.

Henredon, J. *The Way It Spozed to Be.* New York: Simon and Schuster, 1965.

Herrigel, E. *Zen in the Art of Archery.* New York: Pantheon, 1953.

Herrigel, E. *The Method of Zen.* New York: Pantheon, 1960.

Holt, J. *How Children Fail.* New York: Pitman, 1967.

Huizinga, J. *Homo Ludens.* Boston: Beacon Press, 1950. Originally published 1939.

Illich, I. *De-Schooling Society.* New York: Harper, 1971.

Jaspers, K. *Nietzsche.* Chicago: Regnery, 1969.

Jewell, P. A., and Loizos, C. *Play, Exploration and Territoriality in Mammals.* Symposium Vol. 18. London: London Zoological Societies, 1966.

Jones, E. "The Problem of Paul Morphy." *International Journal of Psychoanalysis,* 1931, *12,* 1-23.

Jung, C. G. *Memories, Dreams, Reflections.* New York: Vintage, 1963.

Keniston, K. *The Uncommitted.* New York: Delta, 1960.

Kenyon, G. S. *Values Held for Physical Activity by Urban Secondary School Students.* Madison: University of Wisconsin, School of Education, 1968.

Kenyon, G. S. "Six Scales for Assessing Attitude Towards Physical Activity." In W. P. Morgan (Ed.), *Contemporary Readings in Sport Psychology.* Springfield, Ill.: Thomas, 1970.

Knight, M. *Return to the Alps.* New York: Friends of the Earth, 1970.

Kusyszyn, I. "How Gambling Saved Me from a Misspent Sabbatical." *Journal of Humanistic Psychology,* 1975 (in press).

Laski, M. *Ecstasy: A Study of Some Secular and Religious Experiences.* Bloomington: Indiana University Press, 1962.

Lepper, M. R., Greene, D., and Nisbett, R. E. "Undermining Children's Intrinsic Interest with Extrinsic Rewards: A Test of the Overjustification Hypothesis." *Journal of Personality and Social Psychology,* 1973, *28,* 129-137.

Lukan, K. "Climbers in the Alps." In K. Lukan (Ed.), *Alps and Alpinism.* New York: Coward-McCann, 1968. Pp. 43-93.

Maccoby, E. "Women's Intellect." In S. M. Farber and R. H. Wilson (Eds.), *The Potential of Women.* New York: McGraw-Hill, 1963.

Maccoby, E. *The Development of Sex Differences.* Palo Alto, Calif.: Stanford University Press, 1966.

Maddi, S. R. "The Search for Meaning." In M. Page (Ed.), *Nebraska Symposium on Motivation.* Lincoln: University of Nebraska Press, 1970. Pp. 137-186.

Marcuse, H. *Das Ende der Utopie.* Berlin, 1967.

Maslow, A. *Motivation and Personality.* New York: Harper, 1954.

Maslow, A. *Towards a Psychology of Being.* Princeton, N.J.: Van Nostrand, 1962.

Maslow, A. "Humanistic Science and Transcendent Experience." *Journal of Humanistic Psychology,* 1965, *5* (2), 219-227.

Maslow, A. *The Farther Reaches of Human Nature.* New York: Viking, 1971.

Mason, J. A., and Peterson, G. E. "On the Problem of Describing the Grammar of Natural Languages." *Language and Speech,* 1967, *10,* 107-121.

McGhie, A., and Chapman, J. "Disorders of Attention and Perception in Early Schizophrenia." *British Journal of Medical Psychology,* 1961, *34,* 103-116.

Mead, G. H. *Mind, Self, and Society.* Chicago: University of Chicago Press, 1934.

Mead, M. *Sex and Temperament in Three Primitive Societies.* New York: Morrow, 1935.

Moltmann, J. *Theology of Play.* New York: Harper, 1972.

Montmasson, J. M. *Invention and the Unconscious.* New York: Harcourt, Brace, 1932.

Muller-Schwarze, D. "Play Deprivation in Deer." *Behaviour,* 1968, *31,* 144-162.

Murphy, G. *Personality: A Biosocial Approach to Origins and Structure.* New York: Harper, 1947.

Murphy, G. *Human Potentialities.* New York: Basic Books, 1958.

Naranjo, C., and Ornstein, R. E. *On the Psychology of Meditation.* New York: Viking, 1971.

Nathanson, C. A., and Becker, M. H. "Job Satisfaction and Job Performance: An Empirical Test of Some Theoretical Propositions." *Organizational Behavior and Human Performance,* 1973, *9,* 267-279.

Nelson, B. "Self-Images and Systems of Spiritual Direction in the History of European Civilization." In S. Z. Klausner (Ed.), *The Quest for Self-Control.* New York: Free Press, 1965. Pp. 49-103.

Newell, A., Shaw, J. C., and Simon, H. A. "Chess-Playing Programs and the Problem of Complexity." *IBM Journal of Research and Development,* 1958, *2,* 330-335.

Olds, J. "The Central Nervous System and the Reinforcement of Behavior." *American Psychologist,* 1969, *24,* 707-719.

Olds, J., Disterhoft, J. F., Segal, M., Kornblith, C. L., and Hirsh, R. "Learning Centers of Rat Brain Mapped by Measuring Latencies of Conditioned Unit Responses." *Journal of Neurophysiology,* 1972, *35,* 202-219.

Payne, R. W., and Hewlett, J. H. G. "Thought Disorder in Psychotic Patients." In H. J. Eysenck (Ed.), *Experiments in Personality.* London: Routledge and Kegan Paul, 1960. Pp. 3-104.

Perun, P. "Female Chess Players: Women in a Man's World." Unpublished M.A. thesis, University of Chicago, 1973.

Piaget, J. *Play, Dreams and Imitation in Childhood.* New York: Norton, 1951.

Piaget, J. *The Moral Judgment of the Child.* New York: Free Press, 1965.

Polanyi, K. *The Great Transformation.* Boston: Beacon Press, 1957.

Pushkin, V. N., Pospelov, D. A., and Efimov, I. E. "Psychological Theory of Thinking and Some Trends in the Development of Cybernetics." *Voprosy Psikhologii,* 1971, *17,* 66-79.

Radnitzky, G. *Contemporary Schools of Metascience.* Chicago: Regnery, 1973.

Rahner, H. *Man at Play.* New York: Herder and Herder, 1967.

Rankin, N. "The Effects of Selective Social Deprivation in a Natural Setting." Unpublished doctoral dissertation, University of California, Berkeley, 1969.

Roberts, J. M., and Sutton-Smith, B. "Child-Training and Game Involvement." *Ethnology,* 1962, *1,* 166-185.

Robinson, D. "The Climber as Visionary." *Ascent,* 1969, *9,* 4-10.

Rogers, C. R. *On Becoming a Person.* Boston: Houghton Mifflin, 1961.

Roszak, T. *The Making of a Counter-Culture.* Garden City, N.Y.: Doubleday, 1969.

Sheets, M. *The Phenomenology of Dance.* Madison: University of Wisconsin Press, 1966.

Shield, P. H., and others. "Investigation of Factors Related to Stimulus Overinclusion." *Psychiatric Quarterly,* 1974, *48* (1), 109-116.

Singer, J. L. *Daydreaming: An Introduction to the Experimental Study of Inner Experiences.* New York: Random House, 1966.

Singer, J. L. *The Child's World of Make-Believe.* New York: Academic Press, 1973.

Skinner, B. F. *Science and Human Behavior.* New York: Macmillan, 1953.

Smith, M. B. *Social Psychology and Human Values.* Chicago: Aldine, 1969.

Spitz, R. A. "The Role of Ecological Factors in Emotional Development in Infancy." *Child Development,* 1949, *20,* 145-156.

Steiner, G. "Fields of Force." *New Yorker,* Oct. 28, 1972, pp. 42-117. Also published in book form: *Fields of Force.* New York: Viking, 1974a.

Steiner, G. "The Lost Garden." *New Yorker,* June 3, 1974b, pp. 100-108.

Sutton-Smith, B. "The Expressive Profile." *Journal of American Folklore,* 1971a, *84* (331), 80-92.

Sutton-Smith, B. "Play, Games and Controls." In J. P. Scott and S. F. Scott (Eds.), *Social Control and Social Change.* Chicago: University of Chicago Press, 1971b. Pp. 73-102.

Sutton-Smith, B. *The Folkgames of Children.* Houston: University of Texas Press, 1973.

Sutton-Smith, B., and Roberts, J. M. "Game-Involvement in Adults." *Journal of Social Psychology,* 1963, *60,* 15-30.

Terkel, S. *Working.* New York: Pantheon, 1974.
Thompson, E. P. *The Making of the English Working Class.* New York: Vintage, 1963.
Tikhomirov, O. K., and Terekhov, V. A. "Human Heuristics." *Voprosy Psikhologii,* 1967, *12,* 26-41.
Tucker, G., and others. "Perceptual Experiences in Schizophrenic and Non-Schizophrenic Patients." *Archives of General Psychiatry,* 1969, *20,* 159-166.
Turnbull, C. *The Forest People.* New York: Simon and Schuster, 1962.
Turnbull, C. *The Mountain People.* New York: Simon and Schuster, 1972.
Turner, V. *The Ritual Process.* Chicago: Aldine, 1969.
Turner, V. "Liminality, Play, Flow, and Ritual: Optational and Obligatory Forms and Genres." Paper presented at the Burg Wartenstein Symposium, No. 64, 1974.
Unsworth, W. *North Face.* London: Hutchinson, 1969.
Walker, C. R., and Guest, R. H. *The Man on the Assembly Line.* Cambridge, Mass.: Harvard University Press, 1952.
Weber, M. *The Protestant Ethic and the Spirit of Capitalism.* London: Allen and Unwin, 1930.
Weber, M. *The Theory of Social and Economic Organization.* New York: Oxford University Press, 1947.
Weissberg, A. *The Accused.* New York: Simon and Schuster, 1951.
White, R. W. "Motivation Reconsidered: The Concept of Competence." *Psychological Review,* 1959, *66,* 297-333.
Worsley, P. *The Trumpet Shall Sound.* New York: Schocken, 1968.

Index